AN

HISTORICAL SKETCH
OF
SANSCRIT LITERATURE

AN

HISTORICAL SKETCH
OF
SANSCRIT LITERATURE,

WITH COPIOUS

BIBLIOGRAPHICAL NOTICES
OF
SANSCRIT WORKS AND TRANSLATIONS.

TRANSLATED BY

ADELUNG

(FRIEDRICH VON ADELUNG)

GYAN

Published by

Gyan Publishing House
5, Ansari Road
Daryaganj, New Delhi-110002
Phone: 011-47034999, 9811692060
E-mail: books@gyanbooks.com

Distribution Network
gyanbooks.com
India, USA, Canada, UK, Australia

ISBN: 978-93-6208-385-2 (PB)
First Published, 1832

2nd Impression 2024

Printed at: Gyan Press, Delhi.

AN HISTORICAL SKETCH OF SANSCRIT LITERATURE
Translator: ADELUNG (FRIEDRICH VON ADELUNG)

AN

HISTORICAL SKETCH

OF

SANSCRIT LITERATURE,

WITH COPIOUS

BIBLIOGRAPHICAL NOTICES

OF

SANSCRIT WORKS AND TRANSLATIONS.

FROM THE GERMAN OF ADELUNG,

WITH NUMEROUS ADDITIONS AND CORRECTIONS.

OXFORD, D. A. TALBOYS.

M DCCC XXXII.

CONTENTS.

A CATALOGUE OF SANSCRIT WORKS AND TRANSLATIONS.

SACRED WRITINGS.

JURISPRUDENCE.

PROFANE LITERATURE.

FINE ARTS.

THE DRAMA.

PREFACE.

THE foundation of a professorship of Sanscrit in this University, and the late election, which has raised Mr. Wilson to the professor's chair, could scarcely have taken place without giving, at least for the time, an additional impulse to the curiosity of the learned respecting the nature and literature of that language. Some enquiry began to be made for Sanscrit books. Hence it will appear very natural that a bookseller, who aims at being something more than the mere go-between of author and reader, should desire to gain some information respecting a subject now likely to form a new department of his calling. It was with some pleasure, therefore, that he took up and read the German work of Adelung; and, with the hope of its being interesting and useful to others, he undertook the translation of it into English.

In doing this, he cannot but feel aware that he has, in some degree, laid himself open to the charge of presumption, for attempting to translate a treatise concerning a language of which he knows not even the alphabet. Had he indeed foreseen, at the commencement of his task, the extent of labour, which, from the nature of the work he has had to undergo, the following pages would probably never have seen the light. He trusted too much, however, to the great name of Adelung; and, anticipating but little trouble in turning his German into English, was not aware of the pains and research necessary to correct the mistakes, and supply the omissions, almost unavoidable in a work of this kind. This he has attempted to do as far as lay in his power, and with such helps as he could procure. The corrections and alterations he has made, it would be almost impossible to point out; perhaps there is scarcely a page in which some emendation does not occur.

Besides these corrections, many alterations and additions have been made, which will not perhaps be so readily admitted as improvements. These indeed are so numerous, that they give the work the character rather of a new compilation than of a mere translation. The first part of the essay has been entirely re-modelled; as after the first two sheets had been printed in its original form, their appearance was so crude and foreign, that it was deemed advisable to cancel them. Besides this, full one half of the matter now presented to the public is not to be found in the original German. Of these additions, the greater part relate to subjects essentially connected with the work, and therefore requiring no apology; others, which have been inserted with a view of placing the subjects to which they refer in a stronger light, and of enlivening the dulness of a catalogue, must be left to the taste and indulgence of the reader. They consist, for the most part, of short extracts from the works referred to, and brief sketches of the various departments of Sanscrit learning into which the work is divided. It was intended at one time to distinguish them from the original work; but their number made it inconvenient, and the design was abandoned. Examples will be found under the heads of Philosophy, Poetry, Medicine, the Drama, etc.: reference being invariably made to the sources from which they are taken.

In this part of his work the translator has been greatly assisted by the kindness of Dr. Bandinel in allowing him the use of the Bodleian Library, and by the generous attention of the other gentlemen connected with that establishment. It is to him a pleasing duty to make this public acknowledgement of their liberality.

In the orthography of the Sanscrit and other oriental words, he has been favoured with the assistance of a scholar in this branch of learning, without which he would have been unable to proceed. Still, exact uniformity in this respect is not to be looked for. European scholars seldom agree in the manner of representing Sanscrit sounds by Roman letters; and the writers of different nations vary considerably in their orthography of the language: indeed they are frequently inconsistent even with themselves, and to such a degree, that the same word will often be found written several different ways in the same page. Add to this an observation made by Professor Wilson in the preface to his Sanscrit dictionary; viz. that "the various readings arising from confounding the different nasals and sibilants, and above all from the perpetual interchange of the letters B and V, are innumerable and of almost impracticable adjustment." And when it is known that this arbitrary substitution of one letter for another is further sanctioned by a convenient rule[a], the learned reader will perhaps be more disposed

[a] "The letters R and L, D′ and L, J and Y, B and V, S′ and S, M and N; a final visargah or its omission, and a final nasal mark or its omission, are always optional, there being no difference between them." *Wilson's Dictionary, Preface*, p. 41.

to pardon an occasional error or two in the orthography, and not be surprised should he even find the same word differently written in different places. In the titles of books and quotations, the original orthography has been adopted where it could be ascertained[b], in other cases uniformity has been aimed at, but it is feared with but moderate success.

The usefulness of the present publication must of course chiefly depend upon the importance of the subject of which it treats—a question that seems sufficiently decided by the foundation and intention of the Boden professorship[c], and the new impulse which this has given to the culture of Sanscrit literature. The very fact, indeed, of a gentleman's bequeathing an immense property for the promotion of this object, from a conviction, resulting from his own experience, of its being the best means of extending the knowledge of Christianity to a hundred millions of our fellow-creatures, should, and must engage in its interest every one who feels the value of this blessing; while its recommend-

[b] This has in some instances led to mistakes: as for example at p. 96, etc., where *Damayanti* has been improperly spelt *Damajanti*, in consequence of the compiler trusting to the correctness of the Quarterly Reviewer.

[c] The late Joseph Boden, esq., Colonel in the Honourable the East India Company's service, bequeathed the whole of his property to the University of Oxford for the foundation of a Sanscrit professorship, and the encouragement of Sanscrit learning; being of opinion "that a more general and critical knowledge of the Sanscrit language will be a means of enabling his countrymen to proceed in the conversion of the natives of India to the Christian religion, by disseminating a knowledge of the sacred scriptures amongst them, more effectually than all other means whatsoever." *Oxford Calendar*, 1832, p. 48. Horace Hayman Wilson, esq., perhaps the first Sanscrit scholar of the present age, and highly distinguished for his taste and learning in general literature, was elected to this chair in the present year.

ations of a more worldly nature, though but a feather when weighed against this paramount one, are still otherwise of a high and powerful character. Both, no doubt, have operated in producing the rapid and accelerated motion with which the cultivation of Sanscrit literature has advanced within these very few years in Europe; and it appears a striking argument in its favour, that the interest taken in it has increased in proportion to the information obtained respecting it, and that each step has been regarded but as a new position from which to make a farther advance[d]. Some of its warmest admirers have, indeed, gone so far, as to predict that it would exercise the same influence upon the learning and general tone of European society, as the introduction of Greek did in the fifteenth century; and, though few readers may go so far as these enthusiasts, it must, at least, be admitted, that the curious structure of the language, its close analogy with those already familiar to scholars[e], its great antiquity, and its presumed connection with the religion, the arts, and the sciences of Greece and Rome, are all well calculated to excite a fond and anxious research into its literary remains—remains equally wonderful for their extent and the harmonious language in which they are composed[f],

[d] Adelung, in his preface, mentions it as a matter of surprise, and as proving a great predilection for this language, that in the short space of thirty years seven hundred works should have been published relating to it, while not above a hundred persons in all Europe have applied themselves to its study, and of these there certainly are not fifty who know it accurately.

[e] See below, p. 39, etc.

[f] Professor Wilson says, "The music of Sanscrit composition must ever be inadequately represented by any other tongue." M. Chézy, in his opening discourse, calls it the celebrated dialect, perhaps spoken by the gods of Homer, and if not, worthy to be so. The praise indeed which Sanscrit

and containing treatises, written at various periods from a hundred to three thousand years ago, on philosophy, metaphysics, grammar, theology, astronomy, mathematics, jurisprudence, ethics, poetry, rhetoric, music, and other sciences cultivated among the Hindoos, at a time when Europe lay buried in the deepest shades of ignorance[g].

To those who study the history of man, Sanscrit literature offers a surprising mass of novel information, and opens an unbounded field for speculation and research. A language, (and such a language!) which, upon the most moderate computation dates its origin beyond the earliest records of profane history, and contains monuments of theology, poetry, and science, and philosophy, which have influenced perhaps a hundred millions of human beings through a hundred generations, is a phenomenon in the annals of the human race which cannot fail to command attention. Common sense and experience suggest that these facts only require to be known to excite a more general interest in this new department of literature. The following

scholars bestow on this language is not at all inferior to what Gibbon says of the Greek: "In their lowest servitude and depression, the subjects of the Byzantine throne were still possessed of a golden key that could unlock the treasures of antiquity; of a musical and prolific language, that gives a soul to the objects of sense, and a body to the abstractions of philosophy." *Gibbon's Rome*, vol. viii, p. 162, Oxford edit.

[g] The number of Sanscrit works described in the work of Mr. Adelung, amount to upwards of three hundred and fifty; many others have been added in the following pages. This, however, affords but a faint sketch of the copiousness of Sanscrit literature. The reader may perhaps form a more adequate notion by being informed, that Col. Kirkpatrick, in his account of Nepaul, quotes an instance of a single private library at Blatgŏng, the Benares of the Ghoorkali territory, amounting (according to his information) to fifteen thousand volumes. See also Col. Tod's preface to his splendid work on the Annals of Rajast'han, *passim*.

pages show that it has afforded subjects of sufficient interest to exercise the talents of writers of the highest reputation for taste and genius; and that Sanscrit literature still contains inexhaustible mines of wealth for those who have the industry to work them.

Compilers and translators have been somewhere designated as the pioneers of literature; and it will afford the compiler and translator of the following pages much satisfaction if they should clear the road, or lessen the toil of any more deeply engaged in the study of Sanscrit literature The very liberal indulgence with which his translation of Heeren's Researches has been received, emboldens him to hope for the same favour for the present attempt, which, as Mr. Adelung observes, will at least fill up a gap in bibliography, and abridge the labour of any one who may attempt a more complete work on the subject.

D. A. T.

Oxford, June, 1832.

THE SANSCRIT LANGUAGE, AS A LATER PRINCIPLE OF INTERPRETATION, STANDS AS IT WERE AT THE END OF A WHOLE SERIES OF LANGUAGES, AND THESE ARE BY NO MEANS SUCH AS BELONG TO A COURSE OF STUDY WHICH FOR PRACTICAL PURPOSES IS IN A CERTAIN DEGREE UNSERVICEABLE: ON THE CONTRARY, THEY COMPREHEND OUR OWN MOTHER TONGUE AND THAT OF THE CLASSICAL NATIONS OF ANTIQUITY, AND CONSEQUENTLY THEREFORE THE TRUE AND DIRECT SOURCE OF OUR BEST FEELINGS, AND THE FAIREST PART OF OUR CIVILISATION ITSELF.

W. VON HUMBOLDT.

AN HISTORICAL SKETCH

OF

SANSCRIT LITERATURE.

ORIGIN, ANTIQUITY, AND NAME OF THE SANSCRIT LANGUAGE.

Of the origin of the Sanscrit language, the parent stock of nearly all those now in use among the followers of Brahma, nothing is known with certainty but that it is lost in the gloom of remote antiquity. Historical data are entirely wanting respecting the first peopling of India; hence numerous conjectures have been formed concerning the introduction of the Sanscrit into the plains of Hindoostan.

It is the opinion of Klaproth, that, at a very remote period, Japhetic tribes from the north-west settled in these provinces, into which they carried their own language, the stock of the Sanscrit, and blended with it, or rather absorbed into it, at least in the northern districts of the peninsula, the dialects of the aborigines whom they found there [a].

[a] On the origin of the different written characters of the ancient world, by Klaproth, in Asiatic Journal, April, 1832. See also Edinb. Review, vol. xiii, p. 369.

Some learned men, on the contrary, would derive the Sanscrit from the Semitic family of languages. This opinion, however, is now very generally exploded. The alphabet, as M. Klaproth observes, in reply to Dr. Schleiermacher and others, bears no affinity to those of Semitic origin; but differs from them altogether, as well in the shape and sound of the letters as in their systems of arrangement. Bopp also very pertinently remarks, that whilst in the Semitic family a variation of vowels is of no etymological consequence, in Sanscrit and its cognate dialects such a change totally alters the force of the word: a sufficient proof of there being little or no connection between them [b].

According to Colebrooke, Sanscrit derives its origin (and some steps of its progress may even now be traced) from a primeval tongue, which was gradually refined in various climates, and became Sanscrit in India, Pahlavi in Persia, and Greek on the shores of the Mediterranean [c]. Many scholars, however, in the very highest rank of learning, trace the origin of this language in the Zend. Among these are Sir William Jones [d], the father of Indian learning, Paulinus a St. Bartholomæo [e], and the learned Dr. Leyden.

The Zend, however, would seem to be rather a twin sister of the Sanscrit than its parent; and, according to Hammer, a celebrated oriental scholar, the affinity is so close, that out of ten Zend words, six or seven will be found to be pure Sanscrit [f]. Here too may be noticed an observation cited by Langlès, in

[b] See Klaproth, l. c. and Asiatic Journal, January, 1832, p. 2.

[c] Asiatic Researches, vol. vii, p. 199.

[d] Works, vol. i, p. 26.

[e] In his tract, De Affinitate Linguæ Samscrdamicæ cum Zendica.

[f] Wiener Jahrbuch der Liter. 1818, ii, s. 275, in which he follows Sir William Jones.

the French translation of the Asiatic Researches, from Mohammed Fâny, a Persian writer, "that in very early times the Persians and the Indians formed but one people, and had but one religion, government, and, probably, but one language;" an assertion which Othm. Frank does not fail to quote in his Comment. de Persidis Lingua et Genio.

Later writers on this subject (colonel Vans Kennedy and others) award a still higher honour to the Sanscrit language, and make it the common parent of the Greek, and Latin, and Teutonic languages; and, consequently, of the English, French, German, and all the other modern ones to which these have given birth. They conceive Babylonia to have been the original seat of the Sanscrit, and that Asia Minor was peopled at an early period by a race from that country, whose language became the common parent of the Greek and Latin, and of the Thracian, now extinct, but from which descended the Teutonic languages [h].

A writer also in the Edinb. Rev. No. cii, sums up his observations on this subject by saying, "We are free to confess that the result of our enquiries has been, to produce a conviction in our minds that the affinities known to subsist between the Sanscrit, Greek, Latin, and German languages, are perfectly irreconcileable with any other supposition than that of their having all been derived from a common source, or primitive language, spoken by a people of whom the Indians, Greeks, Latins, and Germans, were equally the descendants". It is certain that intimations are given by ancient historians, that the Babylonians were in possession of a *sacred language;* but it seems almost impossible that this could have been the Sanscrit in its

[h] Colonel Vans Kennedy, On the Origin and Affinity of the Languages of Asia and Europe, 4to. p. 34 and 122. See also Raffles's History of p. 369.

present polished state; and Col. Kennedy, together with Klaproth and many others, believes that it was introduced into Hindoostan by Japhetic tribes from the north-west, where it gradually obtained its high state of perfection[i]. According to Langlès[k], it seems most likely that it was brought into Hindoostan from Western Asia, probably from Bactriana, by the Magians, whom Darius expelled the Persian empire.

But whatever may have been the origin of this language, all writers are agreed in ascribing to it a very high antiquity. Volney calls the Sanscrit, that language of a Scythian race which even the Egyptian acknowledged as its legitimate rival in antiquity[l]. And, extravagant as may be considered the assertions of Mr. Halhed, they still serve to prove the very remote antiquity of this language and its literature; so that few, after a careful examination of the subject, and leaving the inspired writings out of the question, will withhold their assent to his assertion, "that the world does not now contain annals of more indisputable antiquity than those delivered down by the ancient Brahmins[m]."

The whole character of the Hindoo nation and its institutions bears testimony in favour of this remote antiquity of their language. Their religion and laws, their mythology and science, all carry us back to times beyond the reach of history; while their magnificent but ruined temples, appear to be the work of no

[i] Tradition makes the Sanscrit to have travelled from the north to the south of India; hence it acquired in India the name of *Vaddamozhi*, the language of the north. Adelung.

[k] Revue Encyclop. 1820, Août, p. 330.

[l] In his Lettre sur l'Alphabet Phénicien, in the Revue Encyclop. vol. ii, Livr. 6, p. 511.

[m] See Halhed's preface to his translation of the Code of Hindoo Laws; and the preface to his Grammar of the Bengal Language; and Q. Crawford's Researches concerning India, vol. ii, p. 181—183, in which the objections to the high antiquity of the Sanscrit are stated and answered.

superstition more modern than that of Egypt or Assyria[n].

The century before the Christian era is regarded as one of the Augustan ages of this language, which, having been progressively refined, became fixed in the classic writings of many elegant poets, most of whom are supposed to have flourished about this period. It is now become almost a dead language; and, what may seem rather extraordinary, its numerous inflections, which are more anomalous than those of any other language, and still more so in the obsolete dialect of the ancient vedas than in the polished style of the classic poets, have led many persons to believe that it was constructed by the concerted efforts of a few priests, who set themselves about inventing a new language. The rules have been supposed to be anterior to the practice; but the supposition is gratuitous: in Sanscrit, as in every other known tongue, grammarians have not invented etymology, but have only contrived rules to teach what was already established by approved usage[o].

All the enquiries, however, respecting this language prove that it must have obtained fixed grammatical inflections at a very early period. The opinion just cited, and repeated by Crawford in his Researches concerning Ancient and Modern India, that the number of its declensions and conjugations, and the complication of its rules, must have prevented it from having ever been in use as a national language, is opposed to all experience respecting the formation of languages. The Sanscrit was certainly at one time the language of the greater part of India, especially

[n] Edinburgh Review, vol. v. p. 289.

[o] Colebrooke on the Sanscrit and Pracrit Languages, in Asiatic Researches, vol. vii, p. 199.

in the regions near the Ganges; and, above all, in *Bahar*, in which the scene of so many of the most ancient Indian poems is laid. It is revered as the national language; and the oldest works in Indian literature are composed in it. Indeed it bears much the same relation to the vernacular languages now in daily use between the Indus and the Ganges, that the Latin does to the Italian, the classical Greek to the modern, or the Saxon to the English. The names, too, of all the most ancient Indian cities (as Colebrooke observes, l. c.) are derived from it [p].

Further, the Sanscrit may be regarded, with the exception of a few mountain dialects, as the parent of all the Indian languages, from the Indus to the farthest part of Aracan, and from Ceylon to Chinese Tartary. Indeed Hammer [q] says, "so far as the etymological investigations of the Sanscrit have hitherto afforded satisfactory results, it may certainly be considered as the parent stock of all the known languages which form the variation of their words, their declensions, conjugations, etc. by inflection; while the northern and western Asiatic languages, in which these are denoted by the addition of particles, must be derived from another origin than the Sanscrit." Colonel Kennedy accounts for the difference of number in the tenses between the Teutonic verb and the Sanscrit, from the experience we have, "that a rude people prefer the use of auxiliary verbs for the formation of tenses, to the more artificial mode of inflecting the verb for this purpose."

The name of this language has been written and pronounced in various ways: we find, for example,

[p] See Asiatic Researches, vii, p. 199, etc. Thus, for example, the name of *Serampoor* is a contraction of the Sanscrit *S'rírámapura*, the city of the divine *Ráma*.

[q] Wiener Jahrb. d. Liter. 1818, ii, s. 275.

Hanscred, *Samscredam*, *Samscrudon*, *Samscrudam*, *Samscret*, *Sanscrit*, *Shanscrit*, *Sungskrit* [r], *Sungskritu*, *Sonskrito*, *Sanscroot*, *Sankrita*, *Sangskrida*.

In India it is called *Sura bâni*, *Sura bhâk'hâ*, and *Dêwa bâni*, the language of the heavenly regions [s].

The Jesuists, most corruptly, have introduced the word *Grantham*, as well as *Grandam*, *Grandom*, *Granthon*, and *Grandonicum*, which, as Colebrooke remarks, is probably derived from the word *Grant'ha*, a book; and this shows the Sanscrit to be the peculiar language of the sacred writings.

From *Grandonicum* is formed *Kerendum*, as the Sanscrit has been likewise sometimes miscalled.

The word *Sanscrita* is the passive participle of a compound verb, formed by prefixing the preposition *sam* to the crude verb *cri*, and by interposing the letter *s* when this compound is used in the sense of embellishment. Its literal meaning then is, *adorned;* and when applied to language, *polished* [t].

[r] As is most usual in the books printed at Serampoor, according to the early custom of pronouncing the short Sanscrit *a* as a short *o*, which the English express by *u*. *Sanscrit*, as the word was written by Sir William Jones and Dr. Wilkins, is the form now generally adopted.

[s] The Indian writers on poetry, rhetoric, and grammar, make *Sanscrit* the language of the gods; *Prucrit* that of the benevolent genii; *Paisachi* that of wicked demons; and *Magadhi* that of men.

[t] The word Sanscrit is a compound participle, literally signifying, *altogether* or *completely made*, *done*, or *formed* (Lat. *confectus*), from the inseparable preposition *sam*, *altogether* or *together* (Lat. *cum*), and *krita*, *done*, with the interposition of a silent *s*, which letter being a dental, requires that the labial nasal which precedes it should be pronounced as a *dental* also, namely, as *n*. The word in its common acceptation, denotes a thing to have been composed or formed by art, adorned, embellished, purified, highly cultivated or polished, and regularly inflected as a language. WILKINS's S. Gram. p. 1.

WORKS ON THE SANSCRIT LANGUAGE IN GENERAL.

Colebrooke's Dissertation on the Sanscrit and Pracrit Languages, in Asiatic Researches, vol. vii, p. 199. A brief account of this is given in the Monthly Review, 1805, March, p. 265. It is reviewed more at length in the Edinburgh Review, vol. ix, p. 289; and is abridged in Vater's Proben deutscher Volksmundarten u. s. w. No. ix, s. 171. It is everywhere spoken of as a work of great merit.

There is a treatise in Chinese on the origin of the Sanscrit language, written A. D. 1020, and another by the emperor Kien Lung, composed in 1749, on the Sanscrit, Thibet, and Mongul languages. Translations of these it is said would throw much new light on the language and literature of the Hindoos. See Quarterly Review, vol. v, p. 395.

"To acquire a perfect knowledge of the Sanscrita language, requires a longer period of diligence and exertion than to attain a similar degree of proficiency in any vernacular tongue." A declamation by Mr. T. Clerk, at the public disputation at the college of Fort William, July 17th, 1816 (? in Sanscrit).

A Dissertation on the Orthography of Asiatic Words, in Roman Letters, by Sir W. Jones. In Asiatic Researches, vol. i, p. 1.

"It is more probable that the Sanscrit, as it at present exists, is a mixture of various dialects than that it should have descended so rich and artificially formed from one original language," *Calcutta*, 1814, 4to. One of the declamations of the students of the college of Fort William in Bengal. It is written in Sanscrit.

La Croze refers, in his Hist. du Christianisme des

Indes, tom. ii, p. 303, to a Tamulic work, *Divagarum*, written in the twelfth century, which treats of the richness and excellences of the Sanscrit.

Ziegenbalg's Account of the Danish Missionaries, vol. i, p. 116, 429, 627.

Du Pons in the Lettres édifiantes, éd. 2, tom. xiv.

Ueber die Shanscrita von M. Hismann. In the Gotting. Mag. 1780, St. v, p. 269—293.

Ueber die Samskrdamische Sprache, vulgo Samskrit, von Fr. K. Alter, *Wien*, 1799, 8vo.

Mithridates von J. C. Adelung, vol. i. p. 134, etc.; vol. iv, p. 54—62, and 482—485.

Geschichte der neuern Sprachenkunde von Joh. Gotfr. Eichhorn, Erste Abth. s. 228—256.

Ueber die Sprache und Weisheit der Indier, nebst metrischen Uebersetzungen indischer Gedichte von Friedrich Schlegel, *Heidelberg*, 1818, 8vo.; and, Notæ quædam necessariæ ad prima capita libri primi operis Germanici: The Philosophy, etc. of the Indians, in Othm. Frank's Comment. de Persidis Lingua et Genio, *Heidelb.* 1809, 8vo.

De lingua Sanscrit, Diss. auctore Frid. Wilh. Eckenstamm, partes iii, *Lundæ*, 1810, 4to.; pars iv et v, *ibid.* 1811. See Othm. Frankii Chrestom. Sanskrita, vol. i, p. xii.

Heeren's Ideen über den Handel, die Politik u. s. w. vol. ii, s. 394, etc[u].

Discours sur les Avantages, la Beauté, la Richesse de la Langue Sanskrite, et sur l'Utilité et les Agrémens que l'on peut retirer de son étude, par M. A. L. Chézy, in the Mag. Encyclop. Mars, 1815, p. 5—27; see also a review of the same by Silvestre de Sacy, in the Moniteur, 1815, No. xxiii. An English translation

[u] Several volumes of an English translation of this work have been printed and published by the compiler of this essay. The volume here referred to on the Indians is now in progress.

is printed in the Asiatic Journal, May, 1817, p. 334—437.

Ueber das Sanskrit, seinen Zusammenhang mit den davon ausgehenden ostindischen Sprachen und sein Verhältniss zum Latein, Persischen, Germanischen, von J. S. Vater. In his Proben deutscher Volksmundarten u. s. w. s. 169—194.

On the importance of cultivating a knowledge of Sanscrit, in Dr. Wilkins' Grammar of the Sanscrit Language.

Account of the Sanscrit Language, by Q. Crawford, esq. in his Researches concerning the Laws, Manners, etc. of Ancient and Modern India, *London*, 1817, 8vo. vol. ii, p. 161—163, (almost entirely taken from Colebrooke's Essay); and, Importance of the Sanscrit Language as a Key to every other Language, in the same, p. 236—238.

Upon the writing and pronunciation of Hindoo names, in Aug. Wilh. v. Schlegel's Ind. Bibliothek, s. 46—49; and, Heidelb. Jahrb. 1815, No. lvi.

The Hindee Roman Orthoepigraphical Ultimatum; or, a Systematic Discriminative View of Oriental and Occidental Visible Sounds, on fixed and practical Principles, for speedily acquiring the most accurate pronunciation of many Oriental Languages, by John Borthwick Gilchrist, *London*, 1820, 8vo.

Die literarischen Bestrebungen in Indien bis zur Mitte des achtzehnten Jahrhunderts, oder Ubersicht über Europa's allmähliche Bekanntschaft mit der Sanskrit-Literatur bis zum Jahre 1750. Eine Einleitung zu Vorlesungen über die indische Literatur, von N. Nyrup, *Kopenhagen*, 1821, 4to.

Uebersicht sämmtlicher bisher mit und ohne Uebersetzung durch den Druck bekannt gemachter Sanskritischer Schriften, Grammatiken, Wörterbücher u. s. w. by Prof. Bernstein. Leipz. Lit. Zeit, 1820, No. ccxci.

On the present state of Indian learning, by A. W. v. Schlegel, in the Jahrbuche der Preuss. Rhein-Universität, *Bonn*, 1819, I Bd. 2tes Heft. This is also printed separately. In French: in the Bibliothèque Universelle, 1819, Décembre, p. 349—370; and in the Revue Encyclop. 1820. The same essay is likewise inserted in A. W. v. Schlegel's Indischer Bibliothek, St. i, s. 1—28.

On encouraging the cultivation of the Sungskrita language among the natives, in The Friend of India, 1822, *Serampore*, No. v, p. 5.

On the Sanscrit language, in Alex. Murray's History of the European Languages, *Edinburgh*, 1823, 8vo. vol. ii, p. 220.

Ant. Theod. Hartmann's biblisch-asiatischer Wegweiser u. s. w. *Bremen*, 1823, 8vo. s. clxx—clxxvii.

Viasa. Upon the Philosophy, Mythology, Literature, and Language of the Hindoos, by Dr. Othmar Frank, *München*, 1826, 4to.

Die Urwelt, von Link, s. 162—172.

Among the Sanscrit writers the *Suraseni* is considered as a refined sort of Sanscrit, which, according to Dr. Leyden, may be identified with the Zend. See *Vater's* Proben deutscher Volksmundarten u. s. w. s. 216 [x].

[x] The Sanscrit language is now publicly taught in many of the first universities of Europe, namely, in Germany, at Berlin, Breslau, Bonn, etc. At Cambridge it is expounded by professor Sam. Lee, one of the most distinguished linguists of the present day. He is acquainted with Arabic, Latin, Greek, Hebrew, Syriac, Chaldaic, Samaritan, Æthiopic, Coptic, Persian, Hindostan, Malay, Sanscrit, Bengalee, French, German, and Italian, altogether seventeen languages! The Abbé Mezzofante of Bologna speaks or understands thirty-three.

ON THE SANSCRIT ALPHABET AND CHARACTER.

THE Sanscrit differs from all other languages in its alphabet and its structure.

There is no trace in history of the origin of the Sanscrit alphabet; and all that can be said of it is, that the Hindoos having succeeded at a very early period in raising the Sanscrit, their classical and written language, to the highest pinnacle of perfection, wrote it, with an alphabet equally perfect, and so admirable, that they attribute it to divine origin, and call it *Deva-nâgari*, or, the writing of the gods[y]. We are equally uninformed whether those people who brought into India the basis of this language had a written character or not. Colonel Vans Kennedy remarks, that the Sanscrit alphabet is too artificial to have been original and unimproved, and believes that the Brahmins migrating to India probably adapted it to the sounds there in use.

The square character of Hindoostan, which is used in preference to all others for writing the sacred language, the Sanscrit, still retains the name of *Devanâgari*. It is composed of fourteen vowels and diphthongs, and thirty-four consonants. Some authors increase the number of letters to fifty, and make sixteen vowels. The compounds of these letters, called *phala*, form above eight hundred characters. The *Devanâgari* is also called, *Baulobund*[z].

[y] Klaproth on the origin of the different written characters of the Ancient World. In Asiat. Journ. N. S. vol. vii, p. 265. April, 1832.

[z] See Asiatic Journal for April, 1822, p. 317. Professor Schleiermacher laid before the Asiatic Society of Paris a treatise upon the Semitic origin of the Devanâgari alphabet, and some other subjects connected with Sanscrit literature. Volney much earlier had derived the

Sanscrit is also written in the *Telinga* and *Malabar* character, each of which has fifty-three letters. The Sanscrit is said to be most perfectly expressed by the latter, which is also called *Grundrum* (*Grandam?*). See above, p. 7, and Asiatic Journal, April, 1822, p. 317[a].

Besides these, the variety of characters used in the inscriptions, still partly unexplained, in the temple grottos at Salsette, Kennery, Mavalipuram, etc., show that in India various alphabets were in use at a very early period. See Heeren's Ideen, Th. ii, p. 383—386.

All the inscriptions hitherto deciphered are read from left to right, and contain particular signs for the vowels as well as the consonants.

The Sanscrit alphabet is found in the following works:

Athan. Kircheri China illustrata, *Amstelod.* 1661, folio, P. iii, cap. vii, p. 162.

Millii Diss. de Lingua Hindustanica, in his Dissertatt. sel. *Lugd. Batav.* 1743, 4to. p. 455—288.

Th. Siegfr. Bayer's treatise in the Commentatt. Petropol. tom. iii, p. 389.

Sanscrit alphabet from the Phœnician. "If in modern India," says he, "the eighteen or twenty existing alphabets derived from the ancient Sanscrit, are all, like their model, constructed on the syllabical principle, in which the consonant alone expresses the vowel sound necessary to its pronunciation, shall we not be led to believe that the Sanscrit had originally a Phœnician type; and especially as the Sanscrit itself is as indisputably constructed syllabically as the Arabico-Phœnician?" See Lettre de Comte Volney sur l'Antiquité de l'Alphabet Phénicien, in Revue Encyclop. 1819, Août, p. 334. The origin of the Sanscrit alphabet is also traced to the Chaldaic. See Alex. Murray's Hist. of the Europ. Languages, vol. ii, p. 392; and Ulr. Friedr. Kopp in his Bilder und Schriften der Vorzeit, Bd. ii, p. 367—375.

[a] Here also deserves notice that Devanâgari which the Tibetians and Mongols call *Landscha*, and with which are written, in Sanscrit (not in Pali) the sacred records of the Tibetian and Mongol Bauddhas. It is older and far more cursive than the Devanâgari character now in use,

A Code of Gentoo Laws, etc., published by Nath. Brassey Halhed, *London*, 1777, 8vo.

Alex Dow's History of Hindoostan, translated from the Persian of Casim Ferishta, pref. p. xxx.

Crabb's Technological Dictionary.

Alphabetum Grandonico-Malabaricum seu Samscrudonicum, auctore Clemente Peanio Alexandrino, *Romæ*, 1772, 8vo.

Alphabeta Indica, i. e. Granthamicum, seu Samscrudamico-Malabaricum, Indostanicum s. Varanense (Benares), Nagaricum vulgare et Talenganicum, *Romæ*, 1791, 8vo.; with a preface by Frá Paolino a S. Bartholomæo.

Sir William Jones's Dissertation on the Orthography of Asiatic words in Roman letters, in Asiatic Researches, vol. i, and Works.

Mémoire sur les Alphabets et sur les écritures des Indous du Sanscrit, par le Comte Lanjuinais. Lû à l'Institut. in the Mag. Encyclop. 1812, Sept. p. 30[b].

Sur la Valeur des Lettres Sanscrites, in Yadjnadattabada, ou la mort de Yadjnadatta, épisode extrait du Ramâyana, traduit par A. L. Chézy, *Paris*, 1826, 4to. Préface, p. v—xviii.

An Essay upon the best manner of expressing the Indian Language in European characters, by Rask.

though it is evident they are essentially the same. A specimen of it may be found in J. J. Schmidt's Forschungen im Gebiete der Bildungsgeschichte der Völker Mittel-Asiens; and in the Asiatic Museum of Petersburgh there is the Lord's prayer very elegantly written in it, exactly conformable with Dr. Schmidt's interpretation, but which has erroneously been taken for *Multan*.

[b] The author divides the Indian forms of writing into the northern and southern. The former are distinguished by their square and angular shape, the latter by their curve lines. This variety is explained by the difference of the instruments made use of, and the materials written upon. Lanjuinais cites, in his Mémoire, two treatises in the Chinese language, upon the origin of the Indian character. One of these was written in the eleventh century, the other in the year 1749.

Written in English for the first volume of the Acts of the Literary Society at Colombo. See also the preliminary note to *Mrichchakati*, or, the Toy Cart, in professor Wilson's Hindoo Theatre, vol. i.

The Sanscrit alphabet in the Bengalee character, in Chézy's Yadjnadattabada.

Rudimenta lectionis literarum quæ Devanagaricæ dicuntur, in Othm. Frankii Chrestomathia Sanskrita, *Monaci*, 1820, vol. i.

Cognatio literarum Sanskritarum, *ibid.*

Orthoepia vocalium Sanskritarum, *ibid.*

Specimen novæ typographicæ Indicæ. Litterarum figuras ad Codd. Bibliothecæ R. Paris. exemplaria delineavit, cœlandas curavit Aug. Guil. Schlegel. *Lut. Par.* 1821, 8vo.

Besides these, the Sanscrit characters are to be found in the modern grammars of this language already mentioned; and particularly beautiful in that of Wilkins, which have been copied in G. H. Bernstein's Hitopadesi particula, *Breslau*, 1823, 4to. The most beautiful alphabet of the Bengalee language is to be found in Haughton's Grammar, and Chrestomathie.

Respecting the division of certain Sanscrit words, which W. v. Humboldt first brought into notice in the Asiatic Journal, 1827, and which became the subject of much dispute, but was adopted by Bopp and others, the arguments for and against it will be found collected by that ingenious philologist in the Jahrb. für wissenschaftl. Kritik, 1829, No. lxxiii, p. 581—592; No. lxxv, p. 593—595.

The best account of the writing materials of the Hindoos, will be found in the enquiry of Frà Paolino, in his Institutio Linguæ Samscrdamicæ, p. 327, etc.

SANSCRIT GRAMMAR.

THE peculiar and wonderful structure of the Sanscrit language has almost as much recommended it to the notice of the learned, as the interesting literary monuments it is said to contain[c]. "It is the most regular language known, and is especially remarkable, as containing the roots of the various languages of Europe, and the Greek, Latin, German, of Sclavonic[d]."

The Sanscrit possesses one very striking peculiarity. It is that of extending to Syntax the rules for the permutation of letters in Etymology. Similar rules for avoiding incompatible sounds in compound terms exist in all languages; but, in the Sanscrit language, words merely in sequence have an influence upon each other in the change of terminations, and sometimes of initial letters. The rules for this permutation of letters have been more profoundly investigated by Hindoo grammarians than by those of any other nation; and they have completed a system of orthography which may be justly termed euphonical. They require all compound terms to be reduced to this standard; and Sanscrit authors, it may be observed,

[c] Edinburgh Review, vol. xiii, p. 366.—Wilh. von Humboldt (Jahrb. für wissenschaftl. Kritik, 1829, No. lxxiii, p. 580), speaking of the remarkable grammatical construction of the Sanscrit, says, "No language in the world, that we are acquainted with, possesses, in an equal degree with the Sanscrit, the secret of moulding abstract grammatical ideas into such forms, as by means of simple and closely allied sounds still leave evident traces of the root, which often of itself explains the variation of sound (inasmuch as it essentially remains the same) amid the greatest complication of form: nor has any other language, by means of its inherent euphonic amalgamation of inflection, the power of forming such accurate and well-adapted symbols for expressing the conceptions of the mind."

[d] Baron Cuvier's Lectures on the Natural Sciences.

delight in compounds of inordinate length: the whole sentence too, or even whole periods, may, at the pleasure of the author, be combined like the elements of a single word[e].

An excellent and ample history of Indian grammarians is given by Colebrooke in the Asiatic Researches, vol. vii, p. 202, etc. This is copied by Crawford into his Researches concerning Ancient and Modern India, *London*, 1817, 8vo. vol. i, p. 163—176.

A list of the Sanscrit grammars in manuscript, contained in the Royal library of Paris, by Indian writers, will be found in the Catalogue des MSS. Sanscrits, p. 27, 67, 68, 72, 75, 77, 84—87.

The Sanscrit grammars must be divided into *ancient* and *modern*.

1. *Ancient Grammars.*

The grammatical institutes, *Vyâkarana*, in Sanscrit literature are classed among the *Angas*. They belong in a certain measure to the sacred writings, among which they take their place immediately after the *Vedas*.

Upon the Sanscrit grammatical institutes of the Brahmins see Du Pons, in Lettres Edifiantes, tom. xiv, p. 67, second edition; Paulinus a S. Bartholomæo in Vyacarana, p. 14; and Asiatic Researches, vol. vii, p. 119.

The most ancient grammars are named after deities to whom they are ascribed, *Mâheshwara*, *Indra*, and *Chandra*. But the most celebrated of all is the *Sidd' hânta Kaumudi* of Pánini, whom the Hindoos call the father of Sanscrit grammar. He lived in so remote

[e] Colebrooke's Essay—Prichard's Eastern Origin, p. 28.

an age, that he ranks among those ancient sages, whose fabulous history occupies a conspicuous place in the Puránàs, or Indian theogonies. The name is properly a patronymick, indicating his descent from *Pánin;* but, according to the *Pauránica* legends, he was the grandson of Dévala, an inspired legislator.

Whatever may be the true history of Pánini, to him the Sútras, or succinct aphorisms of grammar, are attributed by universal consent. His system is founded on a profound investigation of the analogies in both the regular and anomalous inflections of the Sanscrit language. He has combined these analogies in a very artificial manner, and has thus compressed a most copious etymology into a very narrow compass.

His work consists of three thousand nine hundred and ninety-six *sootras,* or precepts, framed with the utmost conciseness; and this great brevity is the result of very ingenious methods, which have been contrived for this end, as well as to help the student's memory.

Ancient as is the work of Pánini, he still cites the works of Sacalya, Gargya, Casyapa, Galava, Sacatayana, and others who had preceded him[f].

A very learned review and exposition of the system of Pánini will be found in Crawford's Researches, vol. ii, p. 163—166[g].

A copious commentary on the work of Pánini was compiled at a very early period, by an unknown author, but is ascribed to Saptánjali, a fabulous per-

[f] The various ancient grammars of the Sanscrit tongue, as enumerated in a memorial verse, are eight in number, and ascribed to the following authors, viz. *Indra, Chandra, Cásá, Critsná, Pisáli, Sácátáyana, Pánini,* and *Amera Jinéndra.* Colebrooke.

[g] The reader may also consult Colebrooke on the Sanscrit and Pracrit languages, in Asiatic Researches, vol. vii, p. 199, whence Adelung has borrowed the account which I have here amplified, and whence Crawford has copied, verbatim, the account referred to in the text.

sonage, to whom mythology has assigned the shape of a serpent. The title of this voluminous exposition is *Mahábáshya*, or, The Great Commentary [h].

Cátyayána, or, Cattijana, an inspired saint and lawgiver, whose history, like that of all the Indian sages, is involved in the impenetrable darkness of mythology [i], corrected the inaccuracies of the Paniniya grammar. His annotations, entitled *Varticas*, restrict the rules of Pánini where too vague, enlarge others which are too limited, and point out numerous exceptions which had escaped the author. These improved rules of grammar have been formed into memorial verses by Bhartri-Hari, entitled, *Carica*, which have almost equal authority with the precepts of Pánini and the emendations of Cátyayána. The grammar of Pánini, and the two commentaries just mentioned, are among the manuscripts of the Royal Society of London, to whom they were presented by Sir William Jones.

Casica Vritti, a much esteemed commentary on Pánini, composed at Benares, was printed at Serampoor, in the year 1800, in the Devanâgari character; but only the text, without a translation or notes [k].

[h] See also Colebrooke, in Asiatic Researches, vol. vii, p. 205. He says, "In this commentary every rule is examined at great length; all possible interpretations are proposed; and the true sense and import of the rule are deduced through a tedious train of argument, in which all foreseen objections are considered and refuted; and the wrong interpretations of the text, with all the arguments which can be invented to support them, are obviated or exploded."

[i] He is said to have lived in the century before the Christian era; and a beautiful poem has been composed in his name, containing moral reflections, which the poet supposes him to make on the discovery of his wife's infidelity. See Asiatic Researches, vol. vii, p. 204.

[k] Adelung seems to have fallen into a mistake here, as he makes Varanasi the author of this comment. It is spoken of by Colebrooke expressly as the work of an anonymous author. Varanais, I am informed, is the Sanscrit appellation of Benares, from which the common name has been corrupted by transposition.

The anonymous author of this work explains his design in a short preface, "to gather the essence of a science dispersed in the early commentaries, in the *Bháshya*, in copious dictionaries of verbs and nouns, and in other works." He has well fulfilled the task which he undertook. His gloss explains, in perspicuous language, the meaning and application of each rule. He adds examples, and quotes, in their proper places, the necessary emendations from the *Varticas* and *Bháshya*.

These voluminous commentaries upon Pánini's work still left many obscurities unexplained, a defect which numerous modern grammarians have endeavoured to supply. The most celebrated among these are the work of Cairata, a learned Cashmirian, and the *Padamanjari* of Haradatta Misra.

The annotations of the former are almost equally copious with the *Bháshya* itself; yet these, too, are loaded with glosses, among which the old and new *Vivaranás* are most esteemed. The *Padamanjara*, which is a commentary on the *Casica Vritti*, is also much esteemed, and the authority of its author held nearly equal to that of the original work[1].

The Grammatical Sootras, or, Aphorisms of Pánini, with selections from various Commentators, *Calcutta*, 1809, 2 vols. 8vo. in the Nagari character. The following is the title as given in Roebuck's Annals of the College of Fort William, *Calcutta*, 1819. Pánini Sútra Vrittri, the Grammatical Aphorisms of Pánini, with a Commentary in Sanscrit; published by H. T. Colebrooke, esq., *Calcutta*, 2 vols. 8vo. Printed entirely in Sanscrit.

A modified arrangement of Pánini's work for those who study the rudiments of the language, has been

[1] Colebrooke.

compiled within these few centuries by Ramachandra, an eminent grammarian, entitled, *Pracrya Caumudi;* and another still later by Bhattoji Dicshita, called *Sidd' hánta Caumudi.*

An analysis of Ramachandra's treatise will be found in Mr. Colebrooke's Essay on the Sanscrit and Pracrit Languages: he says, the rules are Pánini's, and the explanation of them abridged from the ancient commentaries; but the arrangement is wholly different. The order in which Ramachandra has delivered the rules of grammar, is certainly preferable; but the *sootras* of Pánini, thus detached from their context, are wholly unintelligible. Without the commentator's exposition, they are, indeed, what Sir William Jones has somewhere termed them, 'dark as the darkest oracle.'

Bhattoji Dikshita is also spoken of as an able grammarian. He made some useful changes in the arrangement of the *Pracriya,* amended the explanation of the rules, supplied many omissions, enlarged the examples, and noticed the most important points upon which the elder grammarians disagree.

This author also wrote an argumentative commentary upon his own grammar. It is called *Pránta menórama.* And besides this, he composed a very voluminous commentary on the Eight Lectures of Pánini, and gave it the title of *S'abda Caustubha.* The only portion of it Mr. Colebrooke had seen, reaches no farther than to the end of the first section of Panini's first lecture. But this, he says, is so diffusive, that, if the whole had been executed on a similar plan, it must triple the ponderous volume of the *Mahábhashya* itself; he had reason, however, for doubting whether it was ever completed [m].

The *Sidd' hanta Kaumudi,* a grammar conformable

[m] Colebrooke.

to the system of Pánini, by Bhattoji Dikshita, *Calcutta*, 1812, 4to. in the Nagari character, published by Bâburâm Pandit, proprietor and superintendent of the Sanscrit printing establishment.

The commentaries upon these two works are very numerous: several abridgements also have been attempted, the most valuable of which is, *Mad'hya Caumudi;* and this is accompanied by a similar compendium of annotations, entitled *Mad'hya Menorama.*

The *Laghu Kaumudi*, a Sanscrit Grammar, by Vadaraja, *Education Press, Calcutta*, 1827, royal 12mo.

The most celebrated grammarian after Pánini is Vopadeva, whose popular grammar, which is in high repute at Bengal, is entitled *Mugdhabódha.* It consists of one thousand one hundred *sootras*, or short grammatical rules, accompanied by a commentary entitled *Vrith*, which comprise all that it is necessary for a learner of the language to know[n].

In the whole, eight commentaries upon this work are enumerated. But a great drawback, according to Colebrooke, to the use of Vopadeva's Grammar, is, that he has not been content to translate the rules of Pánini, and to adopt his technical terms, but has, on the contrary, invented new terms, and contrived new abbreviations. Hence, the commentaries and scholia written to elucidate poems and works of science, must be often unintelligible to those who have studied *only* his grammar; and the writings of his scholars must be equally incomprehensible (upon all that relates to grammar) to the students of the Paniniya. Accordingly, the pandits of Bengal are cut off, in a manner, from communication on grammatical topics with the learned of other provinces in India. Even etymological dic-

[n] Adelung: see also Colebrooke in Asiat. Researches, vol. vii, 213; and Catalogue des MSS. Sanscrits, p. 84, where, (p. 85,) is mentioned a commentary on the same, by Râmâna Atcharia, entitled *Mugdabódhatika.*

tionaries, such as the commentaries on the metrical vocabularies, must be unintelligible.

The *Mugdha Bodha*, a Grammar by Vopa Deva, *Serampoor*, 1807, 12mo.; in Bengalee, *Calcutta*, 1826, 12mo. Devanâgari character.

The Sungskrit Grammar, called *Moogdboodha*, by Vopa Deva, *Serampoor*, 1817, 8vo. See Catal. de la Bibl. de M. Langlès, p. 116, No. 999.

The *Mugdabodha*, or Sanscrit Grammar of Vopadeva, in the Devanàgari character, *Calcutta*, 1826, 12mo; 1828.

Carey has published Vopadeva's work at Serampoor in two volumes; and Forster, an English version of it, accompanied with paradigms, and a treatise upon the Sanscrit roots, under the title of, A Translation of the Mugdabodha, a celebrated treatise on Sanscrit grammar, by G. H. Forster, *Calcutta*, 1810, 4to.

Viakarana, or Grammar, a treatise on the formation of simple and compound words of the Sanscrit language, of their changes, and of the manner of using them in speech.

The royal library at Copenhagen possesses a manuscript commentary upon the Mugdabodha, in Sanscrit, by Padmanabadatta, in Bengalee character, under the title of *Subadhini*. See Dansk Litter. Tidende for 1819, p. 122.

Vira Metra daya, a Sanscrit Grammar, *Calcutta*, 1815, 4to. A poem in the Sanscrit language, in Parbury, Allen, and Co.'s Catalogue, for 1831.

The *Rhatta-Kavyà*, a Sanscrit Poem illustrative of Grammar, with a commentary, *Calcutta*, 1826, 8vo. and 1828. The author of this was named Bhartri-Hari. He gives in a poem of twenty-two stanzas, the rules of grammar and rhetoric, the materials for which he has drawn from the history of Rama.

Sabadasacti Prakariti, Tractatus Argumenti Grammatici. A manuscript in the royal library at Copenhagen. See Dansk Litter. Tidende for 1819, p. 122.

Another grammar much esteemed is the *Saraswata*, together with its commentary, named *Chandrica*. It seems to have been formed on one of the Caumudis, by translating Pánini's rules, into language that is intelligible°. There is also the *Náma Parayana*, etc. The Ancient Hindoo literature contains altogether one hundred and twenty-six works upon Sanscrit grammar, ninety-six of which treat only of separate portions of it.

2. *Modern Grammars.*

Sidharubam, seu Grammatica Samscrdamica, cui accedit dissertatio historico-critica in linguam Samscrdamicam, vulgo *Samscret* dictam, in qua hujus linguæ existentia, origo, præstantia, antiquitas, extensio, maternitas ostenditur, libri aliqui in ea exarata recensentur, et simul aliquæ antiquissimæ gentilium orationes liturgicæ paucis attinguntur et explicantur, auctore Fr. Paulino a S. Bartholomæo, *Romæ*, 1790, 4to; in Typogr. congreg. de propag. fide. See Götting. gel. Anz. 1796, p. 1658—1664; Nouv. Melanges Asiat. par M. Abel. Rémusat, vol. ii. p. 306.

Vyacarana, seu locupletissima Samscrdamicæ linguæ institutio, in usum fidei præconum in India orientali, et virorum litteratorum in Europa adornata, a Paulino a S. Bartholomæo, Carmelita discalceato, *Romæ*, 1804, 4to. In Typogr. congreg. de propag. fide.

The author of these two grammars was a German, whose proper name is said to have been *Wesdin*. He resided as a missionary on the Malabar coast of India, from 1776 till 1789, and died at Rome in 1805. Anquetil du Perron, in the French translation of the Travels of Fra Paolini, and professor Chézy, in the

° Colebrooke.

Moniteur, 1810, No. cxlvi, both question his knowledge of the Sanscrit; and Dr. Leyden calls his manner coarse, acrimonious, and offensive, and adds, that the publication of his Vyacarana has given a deathblow to his vaunted pretensions to profound oriental learning, and shown that he was incapable of accurately distinguishing Sanscrit from the vernacular languages of India[p]. It is proper, on the other hand, to state that Paolini himself thankfully acknowledges, in many passages of his Systema Brahmanicum, the great assistance he had received in his labours from P. Hanxleden. But, at all events, it would be a waste of time to study these three grammars now, when they have been so entirely superseded by the more modern and well-established works of English and German scholars; though they are still curious for the undisguised spite and hostility which the author takes every occasion of exhibiting towards the opinions of English Sanscrit scholars, and particularly the learned contributors to the Asiatic Researches. The particular character in which he has chosen to write Sanscrit is a remarkable proof of his obstinate prejudice; as are also the dogmatic, yet groundless assertions, with which he has attempted to support his choice.

A Grammar of the Sungskrit Language, composed from the works of the most esteemed grammarians; to which are added examples for the exercise of the students, and a complete list of the *dhatoos* or roots, by William Carey, teacher of the Sungscrit, Bengalee,

[p] See Asiat. Researches, vol. x, p. 278, where proofs are given of his ignorance of Sanscrit; and Edin. Review, vol. i, p. 30, in which the same opinion had been already published. Paolino's work is also reviewed and criticised in professor Wilson's preface to his Dictionary, in the Götting. gel. Anz. 1805, No. cxlv; in the Moniteur, 1810, No. cxlvi; and in Schlegel's Indischer Bibl. i, p. 9.

and Mahratta languages, in the college of Fort William, *Serampoor*, printed at the *Mission Press*, 1806, 2 vols. large 4to; *Calcutta*, 1808, 4to; *London*, 1813, 4to. This work is compiled from original treatises, and is highly esteemed. It is reviewed in the Quarterly, vol. i, where it is said to be everywhere useful, laborious, and exact. It is now scarce, and its high price, seven guineas, is rather against it. Besides this, as it is principally founded on the grammars called *Mugdabodha*, in use in Bengal, it is liable to the objections, urged above, to the treatise of Vopa deva[q].

An Essay on the Principles of Sanscrit Grammar, with tables of inflections, by H. P. Forster, esq. senior merchant of the Bengal establishment, *Calcutta*, 1810, 4to. vol. i. This work has the merit of being the first written of all the Sanscrit grammars compiled by Europeans; it was not, however, published till the year mentioned. Its continuation was interrupted by the death of the author, in 1815. There is an ample notice of this grammar, by Bopp, in the Heidelberg. Jahrb. 1818, No. xxx.

In the year 1810, a Complete Grammar of the Sanscrit Language, by a Catholic missionary at Sira, was published at *Calcutta*.

A Grammar of the Sanscrit Language, by H. T. Colebrooke, esq. vol. i, *Calcutta*, printed at the *Hon. Company's Press*, 1805, fol.; *London*, 1815, fol.; *Calcutta*, 1825, fol. In his preface to this work the author gives a catalogue of more than a hundred Sanscrit works and treatises on grammar.

A Grammar of the Sanskrita Language, by Charles Wilkins, L. L. D. F. R. S. *London*, 1808, 4to; 1813, 4to; 1815, 4to. Wilkins, the author of this grammar, was

[q] See above p. 22; and Edin. Review, vol. xiii, p. 367.

the first European who successfully studied the Sanscrit language, and the first who introduced its literature to the acquaintance of the western world. The Mugdha-bodha, the Sútras of Pánini, together with the works of Bhattoji Dikshita and Ramachandra, as well as several other native grammarians, have been consulted in the construction of this work, which in all quarters has been spoken of with the highest praise. The author's complete knowledge of the structure of the Sanscrit has enabled him to discard the technical terms and arbitrary arrangements of the Indian grammarians, unless where these really facilitate the study to an intelligent European. In short, Mr. Wilkins's performance seems to unite the appropriate excellences of a grammar—accuracy, conciseness, and perspicuity; and may be regarded as the most clear, methodical, and useful grammar of the Sanscrit language that has yet appeared[r].

Terms of Sanscrit Grammar, with references to Wilkins's Grammar, *London*, 1815, 4to.

Sungskrit Grammar, with examples for the exercise of the student, *London*, 1813, 4to.

A Grammar of the Sungskrit Language, on a new plan, by William Yeates, *Calcutta*, 1820, 8vo. See Classical Journal, No. xlvi, p. 413, etc. An unfavourable opinion is given of this work in Ind. Bibl. II. i, p. 11, etc. and in the Asiat. Journal, Jan. 1832, p. 18, it is said that a more jejune and imperfect grammar was never compiled of a language.

W. S. Majewsky o Slawianach i ich pobratymasch, *Warschau*, 1816, 8vo. Part I, on the Sanscrit language,

[r] See Edin. Review, vol. xiii, p. 366; and Quarterly Review, vol. i, p. 53, where this grammar forms the subject of two interesting essays on the Sanscrit language. Wilkins's work is also noticed at some length by Chézy in the Moniteur, 1810, No. cxlvi: see likewise Götting. gel. Anz. 1815, st. 113.

a sketch of its grammar, tables of Sanscrit characters, a brief vocabulary, etc.; principally taken from Paulinus a S. Bartholomæo.

Institutiones ad fundamenta veteris Linguæ Indicæ, quæ Sanscrita dicitur, auctore Em. Fr. Car. Rosenmüller, *Lipsiæ*, 1818, 4to.

Grammatica Sanscrita, nunc primum in Germania edidit Othmarus Frank, *Wirceburgi et Lipsiæ*, 1823, 4to. with numerous lithographic tables. See Jenaische Allg. Lit. Zeit. 1827, No. cxcix.

Ausführliches Lehrgebäude der Sanskrita Sprache, von Friedr. Bopp, *Berlin*, 1824, large 4to. Erstes Heft; Zweites Heft, 1825; Drittes Heft, 1827. Of this work, which is generally spoken of as an excellent performance, there is a copious review, by Burnouf, fils, in the Journal Asiatique, Cah. xxxiii, p. 298—314; xxxvi, p. 359—372. See also Erganz. Bl. zur Jen. Allg. Lit. Zeit. 1826, Nos. xxviii, xxix. This grammar by Bopp, in the German language, is now out of print and rare; the first part of it, however, has been republished in a language which will render it more generally available to English scholars, among whom it is much recommended, under the following title:

Grammatica Critica Linguæ Sanscritæ, a Francisco Bopp. Fasciculus prior, quo continentur euphoniæ leges una cum declinationis et conjugationis doctrina, *Berol.* 1829, 4to. 15s. The remainder of this work is anxiously looked for. Bopp's grammar, as indeed is the case generally with German philologists, is busied too much about the bare form and grammatical inflections of words, and the philosophy of the language, rather than the objects of the language itself; and on that account, excellent and accurate as it is in the above respects, it is by no means so inviting to general students as those grammars which have been compiled less with a view of exhibiting the abstract niceties of inflection and construction, than with the more useful object of enabling the learner to derive practical information, which is the more legitimate end of studying languages.

Elements of the Sanscrit Language, or an easy Guide to the Indian Tongues, by W. Price, *London*, 1827, 4to.

Tabulæ quædam ad Orthographiam et Grammaticam Linguæ Sanscritæ spectantes. In Othm. Frankii Chrestomathia Sanskrita, *Monaci*, 1821, 4to.

Analyse Grammaticale, en Anglais, du commencement de l'ouvrage Sanscrit, intitulé, *Hitopadesa*, in 4to. vide Catal. de la Bibl. de Mr. Langlès, p. 117, No. 1008.

Under this head must be noticed the following work by Lebedeff, although it does not enter very deeply into the Sanscrit:

A Grammar of the Pure and Mixed East Indian Dialects, with Dialogues affixed, spoken in all the Eastern Countries, methodically arranged at Calcutta, according to the Brahmenian system of the Samscrit language, comprehending literal explanations of the compound words and circumlocutory phrases, necessary for the attainment of the idiom of that language, etc. together with a Samscrit Alphabet; and several specimens of Oriental poetry published in the Asiatic Researches, by Herasim Lebedeff, *London*, 1801, 4to[s].

Grammatica Granthamica[t], seu Samscrdamica. An extract from the *Sidharúbam*, by a missionary named

[s] See Mithridates, vol. iv, p. 59—61. The learned author of the Uebersicht der orientalischen Literatur im Brittischen Indien, which is inserted in the Leipz. Lit. Zeitung, 1817, No. lxxii, pronounces the following judgment upon Lebedeff's performance: this volume contains scarcely anything of what its long title promises. See also Asiat. Annual Register, 1802, p. 41; and Catal. de la Bibl. de M. Langlès, p. 117, No. 1009.

[t] See the explanation of this word above, p. 7.

Joh. Ernst Hanxleden, († 1732) a manuscript in the library of the Propaganda at Rome[u].

Langlès cites in the Catalogue des MSS. Samscrits, p. 94, Grammaire Samscrite et Latine abrégée, suivie de l'*Amara Kôcha*, traduit en Latin en grande partie, et d'un Dictionnaire des Verbes Samscrits, avec leur signification également en Latin. A manuscript in the Royal Library at Paris.

Respecting the announcement of a Sanscrit Grammar, by General Boisserolle, of Paris, see below, p. 37.

3. *Treatises on Particular Parts of Sanscrit Grammar.*

Ueber die Sprache und Weisheit der Indier, von Fr. Schlegel. In the first section.

Ueber einzelne Theile der Sanskrit-Grammatik, in Heeren's Ideen, Indier, p. 93, sqq. edit. 1824.

Grammatical Tables, in Othm. Frankii Chrestomathia Sanscrita, *Monaci*, 1820, 4to.

De la Déclinaison Sanscrite, in *Yadjnadattabada*, ou la Mort de *Yadjnadatta*, épisode extrait du *Ramayana*, traduit par A. L. Chézy, *Paris*, 1826, 4to.; Préface, p. xix—xxi.

Ueber das Conjugationssystem der Sanskrit Sprache in Vergleichung mit jenem der griechischen, lateinischen, persischen und germanischen Sprache. Nebst Episoden des *Ramajan* und *Mahabharat*, in genauen metrischen Uebersetzungen aus dem Originaltexte und einigen Abschnitten aus den Veda's, von Franz Bopp. Herausgegeben und mit Vorerinnerung begleitet von Dr. Karl Jos. Windischmann, *Frankf. a. M.* 1816, 8vo. The same work was published in English by the author himself, improved and enriched with many additions, *Lond.* 1820, in the first part of the Annals of

[u] The report spread abroad in the French and German periodicals, that the celebrated linguist Raske published a newly arranged Sanscrit Grammar, during his abode at St. Petersburgh in 1820, is without foundation.

Oriental Literature, p. 1—65, under the following title: Analytical Comparison of the Sanskrit, Greek, Latin, and Teutonic Languages, showing the original identity of their grammatical structure. The Persian is here omitted, but is promised in a larger work: see Götting. gel. Anz. 1821, St. 54, 55.

De la Conjugaison Sanscrite, in *Yadjnadattabada*, trad. par Chézy, Préface, p. xxi—xxvi.

Tableau comparatif des Supins Latins et des Infinitifs Sanscrits. Par le Compte Lanjuinais, in the Mercure de France, 1814, Juin, p. 490.

Upon the Sanscrit Infinitives in Alex. Murray's History of the European Languages, *Edinb.* 1823, vol. ii, p. 410.

Ueber die in der Sanskritsprache durch Suffixa gebildeten Verbalformen, von Wilh. Freid. von Humboldt; in A. W. von Schlegel's Ind. Biblioth. I. iv, p. 433—467; and ii, p. 71—134.

Ueber die Præfixa die Sanskritsprache, in Fr. Bopp's Ausf. Lehrg. der Sanskrita-Sprache, i, p. 71—83.

On the effect of emphasis on the persons of the subjunctive in Sanscrit verbs, in Al. Murray's Hist. of the Europ. Languages, vol. i, p. 340.

A complete catalogue of the Sanscrit words for the cardinal and ordinal numbers, will be found in Haughton's Bengalee Grammar and Chrestomathie, *Calcutta*, 1825.

Mémoire sur la Séparation des Mots dans les Textes Sanscrits, par M. G. de Humboldt, in the Journ. Asiat. Sept. 1827, No. lxiii, p. 163—172.

Ueber den Dualis in der Sanskrit-Sprache, in Wilh. v. Humboldt Ueber den Dualis, *Berlin*, 1828, 4to.

Sur un Usage Remarquable de l'Infinitif Sanscrit; par Eugène Burnouf, fils, in the Journ. Asiat. vol. v, p. 120.

DICTIONARIES.

For information respecting Sanscrit dictionaries and grammars, see Colebrooke's preface to his edition of *Umuru-Coshu;* Wilson in the introduction to his dictionary; and J. S. Vater in his Proben deutscher Volksmundarten u. s. w. s. 172.

1. *On the Primitive Words of the Sanscrit.*

A treatise upon Sanscrit primitives, written in this language itself, in the royal library at Paris, under the title, *Kavi Kalpa Druma,* i. e. Plant of the Poet's Wish, by *Bopa Dêva,* or *Vopadeva.* See Catalogue des mss. Sanscrits, p. 78. This *Kavikalpadruma* is quoted by Carey in his Sanscrit Grammar.

The number of Sanscrit roots does not amount, according to Langlès, to more than ten thousand: see Catalogue des mss. Sanscrits, etc. p. 25. According to Rosen, there are only about two thousand three hundred and fifty, and, if taken strictly, much less.

Srî Dhâtumanyarî, by *Kasinâtha.* The Radicals of the Sanscrita Language (by Charles Wilkins), *London,* 1815, 4to.

Upon the Sanscrit roots see Bopp's Ausführliches Lehrgebäude der Sanskrita Sprache, i, p. 71—83.

A Dissertation on Sanscrit Roots, by H. G. Forster, in his translation of Mugdabodah, a celebrated treatise on Sanscrit grammar, *Calcutta,* 1810, 4to.

View of the principal significations of the radical words in the European languages, and in the Persic and Sanscrit, in Alex. Murray's History of the European Languages, *Edinburgh,* 1823, vol. i, p. 229—254.

Corporis Radicum Sanscritarum Prolusio. Auctore Frid. Rosen, *Berolini,* 1826, 8vo. Analysed by Eugène Burnouf, fils, in the Journ. Asiat. ix, p. 374.

Radices Sanscritæ, illustratas edidit Fridericus Rosen, *Berolini*, 1827, large 8vo. A detailed review of this work, by P. von Bohlen, is to be found in the Jahrbüchern für wissenschaftliche Kritik, *Berlin*, 1828, No. ix—xii.

2. *Ancient Dictionaries.*

The most ancient Sanscrit dictionary is called *Nama parayana*. It is superseded by the *Amra cosha* or *Ameracasha*, the treasure of *Amara*, a dictionary in verse, according to the order of subjects, with numerous commentaries.

From Wilson (Preface to his Dictionary) and W. Ward (Account of the History of the Hindoos) we learn that there are, altogether, seventy-six ancient Sanscrit dictionaries, many of which are as old as the *Amera cósha* (see Asiatic Researches, vol. vii, 214), whose author, *Amer-Sinh*, or *Amara-Singa*, the immortal lion, resided at the splendid court of *Vicramaditya*. († 56 B. C.[x])

Amarasinha, seu Dictionarii Samscrudamici sectio I, de Cœlo, ex tribus ineditis codicibus Indicis MSS. curante P. Paulino a S. Bartholomæo, Carmelita discalceato, LL. Orient. prælectore, missionum Asiaticarum syndico, etc., *Romæ*, 1798, 4to. Typis congreg. de propag. fide, xii, and 60 p. Containing only the first section, concerning God and heaven, with various passages, or strings of verses.

[x] See the preface to Wilson's Dictionary.

Bentley (Asiat. Researches, vii, 6, 4to.; vi, 578, 8vo.) endeavours to prove that neither *Vicramàditya* nor *Amera Sinha*, lived before the tenth or eleventh century of the Christian era; but his opinions are examined and satisfactorily refuted by professor Heeren. At all events he was an eminent poet, and one of the nine gems (for so these poets were called) who were the ornament of Vicramàditya's court. From Mr. Colebrooke's note, the settlement of the century in which he lived is a subject for the investigation of chronologists. See Asiatic Researches, vol. vii, p. 214, 8vo.

The whole of this dictionary has been since published by Colebrooke, under the following title:

Umuru-Coshu, or, a Dictionary of the Sanscrit Language, by *Umuru-Singhu*, with an English Interpretation, Annotations, and Alphabetical Index, by H. T. Colebrooke, Serampoor, printed at the *Mission Press*, 1803, 4to.; 1808, 4to.; reprinted at *London*, 1811, 4to. and again 1813, 4to. in the Deva Nagari character. This contains about ten thousand roots; and explains, in seventeen chapters, the names of the gods, of men, of the stars, elements, etc[y]. Table alphabétique pour *l'Amara Cosha* publié par M. Colebrooke, par M. Jules Klaproth, in his Table alphabétique du Journal Asiatique, *Paris*, 1829, 8vo. p. 105—111.

An ample description of the work of *Amara-Sinha* will be found in Q. Craufurd's Researches of Ancient and Modern India, every word of which is taken from Colebrooke's paper, in Asiatic Researches, vol. vii, p. 199, so frequently referred to, and in the Catalogue des MSS. Sanscrits, p. 23—26, where other manuscript dictionaries are mentioned; one, for example, under the title of *Viswa-Prâkasa*, i. e. the Enlightened World, by *Maheswara*. Langlès, in the same work, p. 76, describes also a manuscript commentary upon the *Amara-Sinha*, by *Nayan Ananda Dêwa*.

Eleven commentaries upon this great work are mentioned by Wilson, in the Preface to his Dictionary, and four others by Ward, in his Account of the History, etc. of the Hindoos, vol. ii, p. 474, sqq.

A further account of this work will be found in the work of Ward just referred to, p. 576; in the first part of the Indischen Bibliothek, p. 12, by A. W. v.

[y] P. Paulinus holds a different opinion respecting the title and antiquity of this dictionary from the one at present adopted by English scholars.

Schlegel; and in Colebrooke's paper on the Sanscrit and Pracrit Languages, in the Asiatic Researches, vol. vii, 199, and in the preface to his edition of it.

Hema-chandra-Cosha, or, the Vocabulary of *Hémachandra*, Calcutta, 1807, 8vo. 1818, 8vo[z].

The *Umuru-Kôshu, Trikândusheshu, Medinee*, and *Haravulee*, four original vocabularies, Nagree character, printed 1807, at the Shunskrit Press at Khizurpoor near *Calcutta*, 8vo.

Four Sanscrit Vocabularies: the *Amaracosha, Tricánda Sésha, Hárávalì*, and *Médini Cosa*, published by H. T. Colebrooke, esq. *Calcutta*, 1818, 8vo.

These five ancient vocabularies, namely[a], *Hoima*, by Hema Chandra; *Amara Kosha*, by Amara-Singa; *Trikanda-Shesha* and *Haravali*, by Purushottumu, and *Medini*[b], of which some appear to be abridgements, and others supplements of the *Amera-Cosha*, are only printed in the original language[c].

Among the supplements to this Dictionary must also be reckoned *Ecácshara*, a little collection of monograms, by Purushottumu, whom I have just mentioned; the *Dháranicosha*, and the vocabularies of Helaynda Váchespati, and some others.

Amara-Sataka, Ghata Karparam, Sanscrit, *Calcutta*, 1818, 8vo.

Divirupa-Kosha, a dictionary of homonymes, in the Devanâgari character, is the title of a MS. in the

[z] The Cosha of *Hémachandra* is important for explaining the theological terms of the *Jains*, as is the Cosha of *Amarasinha* for those of the *Buddhists*.

[a] The titles here given are taken from Th. Roebuck's Annals of the College of Fort William, p. 32, 33. See also Catalogue de la Bibl. de M. Langlès, p. 116, No. 1005.

[b] See Ward, View of the History, Literature, and Mythology of the Hindoos, vol. i, p. 577.

[c] See Colebrooke on Sanscrit and Pracrit, in Asiat. Researches, vol. vii, p. 218, and Wilson's Sanscrit Dictionary, Pref. p. xxvii.

royal library at Copenhagen; where there is also a vocabulary in manuscript, inscribed with the title of *Sarasvata;* and another by Gada Sinha Nanarthadaanimanjari. See Dansk Litter. Tidende for 1819, p. 124.

3. *Modern Dictionaries.*

Yayadeva, printed entirely in Sanscrit, at *Calcutta,* p. 68, in oblong 8vo. According to Ward (View of the History, etc. vol. i, p. 584) it is a short treatise for the explanation of difficult passages and expressions in ancient writers.

A Catalogue of Indian Plants (419), comprehending their Sanscrit, and as many of their Linnæan generic names, as could with any degree of precision be ascertained, by Sir Will. Jones, in the Dissertations relating to the History and Antiquities of Asia, *London,* 1798, vol. iv, p. 234—238. See also his Works, vol. ii, p. 39, 4to. edit.

Fleming's Catalogue of Indian Medicinal Plants and Drugs, with their Names in the Hindustani and Sanscrit Languages, *Calcutta,* 1825, 8vo.

Dictionary of Mohammedan Law, Bengal Revenue Terms, Sanscrit, Hindoo, and other words used in the East Indies, with full explanations, by S. Rousseau, *London,* 1802, 8vo.

Sanscrit and Hindoo Dictionary, by S. Rousseau, *London,* 1812, 4to.

A Dictionary, Sanscrit and English, translated, amended, and enlarged, from an original compilation, prepared by learned natives for the college of Fort William, by Horace Hayman Wilson, secretary of the Asiatic Society, *Calcutta,* 1819, 4to.[d]. This, as the

[d] A greatly improved and enlarged edition of Wilson's Dictionary is now in the press, and was expected to be out by the end of the past year.

title expresses, is rather a condensation of the best ancient dictionaries than an original work. It is compiled by Raghumani Bhattâ Charya, and corrected, arranged, and translated into English by Wilson. See Bopp's Review of this dictionary, in the Götting. Gel. Anz. 1821, St. 36, and Indische Bibliothek, von A. W. v. Schlegel, i, 3, s. 295—364, ii, 1, s. 2—11.

A Sungscrit Vocabulary, containing the nouns, adjectives, verbs, and indeclinable particles, most frequently occurring in the Sungscrit language, arranged in a grammatical order, with an explanation in Bengalee and English, by William Yates, *Calcutta*, 1820, 8vo. Table alphabétique pour le Vocabulaire Sanscrit de M. Yates, par M. Jules Klaproth, in his Table alphabétique du Journal Asiatique, *Paris*, 1829, 8vo. p. 112—135.

Sabda Kalpa Druma, a Sanscrit Dictionary, by Rada Canta Deb, of which the first part was published, *Calcutta*, 1828. See Asiat. Journ. xxv, 497.

San sifan man meng han sti yao, ou Recueil nécessaire de Mots Sanscrits, Tangutains, Mandshous, Mongols, par M. Abel Rémusat. From a Polyglott Dictionary written in China. In the Fundgruben des Orients, tom. iv, 3, 183.

Vocabularium Malabarico-Samscrdamico-Lusitanum, auctore P. Joan. Em. Hanxleden, a manuscript in the library of the Propaganda at Rome.

Anquetil du Perron left also a Sanscrit Dictionary in manuscript, in his own hand writing, and in a fit state for the press, large folio. See Magasin Encyclop. An v, vol. i, p. 241.

The Royal Asiatic Society of London possesses also a Sanscrit Dictionary, compiled in modern times, which bears the name of *Sabda Calpa Druma*, with

Professor Wilson has also the materials for a Sanscrit Dictionary, arranged upon etymological principles. See Memorial to Convocation.

the words explained in Bengalee. See Asiat. Journ. 1828, April, p. 481.

An Original Dictionary, Sanscrit and English, by Alex. Hamilton, is mentioned among the manuscripts in the Oriental catalogue of Howell and Steward, 1827, Suppl. p. 102, No. 4433. In the Journal Asiat. May, 1825, p. 319, general Boisserole announces his intention to publish a grammar and dictionary of the Sanscrit language, for which new types were already cut, of which he gives a very handsome specimen. So far as I know, however, no portion of the work has yet appeared.

Glossarium Sanscritum, auct. Fr. Bopp, Fascic. i, *Berolini*, 1829, 4to.

COMPARISON OF THE SANSCRIT WITH OTHER LANGUAGES.

THE great number of languages which are said to owe their origin, or bear a close affinity to the Sanscrit, is truly astonishing, and is another proof of its high antiquity[f]. A German writer has asserted it to be the parent of upwards of a hundred languages and

[f] After all, the literary world seem much divided respecting the high antiquity of Hindoo learning. Tennemann says, "Writers who have entered deeply into the study of history, with a view to its bearing on theology, have declared the Hebrews to be the primitive race; others, the Egyptians; and lastly, both these have been displaced by the Hindoos." This opinion, which is supported by Fred. Schlegel, is learnedly and forcibly combatted by Ritter, who has devoted a chapter of his History of Philosophy to the examination of this subject. Those who consult it will not be disappointed; as in it he has condensed, with much ability, all that could be gathered on the subject, and placed it before the reader in an elegant and attractive form. It has been published since the work of Adelung. See Tenneman's Manual of the History of Philosophy, translated by the Rev. Arthur Johnson, *Oxford*, 1832, 8vo. Schlegel (Fred.) Ueber Sprache u. s. a. der Indier; and, Geschichte der Philosophie, von Dr. Heinrich Ritter, *Hamb*. 1829, 8vo. vol. i, p. 58—137.

dialects; among which he enumerates twelve Indian, seven Median-Persic, two Arnautic-Albanian, seven Greek, eighteen Latin, fourteen Sclavonian, and six Celtic-Gallic[g]. It seems a remarkable fact, that the various theories in which learned men have latterly so much indulged respecting the origin and affinities of languages, all tend to confirm this statement; for, however widely they may be opposed to one another in the results of their speculations, they nearly all fix upon the Sanscrit as the basis of some part of their argument; thus all tacitly acknowledging the antiquity and influence of that language. The various vocabularies which we now possess, and the results of the laborious and learned investigations which the next few pages will detail, render it pretty evident, that the Sanscrit has not only furnished words for all the languages of Europe, but forms a main feature in almost all those of the East. A host of writers have made it the immediate parent of the Greek, and Latin, and German families of languages; or regarded some of these as descended from it through a language now extinct[h]. With the Persian and Zend it has been almost identified by Sir William Jones and others. Halhed notices the similitude of Sanscrit and Arabic words; and this not merely in technical and metaphorical terms, but in the main groundwork of language[i]. In a contrary direction the Indo-Chinese, and other dialects in that quarter, all seem to be closely allied to it. One original language seems, in a very remote period, to have pervaded the whole Indian archipelago, and to have spread toward Madagascar on one side, and the islands in the South-sea

[g] Rudiger, in Neuern Geschichte der Evangelischen Missions-Anstalten, st. 66, s. 59.

[h] See above, p. 3.

[i] Preface to his Grammar of the Bengal Language.

on the other; but in proportion," adds the historian from whom I borrow this remark, "as we find any of these tribes more highly advanced in the arts of civilised life than others, in nearly the same proportion do we find the language enriched by a corresponding accession of Sanscrit terms, directing us at once to the source whence civilisation flowed towards these regions [k]."

Further information on this subject will be found in the following works:

Researches into the Origin and Affinity of the principal Languages of Asia and Europe, by Lieut. Col. Vans Kennedy, *London*, 1824, 8vo. See an able review of this work in Asiatic Journal, January, 1832, p. 1, etc; in which much information will be found on this subject.

The Eastern Origin of the Celtic Nations proved by a Comparison of their Dialects with the Sanscrit, Greek, Latin, and Teutonic Languages, by James Cowles Prichard, M. D. F. R. S. etc., *Oxford*, 1831, 8vo.

Ueber die Uebereinkunft des Sanskrits mit den Wörten anderer alten Sprachen, see Adelung, Mithridates, vol. i, p. 149, etc.

A comparison of the Indian words found in ancient writers, in Hadr. Relandi Diss. Miscell. (de veteri lingua Indica), *Traj. ad Rhen.* 1706, 8vo. tom. i, p. 757, vol. iv, p. 424.

Synglosse Indo-Européenne par M. Eichhoff, *Paris*, 1829, containing a comparison of the principal languages of Europe with one another, and with the Sanscrit.

1. *With the Indian Languages.*

La Croze quotes, in his Hist. du Christ. des Indes,

[k] Raffles's Hist. of Java, vol. ii, p. 369.

tom. ii, p. 303, a Tamulic work of the twelfth century, *Divagarum*[l], in which is said to be proved the derivation of all the other Indian languages from the Sanscrit.

Plan of a Comparative Vocabulary of Indian Languages, by Sir James Mackintosh, in the Transactions of the Literary Society of Bombay, *London*, 1819, 4to. vol. i, p. 297.

Familienverwandtschaft der indischen Sprachen, von. G. Blumhardt, *Nürnberg*, 1819, 8vo.

Affinity of the Sanscrit with the Prakrit, Pali, and Zend, in which is described the most holy books of the Jains, by Dr. Leyden, in Asiatic Researches, vol. x, p. 279; and in Essai sur le Pali, etc. par E. Burnouf et Chr. Lassen, *Paris*, 1826, 8vo[m].

Ivar Abel Symphona symphona, seu XI Ling. Orient. discors exhibita concordia, Tamulicæ videlicet, Gran-

[l] See above, p. 8.

[m] These three dialects, the Prakrit, the Pali, and the Zend, are probably the most ancient derivatives from the Sanscrit. The great mass of vocables in all the three, and even the forms of inflection, both in verbs and nouns, are derived from the Sanscrit. The Pali alphabet seems to be derived from the Devanâgari. Leyden's Essay, as above. Again, professor Wilson observes, "There is one question of some interest attaching to the construction of the Prakrit, which seems to merit a fuller enquiry than has yet been given to it; namely, Does it represent a dialect that was ever spoken; or is it an artificial modification of the Sanscrit language, devised to adapt the latter to peculiar branches of literature? The latter," he continues, "seems the most likely." There certainly appears something very mysterious about these languages. If the Prakrit be no more than a modification of the Sanscrit, why may not the Sanscrit be a device, or the modification of some other ancient language? Why, indeed, may not the round assertion of a recent critic be true, who affirms that this language never could have been spoken, and that it is a fabrication from beginning to end? See Wilson's Preface to his Hindoo Theatre, p. 70; and Theological Review, vol. v, p. 360. This opinion, however, is forcibly combatted by Heeren, in his Researches on the Indians; who acutely remarks, that it is not very easy to define what is meant by inventing a language; and asks how it is possible for any literature to be fully developed unless through the medium of vernacular speech.

thamicæ, Telugicæ, *Samscrutamicæ*, Marathicæ, Balabandicæ, Canaricæ, Hindostanicæ, Cuncanicæ, Guzuraticæ, et Peguanicæ non characteristicæ, quibus ut explicativo-harmonica adjuncta est Latina, *Hafniæ*, 1782, 8vo.

History and Languages of the Indian Islands, in Edinburgh Review, vol. v, 23.

Ueber die Verzweigungen der indischen Sprachen mit dem Sanskrit in einer systematischen Aufzählung derjenigen Sprachen, welche in Vorderund Hinter-Indien und in den anstossenden Ländern gesprochen werden, von Joseph von Hammer, in the Wiener Jahrbüchern der Literatur, 1818, vol. ii, p. 276—290.

The affinity of the Sanscrit to several Indian dialects and kindred languages, is also shown by M. Wilhelm Palmblad, in his essays on the origin of the Hindoos, in the Swedish Journal, Svea, für Wissenschaft und Kunst, *Upsala*, 1819, vol. ii, p. 1—168.

Fundgruben des Orients, vol. i, p. 459, 460.

Franz Alter's treatise, already quoted, upon the Sanscrit language.

Concerning the influence of the Sanscrit upon all the languages of the East Indian archipelago, see Crawford's History of the Indian Archipelago, *Edinburgh*, 1820, 8vo. vol. ii, p. 71, and Raffles's Java, vol. ii, 369.

Concerning the Sanscrit and its connection with the East Indian languages which have sprung from it, in Vater's Proben deutscher Volksmundarten u. s. w. p. 169—194.

Elucidation of the Hindoo family of languages descended from the Sanscrit, in Carl Ritter's Erdkunde im Verhältnisse zur Natur und zur Geschichte des Menschen u. s. w. *Berlin*, 1817, 8vo. Anhang, p. 800.

Q. Craufurd's Researches on Ancient and Modern India, vol. ii, p. 182, 183, 190, 236—238.

Indian, and the languages related to the Sanscrit, in Asia Polyglotta von Julius Klaproth, p. 53, 387—415.

2. *With the Bohemian or Gypsy Language.*

Mithridates von J. C. Adelung, Th. i, p. 244.

3. *With the Zend.*

Paulini a Bartholomæo Diss. de Antiquitate et Affinitate Linguarum Zendicæ, Samscritanicæ, et Germanicæ, *Padovæ*, 1798, 4to. Two hundred Zend and sixty German words are here compared with the Sanscrit.

The affinity of the Sanscrit to the Zend, by Dr. Leyden, in Asiatic Researches, vol. x, p. 279.

Investigation of the affinity which the Sanscrit bears to the Zend, in Link's Urwelt, p. 162—172.

4. *With the Persian.*

Halhed in the preface to his Grammar of the Bengal Language.

A Dictionary or Vocabulary of those words in Persian which are derived from, or have Synonymes in the Sanscrit. A manuscript in the Supplement to Howell and Stewart's Oriental Catalogue for 1827, *London*, p. 101[n].

De Affinitate qua Lingua Sanscrdamica cum ea Persarum ita conjuncta est, ut potius ab hac illa, quam ab illa hæc naturali ordine sit derivanda, in Othm. Frankii Comment. de Persidis Lingua et Genio.

Comparaison du Persan avec le Samskrit, in the Tableaux Synoptiques, ou Mots similaires qui se

[n] It is described as a small thick folio, very neatly and plainly written; and is priced at 7*l*. 7*s*.

trouvent dans les langues Persane, Samskrite, Grecque, etc., par H. A. le Pileur, *Leyde*, 1814, 8vo. p. 40.

Franz Bopp über das Conjugationssystem der Samskritsprache, p. 116—136.

Concerning the Sanscrit language and its affinity to the Persian, in J. S. Vater's Proben deutscher Volksmundarten u. s. w. p. 169.

On the identity of the Persian and Sanscrit languages, in Alex. Murray's History of the European Languages, vol. ii, p. 379; and, concerning the light which the Sanscrit throws upon the structure of Persian words, in the same, p. 418.

Letters on India, by Maria Graham, *London*, 1817, 8vo.

Commentatio de Adfinitate priscæ Indorum Linguæ, quam Sanscritam dicunt, cum Persarum, Græcorum, Romanorum, atque Germanorum Sermone, P. i, *Vindobonæ*, 1827, 4to. See Jenaische Allg. Lit. Zeit. 1827, No. 199.

5. *With the Chinese.*

The Chinese letters and language compared with the Sanscrit, in a Dissertation on the Character and Sounds of the Chinese Language, etc. by J. Marshman, *Serampoor*, 1809, 4to., and also in Quarterly Review, vol. v, p. 393, etc. See also vol. xv, p. 367, etc.

6. *With the Arabic.*

See Halhed's preface to his Grammar of the Bengal Language, 1778, 4to.

Many Hebrew and Arabic words are compared with the Sanscrit, Malay, Mahratta, Turkish, Tartaric, Chinese, etc., by Math. Norberg, in his Vater-Unser in den Sprachen Asiens in Nova Acta Reg. Societ. Scientiar. Upsal. vol. ix, p. 207, etc. Only the beginning, however, of Norberg's work has appeared, death having put an end to his labours.

7. *With the Greek.*

Sir William Jones says, (Asiat. Research. vol. i, p. 422,) "The Sanscrit language, whatever may be its antiquity, is of a wonderful structure; more perfect than the Greek, more copious than the Latin, and more exquisitely refined than either; yet bearing to both of them a stronger affinity, both in the roots of verbs and in the forms of grammar, than could have been produced by accident; so strong, that no philologer could examine all the three, without believing them to be sprung from one common source, which perhaps no longer exists." The Rev. Dr. Browne observes, in a letter inserted in the Reports of the Bible Society, "The Sanscrit answers to Greek, as face answers face in a glass. The translation into it of the New Testament will be perfect, while it will be almost verbal: it will be published with the Greek on the opposite page, as soon as we can procure Greek types. You will find the verb in the corresponding mood and tense; the noun and adjective in the corresponding case and gender: the idiom and government are the same; where the Greek is absolute so is the Sanscrit; and, in many instances, the primitives or roots are the same." See Appendix to Barker's edition of Cicero de Senectute, Valpy, 1811, p. xcviii.

Connection between the Sanscrit and Greek, Asiat. Journal, 1830, vol. i, p. 325.

On the grammatical analogy which subsists between the Sanscrit, the Latin, and the Greek, in Philological Conjectures, by Dr. Wait, in Asiat. Journ. May, 1830, p. 15.

Resemblances of the Sanscrit, Greek, and Roman Numerals, in Asiat. Journ. iv, 117.

A comparison of the Sanscrit with the Greek, in Prichard's Eastern Origin of the Celtic Nations.

Sur les Rapports entre le Sanskrit et le Grec et le Latin, tant pour la Construction Grammaticale que pour les Mots. In the correspondence of Barthélemy Anquetil with the missionary P. Cœurdoux. See Mémoires de l'Académie des Inscr. tom. xlix, p. 647—712. As a Supplement to Anquetil's treatise upon the Ganges of the ancients.

Halhed, in the preface to his Bengal Grammar.

A parallel between the Greek, Latin, and Sanskrita languages, in the Classical Journal, No. xii, p. 375—384; No. xvii, p. 219—222; and Suppl. to No. xviii, p. 528—538.

Franz. Bopp über das Conjugationssystem der Sanskritsprache, p. 61, etc. This author's investigations of the affinity of the Sanscrit with the Greek, which he first began in this work, were much amplified in the Vergleichenden Zergliederung des Sanskrit und der damit verwandten Sprachen, Erster Versuch, printed among the treatises of the Berlin Academy of Sciences, *Wiss.* 1824, 4to. In English, Analytical Comparison of the Sanskrit, Latin, and Teutonic Languages, showing the original identity of their grammatical structure, printed in the Annals of Oriental Literature, P. i, p. 1—65, reviewed by Burnouf, fils, in the Journal Asiat. P. vi, p. 52, et 113.

De usu linguæ Brachmanum sacræ in causis linguæ Græcæ et Latinæ indagandis, Programma, auctore A. W. de Schlegel, *Bonn*, 1819, 4to.

A parallel between the Greek, Latin, Celtic, and Sanscrit, in Alex. Murray's History of the European Languages, *Edinburgh*, 1823, vol. i, p. 149; vol. ii, p. 228. In German, Zum Europäischen Sprachenbau, oder Forschungen über die Verwandtschaft der Teutonen, Griechen, Celten, Slaven, und Juden. Nach

A. Murray bearbeitet von A. Wagner, *Leipzig*, 1826, 2 Bde. 8vo.

Comparison of the Sanscrit with the Greek, in A. W. v. Schlegel's Indischer Bibl. ii, 3, p. 285.

Commentatio de Adfinitate priscæ Indorum Linguæ, quam Sanscritam dicunt, cum Persarum, Græcorum, Romanorum, atque Germanorum Sermone, P. i, *Vindobonæ*, 1827, 4to.

Affinity of the Sanscrit and Greek languages, in the third volume of the Elements of the Philosophy of the Human Mind, by Dugald Stewart, *Edinburgh*, 1827.

Beiträge zur allgemeinen vergleichenden Sprachkunde, von G. C. F. Lisch, *Berlin*, 1826, 8vo.; Erstes Heft, p. 6, sqq.

Ursprachlehre von Schmithenner, *Frankf. a. M.* 1826, 8vo.

8. *With the Latin.*

Halhed, in the preface to his Bengal Grammar.

Sir William Jones says, in the Preliminary Discourse to his translation of the Sakontala, " I began with translating it verbally into Latin, which bears so great resemblance to the Sanscrit, that it is more convenient than any other modern language for a scrupulous interlineary version." See also above, p. 45.

Fr. Paulini a S. Bartholomæo Diss. de Latini Sermonis Origine et cum Orientalibus connexione, *Romæ*, 1802, 4to. Contains only fifty-five Sanscrit words bearing affinity to the Latin.

Fr. Schlegel, in his treatise, Ueber die Weisheit und Sprache der Indier.

On the analogy of the Sanscrit with the Latin and other languages, in the Edinburgh Review, vol. xiv, p. 272.

On the conformity of the Latin and Sanskrita Languages, in the Edinburgh Review, 1811, Aug. No. xxxvi, p. 345.

In Tableau Comparatif, quoted above, p. 31, of Count Lanjuinais.

In the correspondence of Barthélemy, mentioned above.

A parallel between the Latin, Greek, and Sanskrita Languages, in the Classical Journal, Nos. xii, xvii, xviii.

Fr. Bopp über das Conjugationssystem der Sanskritsprache, p. 88—155; and his Analytical Comparison of the Sanskrit, Greek, Latin, and Teutonic Languages, in the Annals of Oriental Literature, P. I, p. 1—65.

A comparison of the Sanscrit with the Latin, in Prichard's Eastern Origin of the Celtic Nations.

On the Sanscrit and its affinity to the Latin, Persian, and German, J. S. Vater, in Proben deutscher Volksmundarten u. s. w. p. 169.

Letters on India, by Maria Graham, *London,* 1817, 8vo.

In the first section of Observations sur la Ressemblance frappante que l'on découvre entre la Langue des Russes et celle des Romains, *Milan,* 1817, 8vo.

In the preface to Fr. Bopp's Nalus, carmen Sanscritum, *Londini,* 1819, 8vo.

On the grammatical analogies between the Sanscrit, the Latin, etc., by Dr. Wait, see above, p. 45.

A parallel between the Greek, Latin, Celtic, and Sanscrit, in Alex. Murray's History of the European Languages, vol. i, p. 149.

Commentatio de Adfinitate priscæ Indorum Linguæ, quam Sanscritam dicunt, cum Persarum, Græcorum, Romanorum, atque Germanorum Sermone, Pars i, *Vindobonæ,* 1817, 4to.

9. *With the Celtic.*

Prichard's (Dr.) Eastern Origin of the Celtic Nations, proved by a Comparison of their Dialects with the Sanscrit, Greek, Latin, and Teutonic languages, *Oxford*, 1831, 8vo. A work which will be found very satisfactory on this subject.

Coincidences of the Sanscrit with the Gælic, in Hermes Scythicus; or the Radical Affinities of the Greek and Latin Languages, with the Gothic, etc., by John Jamieson, D. D. F. R. S. etc. *Edin.* 1814, 8vo. p. 218, etc.

They are also compared in Recueil de Monumens Antiques, la plupart inédits, et découverts dans l'Ancienne Gaule, etc. par Grivaud de la Vincelle, *Paris*, 1817, 4to. part i, p. 124.

A parallel between the Greek, Latin, Celtic, and Sanscrit, in Alex. Murray's History of the European Languages, vol. i, p. 149.

10. *With the Irish or Erse, Welsh, &c.*

The similarity between the Irish and the Sanscrit is very striking, and deserves further research, as is observed in Unterhaltungsblättern für Welt und Menschendkunde, 1825, No. xxxvii, p. 617; in the Journey through Ireland in the year 1818, which is there inserted[o].

[o] This has been done with great research, and, as I am informed by one well qualified to judge, with great ability, by Dr. Prichard in his Eastern Origin of the Celtic Nations. In this work the Sanscrit is not only compared with the Erse, or old Irish, and Welsh, but also with the other surviving dialects of the Celtic, namely, the Cornish, the Armorican, the Gælic, and the Manks. Further information on this subject may be found in Vallancy's Prospectus of a Dictionary of the Language of the the Airecoti, or Ancient Irish, compared with the language of the Cuti or Ancient Persians, with the Hindostanee, the Arabic, and Chaldean languages: with a Preface, containing an Epitome of the Ancient

11. *With the Gothic.*

Franz Bopp über das Conjugationssystem der Sanskritsprache, p. 116—157; and in his Analytical Comparison, see above, p. 46.

12. *With the German.*

Paul. a S. Bartholomæo de Antiquitate et Affinitate Linguarum Zendicæ, Samskritanicæ, et Germanicæ, *Padovæ*, 1798, 4to. Only sixty words are here compared with the Sanscrit.

Fr. Bopp über das Conjugationssystem der Sanskritsprache, p. 116—157; and in his Analytical Comparison in the Annals of Oriental Literature, P. i, p. 1—65.

Ueber das Sanskrit und seine Verhältnisse zum Germanischen, von J. S. Vater, in his Proben deutcher Volksmundarten u. s. w. p. 169.

On the identity of the Sanscrit with the Teutonic, in Alex. Murray's History of the European Languages, vol. ii, p. 228; in German, by A. Wagner, *Leipzig*, 1826, 2 Bde. 8vo.

Commentatio de Adfinitate priscæ Indorum Linguæ, quam Sanscritam dicunt, cum Persarum, Græcorum, Romanorum, atque Germanorum Sermone, Pars i, *Vindobonæ*, 1827, 4to.

Ursprachlehre. Entwurf zu einem System der Grammatik mit besonderer Rücksicht auf die Sprachen des indisch-deutschen Stammes: das Sanskrit, das Persische, die Pelasgischen, Slavischen, und Deutschen Sprachen, von Friedr. Schmitthenner, *Frankf. a. M.* 1826, 8vo.

History of Ireland, corroborated by late discoveries in the Puranas of the Brahmins, and by our learned countrymen in the East, etc. *Dublin*, 1803, 4to. See also his Collectanea de Rebus Hibernicis. *Dublin*, 1786, etc., 6 vols. 8vo., and his Grammmar of the Iberno-celtic or Irish Language, etc. *Dublin*, 1773, 4to.

Letters on India by Mrs. Graham; Edinburgh Review, xiii, 272; Prichard's Eastern Origin of the Celtic Nations; Kennedy's Researches into the Origin and Affinity of the principal Nations of Europe.

Origin and Affinity of the Languages of Asia and Europe, in Asiat. Journ. 1832, p. 1.

13. *With the Scandinavian Languages.*

Tableau des Peuples qui habitent l'Europe, etc., par Fréd. Schoell, second edition, p. 14.

On the affinity of the Sanscrit and Scandinavian languages, in La Scandinavie vengée de l'Accusation d'avoir produit les Peuples barbares, qui détruisirent l'empire de Rome, par M. Graberg de Hemso, *Lyons*, 1822, 8vo.

Undersögelse om det gamle Nordise eller Islandske Sprogs Oprindelse, forfattet af R. K. Rask, *Kjöbenhaven*, 1818, 4to.

Magnussen in the Index to the twelfth part of his Edda, *Copenhagen*, 1818, 4to.

14. *With the Sclavonic Languages.*

Aweiar's Kalwiorhuckam, oder Sittensprüche aus Tamulischen Palmblättern, mit Bemerkungen über indische Gelehrsamkeit, von J. C. C. Rüdiger, *Halle*, 1791, p. 26.

De lingua Rossica ex eadem cum Samscrdamica matre orientali prognata: adjectæ sunt observationes de ejusdem linguæ cum aliis cognatione, et de primis Russorum sedibus, auctore Conr. Gottl. Anton, *Vitembergæ*, 1810, 4to.

Rapports entre la Langue Sanscrit et la Langue Russe. Présentés à l'Académie Impériale Russe, par Fréd. Adelung, *St. Petersbourg*, 1811, 4to.; translated into Russian, by Paul v. Friedgang. The introduction has been reprinted word for word by Millin, in the Magasin Encyclop. 1813, Nov., and by Langlès, in the Mercure Etranger, No. xv [p].

Etymologies Slavonnes tirées du Sanscrit, by count T. Golowkin, in Fundgruben des Orients, vol. i, p. 459.

A table of two hundred words bearing some resemblance in sound and meaning in the Sanscrit and Sclavonic languages, by A. v. Mihanovich, in the Archiv für Geschichte, Geographie u. s. w. von Freih. v. Hormayr, 1823, No. 66, 67, and 71. It has also been printed separately.

Comparison of words alike in the Sanscrit and Sclavonic, in Alex. Murray's History of the European Languages, vol. ii, p. 346.

W. S. Majewski o Slavianach i ich probratymsach, *Warschau*, 1816, 8vo. p. 166—180. The comparison is made more particularly with the Polish language.

Comparison of the Sanscrit with the Sclavonian Dialects, etc., by Bopp, in his Vergleichenden Zergliederung des Sanskrits und der mit ihm verwandten Sprachen, Erster Versuch.

Professor Bohlen read a public lecture in German, in 1828, before the Royal German Society of Königsberg, upon the affinity between the Lithuanian and Sanscrit languages.

Pastor Carl Fried. Watson of Courland has noticed a great similarity between the grammatical forms of the Lettish and Sanscrit [q].

15. *With various other Languages.*

Observations sur les Rapports grammaticaux de la

[p] It was for some time doubted whether Adelung was the author of this little work or not; he, however, has now acknowledged it, and also his obligations to M. Julius Klaproth for his assistance in its compilation.

[q] The early death of this amiable scholar has interrupted his more extensive labours upon this subject, which had been announced.

Langue Sanskrite avec la plupart des Langues modernes de l'Europe, par M. Eichhoff. This treatise was presented by the author to the Asiatic Society at Paris. See Rapport de la Société Asiatique, *Paris*, 1828, 8vo. p. 8.

Friedr. Schlegel (Sprache und Weishiet der Indier, p. 58) discovers a resemblance between the language of Peru and the Sanscrit, and particularly in the words which he considers as roots of the ancient language of the Incas, who are said to have emigrated from the regions eastward of China.

On the occurrence of Sanscrit words in the Hebrew, Phœnician, etc. see Indien in s. Hauptbeziehungen, von A. W. v. Schlegel, in the Berlin Taschenbuch für 1829, p. 5. Dr. Hale makes this language a dialect of the ancient Syriac. See Analysis of Chronol. vol. i, p. 421.

Dictionnaire Hindoustani, dans lequel on rectifie un grand nombre d'erreurs répandues en Europe sur la Religion, les Mœurs, les Usages, et les Connaissances des Hindous; précédé d'une Grammaire, et d'un Recueil d'Etymologies Indiennes, *contenant plus de mille Mots Européens dont l'origine remonte jusqu'au Sanskrit*, ou autres Langues de l'Inde, par J. Morenas, *Paris*, 1826, 3 vols. 8vo. Such was the ample prospectus of a work which probably will never see the light.

CHRESTOMATHIES.

Chrestomathia Sanscrita, quam ex codicibus manuscriptis, adhuc ineditis, Londini exscripsit, atque in usum tironum versione, expositione, tabulis grammaticis, etc. illustratam edidit Othmarus Frank, philos. prof. Monachii, typographice ac lithographice sumtibus propriis, 1820, 4to; pars secunda, ibid. 1821. See

Annals of Oriental Literature, part iii, p. 558—562; Götting. gel. Anz. 1820, p. 210; Hall. Allg. Lit. Zeit. 1821, No. ccxxxiii, ccxxxiv; A. W. v. Schlegel's Ind. Bibl, ii, 1, p. 20, etc. A work much recommended.

PROVERBS.

A collection of Proverbs in various languages, Bengalee, Sanscrit, Arabic, Persian, Latin, and English, under the title of *Bhoodursun*, edited by Neelrutten Huldar, *Calcutta*, 1826.

Persian and Hindoostanee Proverbs, compiled by Capt. Roebuck, edited by H. H. Wilson, *Calcutta*, 1824, 2 vols. 8vo. The second volume contains two hundred and seventy-four proverbs, a great many of which are borrowed from the Sanscrit.

ANCIENT INSCRIPTIONS AND BOOKS IN THE SANSCRIT LANGUAGE.

THE remains of the ancient Sanscrit language consist of inscriptions, which are considered to exhibit it in its purest and most genuine form, and of books. The following works give the best information with regard to both these subjects.

1. *Inscriptions.*

These are not only of importance as exhibiting the form of this language at an early date, but as serving to elucidate the history of India. Their utilty in both these respects has been duly appreciated by the learned and indefatigable orientalist Mr. Colebrooke; who was one of the first to call the attention of the literary public to this important branch of Indian antiquity in his dissertation,

On Ancient Monuments containing Sanscrit Inscriptions, by H. T. Colebrooke, esq., published in the Asiatic Researches, vol. ix, p. 398, containing an account of nine inscriptions; with plates of the original Sanscrit, and translations.

Some account of these also will be found in Heeren's Researches upon India, an English translation of which is now in the press.

The monuments of this sort are either inscriptions upon temples, grottos, and single stones; or engraven upon copperplates, and containing grants of land, privileges, diplomas, etc. See Götting. gel. Anz. 1819, St. 107.

The following are the most remarkable of these inscriptions:

Among the most ancient are two inscriptions discovered in a cave, or temple-grotto, near Gya in the Vindya mountains. They were deciphered and translated by Mr. Wilkins, in the Asiatic Researches, vol. i, p. 279; ii, 168, who states that the language is pure Sanscrit, but that the character is the most ancient he had met with, and even differed materially from that found in inscriptions eighteen hundred years old.

Account of Ancient Hindoo Remains, by R. Jenkins, with Translations and Observations by H. H. Wilson.

These consist of three copperplates, united by a ring of the same metal, with a seal embossed; and of an inscription which records the grant of some lands by Tivara Deva, king of Korsala, to certain Brahmins. Professor Wilson, in his observations, remarks, that "the copperplates furnish specimens of a character which has not yet found a place amongst the varieties of monumental writing in India, hitherto offered to the public. This character was unknown to the Brahmins of the place, and equally unintelligible to the pandits of Calcutta; but were deciphered by a Jain of great respectability and learning, who had belonged to the establishment of the late colonel Mackenzie." Professor Wilson concludes by saying, that "a comparison of these inscriptions with those which remain to be deciphered in the province of *Chatsísgerh* (of which a list is given), seems calculated to illustrate the political and religious history of that part of India, in the eighth and ninth centuries: information that cannot but be acceptable in the utter gloom which envelopes almost the whole of Hindoostan history, anterior to the Mohammedan invasion." See Asiatic Researches, vol. xv, p. 499—515.

An inscription on a pillar near *Buddal,* consisting of twenty-eight Sanscrit verses, translated by Charles Wilkins, esq., in the Asiatic Researches, vol. i, p. 131, 8vo. edition. The last ten verses have been translated into German, by Jos. von Hammer, in the Wiener Jahrbüchern der Literatur, 1818, vol. ii, p. 335.

Sanscrit Inscriptions, by the late captain E. Fell; with observations, by H. H. Wilson, esq., Sec. As. S. in Asiatic Researches, vol. xv, p. 437, sqq. These consist of various inscriptions, described and translated by captain Fell, and followed by historical remarks by Mr. Wilson, the present professor of Sanscrit. The first was found at *Garḥa Mandela;* in what situation is not upon record. The *Hansi* inscription was found upon a stone near the fort. The inscriptions from *Benares* consist of seven plates of copper, with Sanscrit inscriptions, found in a field near the town by a peasant. They contain the genealogy of various princes, with occasional sketches of their character and deeds; and seem of importance for the history of India[r]. See Asiatic Researches, vol. xv, p. 436.

[r] These inscriptions are made the subject of two articles in Adelung

Inscriptions upon rocks in *South Bihár*, described by Dr. Buchanan Hamilton, and explained by Henry Thomas Colebrooke, in the Transactions of the Royal Asiatic Society, *London*, 1826, vol. i, part ii, p. 201—206. These are referred to the years 1219 and 1229 of the era of *Vicramaditya*, A. D. 1163 and 1173.

Translation of a Sanscrit inscription on a stone found in *Bundèlc'hand*, by lieut. W. Price, in Asiatic Researches, vol. xii, p. 360, consisting of fifty verses in a character approaching, except in some few letters, very nearly to the Devanâgari now in use, and containing a genealogical table of several princely families.

Inscriptions on the Staff of *Firuz Shah*, (a very singular monument near *Delhi*), translated from the Sanscrit, as explained by Radhacanta Sarman, Asiat. Researches, vol. i, p. 379.

Translations of one of the inscriptions upon the pillar at *Delhi*, called the *Lat of Firuz Shah*, by Henry Colebrooke, esq.; with introductory remarks, by Mr. Harrington, Asiat. Research. vol. vii, p. 175.

The date of this inscription is ascertained to be 1220 of the Samvat era, A. D. 1164. It is considered of great importance in confirming and illustrating the records extant, relative to the history of Hindoostan, immediately preceding the Mahommedan conquest. See Edin. Review, Jan. 1807, p. 284[a].

A copy of the inscriptions in the Pagoda of *Saringam* was obtained by the late Prof. Rudiger, of Halle, from the missionary John. See Neuere Gesch. der evangel, Missionsanstalten, St. 66, *Halle*, 1816, p. 527.

A Royal Grant of Land, engraved on a copperplate, bearing date twenty-three years before Christ and dis-

(p. 72), as are also those described by Mr. Jenkins; but from the way in which he has mentioned them, it is clear that he had not seen the volume to which he refers.

[a] The two above articles are very incorrectly described in Adelung.

covered among the ruins at *Mongueer*, translated from the original Sanscrit, by Charles Wilkins, in the Asiat. Researches, vol. i, p. 123, and 357. Other inscriptions of grants of land are also found in the same work, vol. iii, p. 39; and vol. iii, p. 3; and in the Transactions of the Literary Society of Bombay, vol. iii, p. 391—397; Translation of a Grant of Land in the *Concan*, by Dr. Taylor of Bombay.

Comments on an Inscription upon marble, at *Madhucarghar;* and three grants inscribed on copper, found at *Ujjayani*, by major James Tod, Transact. of the Royal Asiat. Society, vol. i, part ii, p. 207—229.

Three Grants of Land, inscribed on copper, found at *Ujjayani*, translated by Henry Thomas Colebrooke, esq., Transact. of the Royal Asiat. Society, vol. i, part ii, p. 230—239, and 463.

A description and translation of a collection of copies of Sanscrit inscriptions found in the *Aboo* mountains, was presented to the Asiatic Society of Calcutta, by Major Jackson. See Asiatic Journal, 1824, December, p. 605.

The inscriptions amount to above two hundred, and throw much light on early Indian history. They especially illustrate the *Chaulukyæ*, or the succession of the ruling power at *Guzerat*, in the eleventh, twelfth, and thirteenth centuries.

Lettre sur une Inscription Sanscrite à *Gusurate*, in the Journ. Asiat. tom. viii, p. 110.

Note sur les Inscriptions Sanscrites découvertes par M. le lieutenant-colonel Tod, dans le *Râdjasthân*, et données par lui à la Société Asiatique, par Eug. Burnouf, in the Nouv. Journ. Asiat. 1828, No. v, p. 397—400.

These inscriptions are as follows:

1. Inscriptions upon the ancient temple at *Char-Chaomu*, in the district of *Haravati*, dedicated to

Chandra-Ishvara-Mahadeva, from the year 500 of the era *Samvat* (A. D. 444), discovered in 1819.

2. Four inscriptions upon copper, found at *Gwalior*, in the *Decan*, still older than the foregoing, and scarcely to be deciphered.

3. Inscriptions found at *Jayselmer* in the Indian desert. It is referred to king *Bidjy Rae*, who lived in the ninth century, and contains a genealogical table of Brahma down to *Vidyaya Rajah* (*Bidjy Rae*), written by *Somânathaka*: without date.

4. An inscription found upon the walls of the ancient city of *Chitore*: very ancient, and almost illegible.

5. Many inscriptions upon marble, which refer to the princes *Solanki* or *Châloûka* in the thirteenth century, and found in the district of *Mandelgurh*.

The greater part of these inscriptions are pure Sanscrit, and written either in the Devanâgari character, or so that they may be understood by it; but the inscriptions in the temple grottos of *Salsette*, *Mavalipuram*, and others, have not yet been deciphered.

Respecting the tables which record the privileges obtained by the Jews in *Cochin*, and by the Christians on the *Malabar* coast, see the extract from Tychsen's treatise De Inscriptionibus Indicis et Privilegiis Judæorum et Christianorum S. Thomæ in ora Malabarica, cum explicatione Inscriptionis trilinguis a Buchanano adlatæ, in the Götting. gel. Anzeigen, 1819, St. 107.

The copies, drawings, etc. of inscriptions upon stone and copper found in the East Indies, by lieut.-col. C. Mackenzie, surveyor-general of India, amounted to 8076, and were bound up in seventy-seven volumes. See Asiat. Journal, 1823, Aug. p. 137.

WORKS IN SANSCRIT.

THE best information respecting Sanscrit literature will be found collected in the following works:

On the literature of the Hindoos, from the Sanscrit, communicated by Goverdhan Caul, translated, with a short commentary, by the president Sir William Jones, first printed in the Asiat. Research. vol. i, p. 340; and again, in the works of Sir William Jones, vol. i, p. 349[t].

Remarks upon Ancient Sanscrit Literature, the *Vedas*, *Puranas*, and *Shastras*, in the German translation of Sonnerat's Voyages to the East Indies and China, *Zurich*, 1782, 4to.

Account of the History, Literature, and Religion of the Hindoos, including translations from their principal works, by William Ward, *Serampoor*, 1811, 4to. 4 vols. Again, shortened and improved, with the following title, A View of the History, Literature, and Mythology of the Hindoos, including a minute description of their manners, and customs, etc., by the Rev. William Ward. The second edition, carefully abridged and greatly improved, *Serampoor*, 1815, 2 vols. 4to.; the third edition, *London*, 1817, 2 vols. 8vo.; 1821, 3 vols. 8vo.

This work is reviewed at length in the Asiatic Journal for 1817, January and February, where a very favourable opinion is given of it. The virtuous indignation of the missionary seems to have led him to paint the moral character of the Hindoos, in colours almost too dark to belong to human nature; the work, however, is undoubtedly very valuable.

Sketches relating to the History, Religion, Learning, and Manners of the Hindoos, by Quint. Craufurd, *Lond.* 1792, 2 vols. 8vo.

Catalogue and Detailed Account of a Valuable and

[t] These are given as two distinct works by Adelung, p. 78 and 80.

curious collection of mss. collected in Hindoostan, including all those that were procured by Monsieur Anquetil du Perron, relative to the religion and history of the Parsees, etc , by S. Guise, esq., *Lond.* 1800, 4to.

On the literature of the Hindoos, in the Preface to Selections of Popular Poetry of the Hindoos, by Thomas Broughton, *London*, 1814, 8vo.

Upon the different ages of Indian literature, in Mélanges de Littérature Sanscrite par A. Langlois, *Paris*, 1827, 8vo. p. 40—48.

On the advantage of Sanscrit literature to science and learning, in *Vijasa*, a journal, by Othm. Frank, vol. i, p. 1—45.

Mackenzie Collection. A Descriptive Catalogue of the Oriental Manuscripts, and other articles illustrative of the literature, history, statistics, and antiquities of the south of India; collected by the late lieut.-col. Colin Mackenzie, surveyor-general of India, by H. H. Wilson, esq., secretary to the Asiatic Society of Bengal, etc., *Calcutta*, 1828, 2 vols. 8vo.

This collection consists of 1568 mss. of which six hundred and sixty-seven are in Sanscrit, written in various characters; of 2070 local tracts, in two hundred and sixty-four volumes; of 8076 inscriptions, in seventy-seven volumes. Of translations and tracts, in loose sheets, six hundred and seventy-nine, and 1480 in seventy-five volumes. Plans, seventy-nine; drawings, 2630; coins, 6218; images, one hundred and six; antiquities, forty; Wilson's Preface, p. xxii. Besides these, col. Mackenzie left an immense collection of notes, observations, journals of thirty-four years, inscriptions, drawings, etc. amounting to many volumes, of which forty, in folio, form but a part. An account of these is given in two articles in the Asiat. Journal for 1822, March and April, which concludes with the following observation: "Col. Mackenzie has done more than could reasonably be expected from human industry; and there is something so vast in the discoveries he has made, that they remind us of the protracted life of an antediluvian, and seem totally unsuited to the limited span allotted to our present existence."

Catalogus Bibliothecæ Regiæ Parisiensis, *Parisiis*, 1739, fol. by Etienne Fourmont.

Versuch einer Ostindischen Literatur-Geschichte, von Henning, *Hamburg*, 1786, 8vo.

Systema Brahmanicum Liturgicum, Mythologicum, Civile, ex Monumentis Indicis Musæi Borgiani Velitris. Diss. notis historico-criticis illustravit Fr. Paulinus a S. Bartholomæo, *Romæ*, 1792, 4to. See Nouv. Mélanges Asiat. par M. Abel-Remusat, vol. ii, p. 307.

Paul. a S. Bortholomæo Examen Hist. Criticum Codd. Ind. Bibliothecæ Congregationis de propag. Fide, *Romæ*, 1792, 4to. The author at p. 23, gives rules for distinguishing genuine Indian manuscripts from spurious.

De manuscriptis Codicibus Indicis R. P. J. Eman. Hanxleden S. J. Epistola, edidit Paul. a S. Bartholomæo, *Vindobonæ*, 1799, 4to.

Ejusd. Musæi Borgiani Codices Avenses, etc. *Romæ*, 1793, 4to.

Ejusd. Lettera su' Monimenti Indici del Museo Borgiano, *Roma*, 1794, 4to.

Ejusd. Viaggi alle Indie Orientali, *Roma*, 1796, 4to. p. 269, sqq.

A Catalogue of the principal Sanscrit works in the Asiatic Researches, and in the treatises of Sir William Jones, translated by Kleuker, and in Friedr. Hermann's Gemälde von Ostindien, Th. ii, p. 342, etc.

Sur la Poésie Mystique des Persans et des Hindous, extrait de l'Anglais de W. Jones. From the Archives Littéraires in the Moniteur, 1806, No. cclvii.

A Catalogue of Sanscrit and other Oriental Manuscripts presented to the Royal Society by Sir William and Lady Jones, in Sir William Jones's Works, vol. vi, 4to[u].

Specimens of Hindoo Literature, consisting of translations from the Tamoul language, of some Hindoo works of morality and imagination, with explanatory notes, to which are prefixed introductory remarks on the mythology, literature, etc. of the Hindoos, by N. E. Kindersley, *London*, 1794, 8vo.

Sanscrit Fragments, or extracts from the sacred books of the Brahmins, on subjects important to the British isles, by the Rev. Thomas Maurice, *London*, 1798, 8vo.

The Oriental Miscellany, consisting of original productions and translations, vol. i, *Calcutta*, 1798, 8vo.

The Asiatic Miscellany, consisting of original productions, translations, fugitive pieces, imitations, and extracts from curious publications, *Calcutta*, 1785, 1786, large 4to. 2 vols.

The New Asiatic Miscellany, *Calcutta*, 1789, small 4to. 2 parts.

Ancient Indian Literature, illustrative of the researches of the Asiatic Society of Bengal, from original mss., *London*, 1807; 4to. 1809.

Catalogue des Manuscrits Sanscrits de la Bibliothèque Impériale avec des notices du contenu de la plupart des ouvrages, etc. par MM. Alex. Hamilton et L. Langlès, *Paris*, 1807, 8vo[x]. This catalogue contains the title, and occasional extracts, from one hundred and seventy eight treatises in Sanscrit, and four-

[u] Comprising fifty-nine articles (in seventy-one vols.) in Sanscrit; nine in Chinese; seventy-seven Persian; thirty-four Arabic; and two Hindostani. It is also given in the Philosophical Transactions, abridged by Hutton.

[x] Hamilton was the real author; Langlès did no more than translate his English manuscript.

teen in Bengalee. A very ample review of this work will be found in the Moniteur, 1808, 31 May and 25 June.

Vijasa, Ueber Philosophie, Mythologie, Litteratur, und Sprache der Hindu. Eine Zeitschrift von Dr. Othmar Frank, Erstes Heft, *München,* 1826, 4to.

Monumens Littéraires Sanscrite; contenant une exposition rapide de cette littérature, et un aperçu du systême religieux et philosophique des Indiens d'après leurs propres livres; par A. Langlois, *Paris,* 1827, 8vo. A very ample review of this work is given in the Journal des Savans, Avril, 1827, p. 231, etc., and Asiatic Journal.

The Sanscrit Reader, *Calcutta,* 1821, 8vo.

Mithridates von J. C. Adelung, Th. i, p. 134—143; iv, p. 53—56.

Geschichte der neuern Sprachenkunde, von J. G. Eichhorn, Erste Abtheil, p. 228—256.

Specimens of Hindoo Literature, *London,* 1813, 8vo. Query if not a new edition of Kindersley's Work, see above, p. 63.

Letters on India, by Maria Graham, *London,* 1817, 8vo.

Description of the Character, Manners, and Customs of the people of India, and of their Institutions, Religious and Civil, by the Abbé J. A. Dubois, missionary in the Mysore, *London,* 1817, 4to. An edition of the original French, much improved by the author, appeared at Paris, 1825.

Essays relative to the Habits, Character, and Moral Improvement of the Hindoos, *London,* 1823, 8vo. first printed in the Friend of India.

General View of the Literature of the Hindoos, in the Oriental Herald, June, 1825, p. 859, sqq.

The Progress of Inquiry into the Learning of India, in the Quarterly Oriental Magazine of Calcutta, and again in the Asiat. Journal, No. cxxxiii, Jan. 1827, p. 30—34; Feb. p. 189—196.

Catalogus Librorum Sanskritanorum, quos Bibliothecæ Univers. Havniens. vel dedit vel paravit Nathan. Wallich. Auct. Erasmo Nyerup, *Hafniæ*, 1821, 8vo.

Indische Bibliothek. Eine Zeitschrift von Aug. Wilh. v. Schlegel. Erster Band, *Bonn*, 1823, 8vo. sqq.

A general View of the Language and Literature of the Hindoos, in Niklas Müller's Glauben, Wissen und Kunst der alten Hindoos in ursprünglicher Gestalt und im Gewande der Symbolik u. s. w. *Mainz*, 1822, 8vo. I. Bd. I[r] Abschn.

Quelques lignes sur les Sciences des Indiens, extraites de l'Araïch-i-mahfil, de Mir Cher Aly Assos et traduites de l'Hindostani par M. Garcin de Tassy, in the Journ. Asiat. 1826, Cah. l. p. 97.

Notice des Manuscrits Sanskrits laissés par Sir Robert Chambers, in the Journ. Asiat. vol. vii, p. 62.

Ueber religiöse Bildung, Mythologie und Philosophie der Hindus, mit Rücksicht auf ihre älteste Geschichte, von J. G. Rhode, *Leipzig*, 1827, 2 B. 8vo. m. Kfp.

Fraser, James, Catalogue of Manuscripts in the Persic, Arabic, and Sanscrit Languages, *London*, 1742, 8vo.

A Succinct Account of the Sanscrit, or learned language of the Brahmins; in the Way to Things by Words, by John Cleland, *London*, 1767, 8vo.

Catalogue of Sanscrit Books, and of Translations from the Sanscrit, in Parbury, Allen, and Co.'s Catalogue of books in Oriental literature, 1832.

Very interesting accounts of Sanscrit literature will also be found in Heeren's Ideen, Inder, the first section *passim;* Cousin, Victor, Histoire de la Philosophie du xviiime Siècle; in Ritter, Geschichte der Philosophie, Th. i, p. 58, sqq.; and in the Discours prononcé au

Collége Royal de France à l'ouverture du Cours de Langue et de Littérature Sanscrite, par M. de Chèzy, *Paris*, 1815, 8vo.

A CATALOGUE OF SANSCRIT WORKS, AND TRANSLATIONS.

SACRED WRITINGS [x].

1. ON THE VEDAS IN GENERAL.

THE whole circle of Hindoo knowledge and science is divided into eighteen parts, of which the first four are the *Vedas*, from *Ved* or *Bed*, the law.—*Bed, Beid, Bedam, Bedang, Bedaos, Vedam, Vidya*, etc., according to the different modes of writing and pronunciation observed by Europeans in India. These are regarded as an immediate revelation from heaven; and as containing the true knowledge of God, of his religion, and of his worship, disposed into one harmonious composition. Next to the Vedas rank four *Upavedas*, which comprise the knowledge of medicine, music, and other arts; after these follow six *Vedangas*, which relate to pronunciation, grammar, prosody, religious rites and ceremonies, etc.; and finally, four *Upangas*, which treat of logic, philosophy, jurisprudence, and history.

Each *Veda* consists of two parts; the *Mantras*, consisting of prayers, hymns, and invocations; and the *Brahmanas*, comprising precepts which inculcate re-

[x] The usual division of these works into prose and verse is not observed here, because even the first are written in metre, and the poetical form of the latter does not seem to give a sufficient reason for dividing them.

ligious duties; maxims explaining these precepts; and theological arguments. The complete collection of the hymns, prayers, and invocations, belonging to one *Veda*, is called its *Sanhita*. The *Sanhitas* with their various commentaries are subdivided into *Sahas*, that is, branches of the *Vedas*. The theology of the Indian scripture, comprehending the argumentative portion, entitled *Vedanta*, is contained in tracts called *Upanishads;* that is, the *sacred science*, the knowledge of God.

The *Vedas* are undoubtedly the most ancient compositions in the whole range of Sanscrit literature. Their obscurity, and the obsolete dialect in which they are written, are such as to render the reading of them difficult even to a Brahman[y]. Ramachandra explains, in his treatise on the grammar of Pánini called *Pracriya Caumudi*, the anomalies of the dialect in which the *Vedas* are composed. See Q. Craufurd's Researches on Ancient and Modern India, vol. ii, p. 171.

Sir William Jones fixes the date of the *Vedas* at 1500 years before the birth of Christ; but colonel Kennedy remarks, in his Researches into the Nature and Affinity of Ancient and Hindoo Mythology, that Sir William Jones was misled in his notions of Indian

[y] When the study of the Indian scriptures was more general than at present, especially among the *Brámanas* of *Canyacubja*, learned priests derived titles from the number of *Vedas* with which they were conversant. Since every priest was bound to study one *Veda*, no title was derived from the fulfilment of that duty; but a person who had studied two *Vedas*, was surnamed *Dwivedi;* one, who was conversant with three, *Trivedi;* and one, versed in four, *Chaturvedi:* as the mythological poems were only figuratively called a *Veda*, no distinction appears to have been derived from a knowledge of them, in addition to the four scriptures. The titles above-mentioned have become the surnames of families among the *Brahmans* of *Canoj*, and are corrupted, by vulgar pronunciation, into *Dobé*, *Tiwáré*, and *Chaubé*. Colebrooke, in Asiatic Researches, vol. viii, p. 381.

chronology, by taking the religious personages which occur in the Hindoo sacred books for real historic characters, and by attempting to define the exact age at which they are supposed to have lived[a]. The same author observes, that the sacred books of the Hindoos afford no data from which the period of their composition may be determined, even by approximation; the writers apparently never having intended them to be the subject of chronological computation. The first historical era is that of *Vicràmiditya* (fifty-six years B. C.), preceded by a period of three thousand years, in which the Hindoos pretend to no "continuous accounts either religious, traditional, or historical." This three thousand years is a chasm which cannot be filled up. Various other circumstances, however, conspire to prove the antiquity and authenticity of the Hindoo scriptures; and particularly an unvaried uniformity of conception, and a total absence of all foreign modes of thinking and extraneous interpolations. The descriptions which the *Vedas* contain of manners, customs, and faith, are too accurate to be spurious; and, as Mr. Colebrooke says, no system of forgery would be equal to the task of fabricating large works to agree with the very numerous citations pervading thousands of volumes, in every branch of literature, dispersed among the various nations of Hindoos inhabiting India. Colonel Kennedy believes the period at which they began to be composed to have been at least one thousand one hundred, or one thousand two hundred years B. C.; and Mr. Colebrooke, in pronouncing them to be genuine, adds, "I mean to say that they are the same compositions which, under the same title of *Veda*, have been

[a] Researches into the Nature and Affinity of Hindoo Mythology, by lieut.-col. Vans Kennedy, *London*, 1831, 4to. p. 494.

revered by Hindoos for hundreds, if not thousands of years[a]."

The original Veda is believed by the Brahmans, the most learned of the Indian philosophers, to have been revealed by Brahma; and to have been preserved by tradition, until it was collected and arranged into books and chapters by the sage *Dwápáyana*, who thence obtained the surname of *Vyasa*, or *Veda vyasa*, the compiler of the Vedas. See Colebrooke in the Asiat. Research. vol. viii, p. 378, etc. 8vo. ed. Hamilton makes this Vyasa to have lived in the eleventh century after Christ. Ritter, the latest writer on this subject, who certainly has examined with much attention all the authorities on the subject, and who betrays his inclination to place the date of the *Vedas* as low as possible, admits that they are certainly the most ancient writings in the whole range of Hindoo literature; "as it would not," he observes, "be easy to find an Indian work in which they are not mentioned." He supposes they were either collected or composed one thousand four hundred, or one thousand six hundred years before the Christian era[b].

But another strong argument for the high antiquity of the *Vedas*, is, that in the greater part of them the common *sloka* is not to be found, but a more ancient iambic metre of eight syllables, which may be justly regarded as the more simple and ancient, and indeed

[a] See Colebrooke on the Vedas, in Asiatic Researches, vol. viii.: the main authority on this subject. This treatise of Colebrooke is noticed in the Edinburgh Review, vol. xii, p. 47; it is there said that "from its subject it is the most curious, and from the ability, candour, and research displayed by its author, the most entitled to approbation of any paper that has appeared in the Asiatic Researches."

[b] Ritter, Geschichte der Philosophie, tom. i, p. 70, etc. Much information, research, and close reasoning, will be found in the part of Ritter's work here referred to, which has been published since the work of Adelung.

as the true origin of the usual *sloka* of sixteen syllables. See Asiatic Researches, vol. xiv, p. 1.

The very existence of the *Vedas* was formerly regarded as a fable; and even Paulinus a S. Bartholomæo, in his Systema Brahman. p. 281, derides the English and French for supposing them real compositions.

It was not only a question whether the *Vedas* were extant; but whether, if portions were still preserved, any person would be found capable of understanding their obsolete dialect. It was also doubted, whether, supposing a Brahman really possessed these Indian scriptures, his religious prejudices would not prevent his imparting the sacred knowledge to any but a regenerate Hindoo[c].

These doubts were not removed until colonel Polier obtained from *Jypoor* a transcript of what purported to be a complete collection of the *Vedas.* This is now deposited in the British Museum, bound in eleven large folio volumes. Europe, therefore, propably possesses a complete collection of these important documents in the original language. They still, however, remain untranslated; and, from their vast extent, the greater part of them will probably always remain so[d]. See Asiatic Researches, vol. i, p. 347, and vol. viii, p. 497.

Ample information respecting the *Vedas* in general

[c] Colebrooke, in Asiatic Researches, vol. viii, p. 377.

[d] Mr. Wilson, in his interesting Memorial to Convocation, as candidate for the Boden professorship, which chair he has, to the honour of the university, been since elected to fill, says, "I have much at heart the printing of the text, with a translation of the Ritual of the *Vedas.* I have made some progress in one of them, the *Rig Veda,* but the execution of this and my other projects, will essentially depend upon my being enabled shortly to resign all public employment, and to devote the remaining portion of my life, as I could be well content to do, to the cultivation of Sanscrit literature."

will be found in the essay of Colebrooke[e], and the works of Ritter and colonel Vans Kennedy already quoted; as well as in the following:

A. H. L. Heeren's Ideen, fourth edition, 1824, part i, vol. iii, p. 3—237, where will be found an interesting assemblage of all that is known upon this subject. See also the ample review of this classical work in the Hall. Allg. Lit. Zeit. 1816, Oct. No. 232—234, 247, and 248[f].

Du Pons in the Lettres édifiantes, second edition, tom. xiv, p. 74.

Hollwell's Interesting Historical Events relative to the Provinces of Bengal, etc. *London*, 1765, 2 vols. 8vo.

Dow's History of Hindostan, *London*, 1768, 3 vols. 8vo.

Sonnerat, Voyages aux Indes Orientales, vol. i, p. 211.

Ezour-Vedam, traduit par Ste. Croix, in the Observations préliminaires, vol. i, p. 111.

Catalogue des Manuscrits Sanscrits de la Biblioth. Imp. par MM. Hamilton et Langlès.

Eichhorn's Geschichte der schönen Literatur, § 248.

Craufurd's Researches on Ancient and Modern

[e] The notes of Langlès to this essay, in the French translation of the Asiatic Researches, are also referred to by Adelung. But this work, which was only continued to the end of the second volume, is not very well spoken of by English critics.

[f] This interesting portion of professor Heeren's Ideen has been ably translated into French by M. Suckau, with some original notes of the author, as well as of the translator. The English reader, I hope, will very shortly have an opportunity of consulting it in his own language, as the Rev. Alfred Browne of Christ Church is at this moment occupied with a translation. It will contain the improvements of the French translation, and original notes by the translator; some new additional matter, furnished by the professor, on the ancient commerce of the island of Ceylon; on Palmyra; and an unedited account of the progress made in Sanscrit literature since the publication of the last edition of his works.

India, *London*, 1817, 2 vols. 8vo. vol. i, p. 185—187, 241. Taken from Colebrooke's treatise already mentioned.

Brahma, von Friedr. Mayer, *Leipzig*, 1818, 8vo. p. 99, etc. 231, 237.

Horæ Biblicæ: part the second: being a connected series of miscellaneous notes on the Koran, Zend-Avesta, the *Vedas*, the Kings, and the Edda, by captain Butler, *London*, 1802, 8vo. Upon this work see Catalogue de la Bibliothèque de M. Langlès, p. 31, No. 255.

Account of a Discovery of a Modern Imitation of of the *Vedas*, with Remarks on the Genuine Works, by Fr. Ellis, esq. in Asiatic Researches, vol. xiv, 1—59.

Précis des Livres sacrés des Gentils de l'Inde Orientale et de leurs coûtumes, in the Collecções de noticias para e historia e geografia das nações ultramarinas, *Lisboa*, 1827, tom. i, p. 1—3. See Bulletin univ. 1828, Juillet, Sciences Hist. p. 39.

Though the Vedas form altogether but one work, they are subdivided, according to the *Baghavata*, into four parts, each of which is again considered as a separate Veda. These are, 1. *Rig Veda; 2. Yajur Veda; 3. Sama Veda; 4. Atharvana Veda*[g].

1. *Rig Veda.*

Rig Veda, from *Rig* or *Rich*, abounding in prayers and texts, and also praises, in sixteen *Sanhitas*, or collections of hymns or invocations. In the *Ezur-Vedam*, the contents of this Veda is stated as follows: It

[g] Anquetil du Perron calls them in his *Oupnek'hat*: *Rak*, *Djedir*, *Sam*, and *Athrban*. In the *Ezur-Vedam*, these names are written *Rick*, *Zozur*, *Chama*, and *Adorbo*. It is moreover said that a fifth *Veda* exists, formed out of the *Ithiasas* and other *Puranas*, and bearing the name of *Vavadam*.

treats of the first cause, of the creation of matter, of the formation of the world, of angels, of the soul, of rewards and punishments, of the bringing forth of all creatures, of their corruption, of sins, etc. See Ith's translation of the *Ezur-Vedam*, vol. i, p. 75.

The hymn, *Mantra*, to the sun, translated from the *Rig Veda*, in Colebrooke's Disquisition on the *Vedas*, in Asiat. Research. vol. viii. In this paper the learned author gives an analysis of the whole *Veda*, with various extracts from it in English. Some of these will be found translated into German in Fr. Bopp's Conjugationssystem der Sanskrit-Sprache, p. 273 and 290.

Rigvedæ Specimen, edidit Fred. Rosen, *London*, 1830. This work, by the professor of the London University, contains a specimen of the *Rig Veda* in the original text, with a translation and notes. It consists of several short hymns, chiefly addressed to Agni, the god of fire, and may be compared, with some interest, with the Pseudo-Orphic Hymns of Greek poetry; consisting, like them, of appellations and descriptions of the attributes of the different deities[h].

2. *Yajur Veda.*

The *Yajur Veda* relates chiefly to oblations and sacrifices, as the name implies, which is derived from *Yaj*, to worship or adore.

This Veda contains instructions respecting religious exercises, the castes, feasts, purifications, expiations, pilgrimages, gifts, various sacrifices, the particulars re-

[h] See Quarterly Review, vol. xlv, p. 6. Professor Heeren also, in an unedited addition to his work on Ancient India, with which he has favoured me, observes, "The only copy of the Vedas, (as far as my information extends,) the one brought to England by Polier, has been lying many years unnoticed in the British Museum. Professor Rosen has now commenced drawing it from obscurity; and although his specimen is but of limited extent, yet it is sufficiently ample to give us an insight into the language, the poetry, and, to a certain degree, the contents of the Vedas.

quired in the animals offered, the building of the temples, the usual ceremonies at births, marriages, and deaths of men of all ranks, etc. See *Ezour-Vedam*, translated by Ith, part i, p. 72[1].

Isávásyam, or an Upanishad from the *Yajur Veda*, translated in the Works of Sir William Jones, tom. vi, p. 423. A part of this Veda, *Ukad Arangak*, together with a commentary on the same by *Sankara-Acharya*, was in the possession of Sir William Jones, and is now in the library of the Asiatic Society of London.

Yajur Veda, translated into German in the fifth volume of the Danischen Missionsberichte, *Halle*, 1742, 4to. p. 1251, sqq.

Translations of many of the hymns and detached portions of this Veda will be found in Mr. Colebrooke's papers on the Religious ceremonies of the Hindoos, and of the Brahmans especially, in Asiat. Research. vol. v and vii.

The beginning of the prayers of the *Sarvamedha* from the *Yajur Veda*, translated in Colebrooke's Essay on the *Vedas*, in Asiat. Research. vol. viii, p. 431, 8vo. edit. and in Fr. Bopp's Conjugat. System der Sanscrit-Sprache, p. 280.

Eighteen *Distichs*, from the *Yajur Veda*, in Carey's Grammar of the Sungscrit Language, p. 903, 904.

Translation of the *Isopanishad*, one of the chapters of the *Yajur Veda*, according to the commentary of the celebrated *Sankara-Acharya*, establishing the unity and incomprehensibility of the Supreme Being, and that his worship alone can lead to eternal beatitude, by Rammohun Roy, *Calcutta*, 1816, 8vo. See Asiat. Journ. 1818, May, p. 465, 468; Journal Asiat. Cah. xvi, p. 244.

Translation of the *Kuth-Opunishud* (*Keth Upanis-*

[1] See below, p. 76.

chada) of the *Ujoor Ved* (*Yajur Veda*) according to the gloss of the celebrated *Sankaracharya*, by Rammohun Roy, *Calcutta*, 1819, 8vo. See Journ. Asiat. Cah. xvi, p. 245.

Sankaræ Atsharjæ præfatio ad *Jadshurvædæ Brihadarànjakun*, cum versione et *Anandæ* animadversionibus, in Othm. Frankii Chrestomathia Sanscrita, vol. i, p. 149. Sancara, one of the most celebrated expositors upon the Vedas, flourished above a thousand years ago at Sringagiri, in the Carnatic. One of his most esteemed works is called *Bhashyum*, an explanation of the most difficult passages of the *Vedas*. Frank has selected the *Upanishad*, entitled *Urihadaránykai*, forming part of the *Yajur Veda*. Sancara is also the author of many other works, among which, one of the best known is *Upadesa-Sahasri*, a metrical epitome of the doctrines of the *Upanishads* and *Brahma-Sootras*. There is an explanation of the same under another *Rama Tirt'ha*, entitled *Pada Yo'janicà*.

I'sávasyam, or an *Upanishad* from the *Yajur Veda*, translated by Sir William Jones, in his Works, vol. vi, p. 423, and by W. Carey in his Sungskrit Grammar, p. 903[k].

Equus mundi Mundus animans. Ex *Jadshurvedæ Brihadaranjako*. Sanskrit und Lateinisch, in *Vjasa*, von Othm. Frank, part i, vol. i, p. 51.

A pretended translation of the whole of the *Yajur Veda* appeared in 1778, under the following title:

L'Ezour Vedam, ou anciens Commentaires du *Vedam*, contenant l'exposition des opinions religieuses et philosophiques des Indiens. Traduit du Samscretan par un Brahme (à Pondicherry). Revu et publié (par le Baron de Sainte-Croix), avec des observations préliminaires, des notes et des éclaircissemens, *Yverdun*, 1778,

[k] See below, under Extracts from the Vedas; p. 79.

2 vols. 12mo. Reprinted verbatim in the Encyclopédie Méthodique Philosophique, ancienne et moderne, par Naigeon, *Paris,* 1792, p. 790—871. In German, *Ezour-Vedam* oder der alte Commentar über den *Vedam.* Von einem Bramen aus dem Samskretanischen ins Französische und aus diesem ins Deustche übersetzt. Mit einer Einleitung und Anmerkungen, nebst einem ungedruckten Fragmente des *Bagavadam,* von J. Ith, 1779, 2 Bde. 8vo.

Upon the appearance of this work its authenticity was much disputed, particularly by Sonnerat, in his Travels to the East Indies, p. 180, etc., and by others. It is said in the preface, that the work was originally among the papers of M. Barthelmy; that a copy was brought from India and presented to Voltaire, who sent it, in 1761, to the Royal Library of France. The forgery, thus manufactured at the instigation of the Jesuits, (it is said by father Roberto de Nobili, in the seventeenth century,) has been lately exposed in the following paper: Account of a Discovery of a Modern Imitation of the *Vedas,* with remarks on the genuine works, by F. Ellis, in the Transactions of the Literary Society of Bombay, vol. iii, p. 1—59: see also Asiat. Researches, vol. xiv, p. 1; Schlegel's Ind. Bibliothek, ii, 1, p. 50, etc.; and Asiat. Journal, Feb. 1818, p. 188[1].

Extracts from the *Ezur-Vedam* are found in Mignot sur les Anciens Philosophes de l'Inde; in the Mémoires de l'Académie des Inscript. tom. xxxi, p. 8; and in Anquetil du Perron's Zend-Avesta, tom. i, in the Discours prélimin. p. 83.

[1] This interesting paper of Mr. Ellis's displays a profound knowledge of Sanscrit literature. It contains an elaborate analysis of the genuine *Vedas;* and compares them with the forgeries, of which it appears copies were found of the other three, in Sanscrit, written in the Roman character, and in French, among the manuscripts of the catholic missionary at Pondicherry; where the one in question was discovered.

3. *The Sama Veda.*

The *Sama Veda*, from *Saman*, a prayer arranged for singing, consists of more than a thousand *Sanhitas*[m]. Colebrooke says, a peculiar degree of holiness seems to be attached to it, according to Indian notions, if reliance may be placed on the inference suggested by the etymology of its name, which indicates, according to the derivation usually assigned to it[n], the efficacy of this part of the *Veda* in removing sin. The prayers belonging to it are composed in metre, and intended to be chanted; and their supposed name is apparently ascribed to this mode of uttering them.

This *Veda* is divided into several parts: a principal division is entitled *Archica*, another portion is called *Aranyagana;* both these are arranged for chanting. Another principal division is *Bráhmana Sama*. It comprises all religious and moral duties, hymns in praise of the Supreme Being, and to the honour of subordinate spirits; commandments to be observed by all the castes, and others relating to separate ones, etc.

Upanishad, Commentar über den *Sama Veda*, in Sanskrit mit Bengali-Schrift gedruckt und herausgegeben, von Rammohun Roy, *Calcutta*, 1818, 8vo. See Revue Encyclop. tom. vii, année 1820, p. 326.

Translation of the *Cena* (*Kena*) *Upanishad*, one of the chapters of the *Sama Veda;* according to the gloss of the celebrated *Sankaracharyá*, establishing the unity, and the sole omnipotence of the Supreme Being, and that he alone is the object of worship, by Rammohun Roy, *Calcutta*, 1816, 8vo; and again, 1817; Asiat.

[m] Asiat. Researches, vol. viii, p. 458, 8vo. edit. Here, as in many places, I have translated all that is said by Adelung, and made considerable additions from Colebrooke, etc.

[n] From the root *Shó*, convertible into *só* and *sá*, and signifying *to destroy*. The derivative is expounded as denoting something which destroys sin.

Journ. 1818, Aug. p. 141—145; see Journ. Asiat. Cah. xvi, p. 245.

A Hymn from the *Sama Veda*, translated in Colebrooke on the *Vedas*, and in Fr. Bopp's Conjugat.-System der Sanskrit-Sprache, p. 293.

4. *Atharvana Veda.*

Atharva, or *Atharvan Veda*, in four *Sanhitas*, contains subjects of mystic theology and metaphysics. Several scholars, learned in Indian literature, have supposed this fourth *Veda*, from its more modern dialect, to be of less authority than the others, and will only acknowledge the first three as genuine. Passages of the Indian scripture itself, says Colebrooke, seem to support the inference; for the fourth *Veda* is not mentioned in the passage, cited by me in a former essay (on Religious Ceremonies, Asiat. Researches, vol. vii, 251), from the white *Yajush;* nor in the following text quoted from the Indian scripture, by the commentator of the *Rich.* "The *Rig Veda* originated from fire; the *Yajur Veda*, from air; and the *Sama Veda* from the sun." Hence some hold the *Atharvana* for no more than a supplement to the others [*].

Translation of the *Moonduk*-(*Mandhaka*) *Opinishud* of the *Uthurva-Ved*, according to the gloss of the celebrated *Shunkara-Charyu*, by Rammohun Roy, *Calcutta*, 1819, 8vo; see Journ. Asiat. Cah. xvi, p. 245.

Verses from the *Athar Veda*, translated by Colebrooke, in his Treatise on the *Vedas*, Asiat. Research. vol. viii, p. 359—476; and by Fr. Bopp, in his Conjug.-System der Sanskrit-Sprache, p. 310.

[*] The popular dictionary *Amerasina* notices only three *Vedas*, and mentions the *Atharvana* without calling it one. From these circumstances, and the received notions of the Hindoos themselves, it appears that the *Riga*, *Yajur*, and *Sama*, are the three principal portions of the *Vedas*; that the *Atharvana* is commonly admitted as a fourth; and that some supplementary matter and poems are reckoned as a fifth.

5. *Extracts from the Vedas.*

Sirr-i-Akbar; the greatest secret, being the essence of four Veds of Hindoo scriptures, compiled by prince Dara Shekoh, manuscript, in Howell and Stewart's Catalogue of Oriental Literature, for 1828.

Extracts from the *Vedas,* in the works of Sir William Jones, tom. vi, p. 313—423, and 427; and in Asiat. Researches, vol. i, p. 33—36, etc.

These are imitations rather than translations; and consist of hymns in verse, preceded by a summary of their contents in prose. Besides these, there are versions of various passages from the *Vedas* in prose, and fragments which appear to be materials towards a dissertation on the primitive religion of the Hindoos. I cannot resist giving the following extracts:

THE GAYATRI, OR HOLIEST VERSE OF THE VEDAS.

"Let us adore the supremacy of that divine sun, (opposed to the visible luminary,) the godhead who illuminates all, who recreates all, from whom all proceed, to whom all must return, whom we invoke to direct our understandings aright in our progress towards his holy seat."

"What the sun and light are to this visible world, that are the *supreme good and truth* to the intellectual and invisible universe; and, as our corporeal eyes have a distinct perception of objects enlightened by the sun, thus our souls acquire certain knowledge, by meditating on the light of truth, which emanates from the BEING OF BEINGS: that is the light by which alone our minds can be directed in the path to beatitude."

There is one beautiful hymn, beginning, "May that soul of mine, which mounts aloft in my waking hours as an ethereal spark, and which even in my slumber has a like ascent, soaring to a great distance, as an emanation from the light of lights, be united by devout meditation with the spirit supremely blest, and supremely intelligent!"

It ends: " There is one living and true God, everlasting, without body, parts, or passion; of infinite power, wisdom, and goodness; the maker and preserver of all things, both visible," etc. Sir William Jones's Works, vol. vi, p. 421, etc.

W. Jones, Abhandl. über die Geschichte, Alterthümer u. s. w. Asiens, *Riga*, 1795—1797, 4 Bde. 8vo; vol. i, p. 265; vol. iv, p. 14—28.

6. *Vedantas.*

The word *Vedanta*, signifies view, or object of the *Vedas*. Under this name there is an ancient work in Sanscrit, by *Vyasa* or *Jaimini*, said to have been composed above 2000 years ago, and to contain an abstract and a *quintessence* of all the Vedas brought together. This work is also known in India, under the title of *Purva Mimansa*, that is, the first, most ancient enquiry, in opposition to the *Uttera Mimansa*. The latter *Mimansa*, which is called *Brahma Mimansa*, is a philosophical-religious system.

The great authority for its doctrine is the collection of Sootras or Aphorisms, bearing the title of *Bramha-Sootra*.

The scholiasts, who have commented upon the *Brahma-Sootras*, are, *Baudhayana*, called the sacred *(Rishi)*; *Upavarsha*, the venerable *(Bhagavat)*, and others. The most celebrated is, *Sankara Acharya*, (see above page 74) placed by Colebrooke at the beginning of the ninth century. His commentary bears the title of *S'áríraca*[p] *Mimansa Bhashaya*. This has had many expounders, among whom we may mention

[p] *S'árira* signifies incorporated.

V'achespati as one of the most esteemed. His treatise is entitled *Bhamati*, or *S'áríraca Bhashya Vibhága*. This commentary is again illustrated by *Analananda*, surnamed *Vyásásrama*, in his *Védánta Calpataru*. Many other commenters are mentioned by Colebrooke in his Essay on the Philosophy of the Hindoos, in the Transact. of the Royal Asiatic Society, vol. ii, p. 7, 8.

These religious dogmas are ascribed to *Badarayana*, the same with *Vyasa*, *Veda Vyasa*, *Dwaipayana* and *Crishna Dwaipayana*[q]. The *Sootras* of *Badarayana* are divided into four books, *Adhyaya*, and each of these into four chapters, *Pada*.

The principal works upon the *Vedanta* are *Védánta Paribháshá*, by Dharma Rája Díkshita; A commentary upon the same by the author's son, Ráma Crish'na Dikshita, under the title: *Védánta Sic'hámani*.

Védanta Vára, a very familiar exposition of the *Vedanta*, by Sadánanda.

Preface, by a Brahmin, to a translation of an abridgement of the *Vedant*, in Asiat. Journ. 1818, Nov. p. 468—474; and 1827, Oct. p. 464—466.

The Bengalee translation of the *Vedant*, or resolution of all the *Veds*, the most celebrated and reserved work of Brahminical theology, establishing the unity of the Supreme Being, and that he is the only object of worship, together with a preface by the translator (Rammohun Roy), *Calcutta*, 1815, 8vo; 1816, 4to; 1817, 4to. A German translation was published in Bran's Miszellen, 1814, under the title Remmohon Roy Auflösung des *Wedant* oder aller *Weds*, des berühmtesten und verehrtesten Werks braminischer Gottesgelehrtheit u. s. w. Auch besonders daraus abgedruckt, *Jena*, 1818, 8vo; and Journ. Asiat. Cah. xvi, p. 243—249.

[q] In an earlier state, as Brahman, he was called *Apántara Tamas*.

Under the title of An Enquiry into the Spiritual Organisation or Soul of the World, there was published at *Calcutta*, 1818, 8vo. in Sanscrit, the *Vedanta Mimansa* according to *Vyasa* and *Sankara Acarya*, by Lallulala Sarma Kavi.

Vedanda Sàra; or Essence of the *Veda*, Sanscrit, *Calcutta*, 1818, 4to.

Vedanta Sara: Elements of Theology, according to the *Vedas*, by *Sadánanda Parivrajakácháryya*; with a commentary by Ramakrishna Tírtha, *Calcutta Education Press*, 1829. From Parbury, Allen, and Co's Catalogue.

Extract from the *Brahma Mimansa*, by H. Th. Colebrooke, esq. in Transact. of the Royal Asiatic Society, vol. ii, p. 1—39.

7. *Upanishads.*

The literary history of India enumerates fifty-two *Upanishads*, or extracts of such portions of the *Vedas*, as relate to argumentative theology. Among these numerous *Upanishads* those most frequently quoted, are, *Ch'hándógya, Caushítací, Vrihad-Aran'yaca Aìtaréyaca, Taittiríyaca, Cát'haca, Cat'havalli, Mund'aca, Pras'na S'wétás'watara, I'sá Vásya*, and *Kena.*

The four *Upanishads, Katha, Îsa, Kaena*, and *Mundaka*, edited by Rammohun Roy, and printed at Calcutta in the Bengalee character, with an English translation, have already been noticed under the *Vedas.*

Upanishad, in Bengalee character, *Madras*, 1818, 8vo.

Copious extracts from this portion of the *Vedas* may be found in Anquetil du Perron's *Upnek'hat;* but these were made from the Persian, and cannot be altogether relied on. The *Upnek'hat*, the Persian term for *Upanishad*, consists of fifty sections, subdivided into eighty-three *Brahmes*, or instructions, which explain, under the form of dialogues and narrations, particular points of theology.

Oupnek'hat, i. e. secretum tegendum, opus ipsa in India rarissimum, continens antiquam et arcanam s. theologicam et philosophicam doctrinam e quatuor sacris Indorum libris, *Rak Beid*, *Djedir Beid*, *Sam Beid*, *Athrban Beid* excerptam; ad verbum e Persico idiomate, Samscreticis vocabulis intermixto, in Latinum conversum. Dissertationibus et annotationibus difficiliora explanantibus illustratum; studio et opera Anquetil du Perron, Indicopleustæ, R. Inscript. et human. liter. Academiæ olim Pensionar. et Director. *Argentorati et Parisiis* an. ix, 1801—1802, 4to. 2 vols. Translated into German under this title, Versuch einer neuen Darstellung der uralten indischen All-Eins-Lehre; oder der berühmten Sammlung *τῶν Oupnekhaτῶν* erstes Stück: *Oupnekhat Tschehandouk* genannt. Nach dem lateinischen der persischen Uebersetzung wörtlich getreuen Texte des Hrn. Anquetil du Perron frey ins Deutsche übersetzt und mit Amnerkungen versehen von Th. A. Rixner, *Nürnberg*, 1808, 8vo[r].

The original Indian text of this body of Indian

[r] In the Transactions of the Literary Society of Bombay, *London*, 1819, p. 207, the following judgment is pronounced upon Anquetil du Perron: "Anquetil's great merit was that of an enterprising traveller: as an oriental scholar his rank is very low. The nation which possesses Silvestre de Sacy may easily resign Anquetil du Perron." See also Fr. Schlegel's Gesch. d. Liter. vol. i, p. 180. A milder sentence is passed upon him by Lanjuinais, in the Mag. Encyclop. an 8, tom. iii.

There is a notice of this work also in the Edinburgh Review, vol. i, p. 412. The critic therein does full justice to M. Anquetil's knowledge of the Persian, but questions his knowledge of the Sanscrit, or rather announces his total ignorance of that language. Ritter also remarks, that it contains so many mistakes and false interpretations, as to be quite useless in a work of investigation. See Geschichte der Philosoph. vol. i, p. 75; and Rhode uber Relig. Bildung, Mythol. and Philos. der Hindus, vol. i, p. 99, f.

theology, was translated into Persian by *Mohammed Darah Shekuh,* the brother of *Aurengzeb,* and thereby first made known to the profane. A specimen of this is given in Anquetil du Perron, Recherches historiques et geographiques sur l'Inde, tom. ii, and in German in the Sammlung asiatischer Originalschriften, Bd. i, p. 273—315. Another fragment of it is found in White's Institutes of Tamerlane, *Oxford,* 1783, 4to. translated from two Persian manuscripts in the possession of Sir Broughton Rouse, formerly governor of Bengal, and another in the preface to Halhed's Code of Gentoo Law, *London,* 1781.

An extract from the *Upnek'hat* is given by Lanjuinais, in the Mag. Encyclop. an ix, tom. iii, v, vi, under the title of Analyse de *l'Oupnek'hat,* par M. le Comte Lanjuinais, which is reprinted in the Journ. Asiat. Cah. x, p. 213—236, vol. xi, p. 265, vol. xii, 344, vol. xiii, 15, and vol. xiv, 71; and again, separately, La Religion des Indoux, selon les *Védah,* ou Analyse de *l'Oupnek'hat,* publiée par M. Anquetil du Perron en 1802, par M. le Comte Lanjuinais, *Paris,* 1823, 8vo.

A word in favour of the authenticity and value of the *Upnekhata,* by Niklas Müller, in his Appendices to his treatise on the Glauben, Wissen und Kunst der alten Hindus, Bd. i.

Considerations upon the *Upnek'hat,* and the formation and character of this theological treatise of the Hindoos, by Friedr. Mayer, in his *Brahma,* oder die Religion der Indier als Brahmaismus, *Leipzig,* 1808, 8vo. p. 7—15. See again, J. G. Rhode über relig. Bildung, Mythologie und Philosophie der Hindus, *Leipzig,* 1827, 2 B. 8vo.

In this place also we may introduce the three following works, by Rammohun Roy.

A Defence of Hindoo Theism, in reply to the attack of an advocate for idolatry at Madras, *Calcutta*, 1817, 8vo. in Bengali.

A Second Defence of the Monotheistical System of the *Veds*, in reply to an apology for the present state of Hindoo worship, *Calcutta*, 1817, 8vo. in Bengali.

An Apology for the Pursuit of Final Beatitude, independently of Brahmanical Observances, *Calcutta*, 1820, 8vo. in Bengali.

8. *Upavedas.*

The *Upavedas*, from *Upa*, joined to, appended to, are a kind of supplementary *Vedas*, said to be immediately deduced from the *Vedas*. There are four of them. The first comprises the theory of disorders and medicines, with the practical method of curing diseases. The second on music, in the more extensive sense of the word: it is chiefly useful in raising the mind by devotion to the felicity of the divine nature. The third treats on the fabrication and use of arms and implements of war. The fourth explains sixty-four mechanical arts and handicrafts, for the improvement of such as exercise them. Of their more minute contents, however, we have as yet no accurate information; indeed it is believed that they are lost. Sir W. Jones's Works, tom. i, p. 358.

Upon music, as forming a part of the religion of the Hindoos, there is a treatise by Sir William Jones, On the Musical Modes of the Hindoos, in Asiatic Researches, tom. iii, p. 55, and in his Works, vol. i, p. 413, From this a German translation has been made, under the title of Ueber die Musik der Inder, von F. H. v. Dalberg, *Erfurt*, 1802, 8vo., with a collection of popular Indian ballads.

9. *Vedangas.*

Angas, member, or *Vedangas,* members of the *Vedas,* supplements to the body of the *Vedas,* six in number, teach the art of pronunciation, grammar, prosody, the explanation of obscure and unusual expressions of the *Vedas,* astronomy, and the rites and ceremonies to be observed in religion. To these belong the prosody of Pingala, the grammar of Pánini, the treatise upon astronomy called *Surya, Lilâwati,* by *Bhânarâ Chârууа,* etc.

10 *Upangas.*

The *Upangas,* four in number, contain the Hindoo learning upon logic, moral philosophy, jurisprudence, and history.

PURANAS.

Purana, Puranam, Puranon, history of life, poetical representations of Indian mythology, and fabulous history. The *Puranas* hold an eminent rank in the religion and literature of the Hindoos. Possessing, like the *Vedas,* the credit of a divine origin, and scarcely inferior to them in sanctity, they exercise a more extensive and practical influence upon Hindoo society. They regulate their ritual, direct their faith, and supply in popular legendary tales materials for their credulity. To European scholars they recommend themselves on other accounts; as they have been considered to contain not only the picturesque and mythological part of Indian superstition, but as the treasury of extensive and valuable historical remains, whose data reach back at least nearly to the deluge. The *Puranas* include ancient traditions respecting the gods, religious doctrines and rites, the creation, the ages of the world, cosmography[s], and the genealogy and history of the ancient kings, as well as the deeds of their successors[t]. Many of these *Puranas* or traditions treat only of some part of these subjects, while others take in the whole circle. Most of them relate a portion of the history of the gods, which they narrate very circumstantially.

The *Puranas* are considered nearly as ancient as the *Vedas*. They are divided into two classes, containing eighteen each. The *Puranas* of the first and higher class set forth in detail the attributes and powers of *Krishna Dwaipayana*. The *Puranas* belonging to this class are said to contain four hundred thousand *slokas*, or one million six hundred thousand lines. Ten of them comprise the love and history of *Shivêa*, four of *Vishnu*, and two of *Brahma*. Two others, named *Agni*, sing the praises of the sun and of fire. The eighteenth is the *Bhagavata*, or Life of Crishna, which crowns the whole series[u].

The actual operation of these works upon the minds of a vast portion of mankind, and the reputation they bear for high antiquity and historical worth, entitle them to a full and candid investigation. A plan has accordingly been adopted for submitting the whole of them to analysis, the result of which, as regards one of

[s] The section of the *Puranas* relating to geography is called *Bhu-Chanda*, or *Bhuvana-Cosa*.

[t] Five of the most important of these are called the *Pantschalakchana*.

[u] Every *Purana* treats of five subjects: the creation of the universe, its progress, and the renovation of worlds; the genealogy of gods and heroes; chronology, according to a fabulous system; and heroic history, containing the achievements of demigods and heroes. Since each *Purana* contains a cosmogony, with mythological and heroic history, the works which bear that title may not unaptly be compared to the Grecian theogonies. See Colebrooke's Essay on the Sanscrit, etc. in Asiatic Researches, vol. vii, p. 202; and Sir William Jones's Works, vol. i, p. 360; or Asiatic Researches, vol. i, p. 351.

them, was communicated to the Asiatic Society of Calcutta by its secretary, the present Boden professor. The *Vishnu Purana*, it appears from this account, is a work of sectarial character, inculcating the preferential adoration of *Vishnu*. The legendary portion, although considerable, is less extravagant than in most of the *Puranas;* and the genealogical and historical sections, contain much curious and valuable matter. Professor Wilson does not consider this *Purana* to be older than the middle of the tenth century, though avowedly compiled from older materials. The historical portion is referred to ancient and apparently traditionary memorials. Upon the whole, it is considered as perhaps the most rational and valuable of the class of works to which it belongs [x].

The names of single *Puranas* are given in detail by Sir William Jones (Works, vol. i, p. 360; or, Asiatic Researches, vol. i, p. 352, 8vo. edition); by Sainte Croix, in his translation of *Ezur-Vedam*; and Hamilton and Langlès, in the Catalogue of manuscripts. Their statements, however, differ.

Catalogue of ten *Puranas*, presented to the London Asiatic Society, by colonel Tod. See Transactions of the Royal Asiatic Society, vol. i, p. 613.

For a general account of the *Puranas* the reader may consult Asiatic Researches, vol. viii, p. 480, (Hall. Lit. Zeit, 1816, Oct. No. 247), and Craufurd's Researches on India, vol. i, p. 187.

For a long time only four complete *Puranas* were accessible to Europeans, through a Tamulic translation from the Sanscrit: namely *Saywon, Kandon, Kurmon*, and *Bagavadon*. To these have been added, in something less than sixteen years, the *Mahabbhrata* and *Ramayana*, which, with the *Bhágavata*, are among

[x] Asiatic Journal, April, 1825, p. 458.

the most celebrated; and are now well known to Europeans by translations of long extracts and complete episodes.

1. *Bhagavata.*

Bagavadon, or *Bhagavata*, takes its name from *Bhagavat*, the ruler, one of the appellations of Krishna. The poem consists of twelve *Skandhas*, or books, and contains the history of *Vishnu*, as *Krishna*, who bore that surname. They are attributed to *Krishna Dwaipâyana*, under the appellation of *Veda-vyâsa*, or merely *Vyâsa*, the compiler, who is said to have lived in the ninth century. Colebrooke, however, from its style, considers it of later date, and ascribes it to Vopadeva.

A copy of the *Bhagavata* in Devanâgari, of 1528, as well as two others in Bengalee, are in the Royal Library at Paris. See Hamilton and Langlès Catalogue des mss. Sanscrits, p. 9, and Notice sur un manuscrit du *Bhagavata-Pourana*, envoyé par M. Duvancel à la Société Asiatique, par M. Burnouf, fils, in the Journal Asiatique, tom. vii, Juillet, 1825, p. 46, et Octobre, p. 193.

Réflexions sur *Bagavadam* par Deguignes, in the Mémoires de l'Académie des Inscriptions tom. xxxviii, p. 312;—see likewise the Monthly Review, 1788, vol. lxxix, p. 591—600, and Fr. Schlegel's Geschichte der Literatur, vol. i, p. 180.

Specimens of the *Bhagavat-Purana* will be found in Asiatic Researches, in the Voyages de Sonnerat, and the first thirteen strophes in Paul. a. S. Bartholomæo. *Sidharúbam*, p. 171.

Bagavadam, ou Doctrine Divine, Ouvrage indien Canonique, sur l'être Suprême, les dieux, les géans, les hommes, les diverses parties de l'univers, etc. (Traduit du Sanscrit en Tamoul, et du Tamoul en Français, par un Malabar chrétien, nommé Maridas Poullé, en 1769). Publié par M. Foucher d'Obsonville, *Paris*, 1788, 8vo. According to Hamilton this is only an extract, of which the beginning alone is tolerably faithful. It is translated into German in the Sammlung asiatischer Originalschriften, *Zürich*, 1791, B. i, p. 1—216.

α. Dialogue of Narada with Brahma.

Uebersetzung eines ungedruckten Fragments des *Bagavadam* (Dialogue of *Narada* with *Brahma*), by J. Ith, in his translation of the *Ezour-Vedam* from Ste. Croix, *Bern*, 1779, 2 Bde. 8vo. vol. ii, p. 229—242.

β. Marriage of Rukminî.

Mariage de *Rukminî*, tiré du *Bhaghavata*, in Mélanges de Littérature Sanscrite par A. Langlois, p. 85—119. *Rukminî*, the golden, was the daughter of king *Bhishmaka*, in her shape *Lakshmî* descended to the earth, when her husband *Vishnu*, as *Krishna*, dwelt among mankind. This episode recites the espousals of these deities upon the earth.

2. *Mahabharat.*

Mahâ Bhârata, or, as Ward writes it, *Muhabharutu*, that is, the great *Bhârata*, is a gigantic Epic poem in eighteen cantos, and of more than one hundred thousand *slokas*, generally of two lines each. It is ascribed to the *Brahman Krishna Dwaipayana Vyasa*, and said to be about four thousand years old[y].

[y] Between the *Vedas* and *Puranas*, in point of antiquity, or, at least, older than parts of the latter, rank the two great epic poems, the *Ramayana* and *Mahâ Bharata*, the Iliad and Odyssey of Sanscrit poetry. Quarterly Review, vol. xlv, p. 6.

Whether this be the case or not, it appears certain, from the various translations of separate parts of it which have been made, that it is a composition not more remarkable for the information it affords respecting ancient manners, and habits of feeling, than for the grandeur of conception, and spirit of poetry, which, notwithstanding much that is offensive to our ideas of good taste, are everywhere manifest [z].

Its principal subject is a history of the misfortunes of a race of kings, descended from the great *Bhârata*, who was banished the city of *Hastinapura*, and wandered about for a long time in misery; but at length, by the assistance of *Krishna*, became victorious, and again happy.

A number of beautiful episodes are interwoven; and what the pandits say of the Sanscrit language, in which it is preserved, may be said of the *Mahâ Bhârata*, "It is a deep and noble forest, abounding in delicious fruits and fragrant flowers, shaded and watered by perennial springs [a].

The contents of this poem are given in detail in the Catalogue des mss. Sanscrits, by Hamilton and Langlès, p. 62—64, and in Will. Ward's View of the History, etc. of the Hindoos, second edition, vol. i, p. 543—557.

Anquetil du Perron Recherches historiques et géographiques sur l'Inde, *Berlin*, 1787, 4to. tom. ii, p. 297, 553.

Polier Mythologie des Indiens, vol. i, p. 395.

Heeren's Researches on the Indians, last edition, in the original German, or in the French and English translation [b].

[z] See Asiatic Journal, 1817, p. 425. [a] Ibid.

[b] The other great epic too of the Mahabharata is coming gradually to light. In addition to the episode of Nalus, which had already appeared, professor Bopp of Berlin has added to our list the episode of the Deluge,

Craufurd's Researches on India, vol. i, p. 187.

Asiatic Journal, 1817, May, p. 425.

This poem is held in high esteem throughout India, and translated into many of the oriental languages. It was rendered into Persian at the command of Acbar the Great, and from this version the contents are given in English in the *Ayeen-Akberi*, vol. ii, p. 100.

Aperçu d'un Mémoire sur la traduction Persane du *Mahabharata*, faite par ordre de l'empereur *Djelal-eddin Mohammed Akbar*, par M. Schulz, in the Journal Asiatic, 1825, Août, p. 110—117; Sept. 129—138. This translation is by Abou'lfazl, Visir to Acbar, and exists in manuscript in the Bibliothèque du Roi. In the notice of Sanscrit manuscripts it is quoted under the title of *Kitab Muhaberat*, i. e. liber ingentium prœliorum.

An extraordinary beautiful Sanscrit manuscript of the *Mahabharata*, in twelve volumes, is described in the Supplement to Howell and Stewart's Oriental Catalogue, for 1827, p. 96.

The History of *Ferishta*, translated by Dow, contains an extract from the *Mahabharat*.

Mahabharat (in Sungskrit), *Calcutta*, 1801—1806, 4 vols. in 12mo.

a. Introduction and Separate Books.

Mahabhàrati exordium cum versione, in Othm. Frankii Chrestomathia Sanscrita, vol. i, p. 3.

The first book of the *Mahabharat*, translated into the Bengalee, *Calcutta*, 1812, 2 vols. 4to; also 4 vols. in 8vo.

A literal translation of the first section of the first book, by Mr. Charles Wilkins, will be found in the

the mythic histories of the Savitri, the Rape of Draupadi, and Arjuna's Journey to Indra's Heaven. Professor Heeren, in a manuscript addition received from him for the English translation of his Asiatic Nations now in the press.

Annals of Oriental Literature, *London*, 1820, vol. i. p. 65—86; vol. ii, p. 278—296; vol. iii, p. 450—461; and a notice of it by Bopp, in the Götting. gel. Anz. 1821, St. 54, 55.

The first four books of the *Mahabharat*, translated into Bengalee, and printed at *Serampoor*, 1801, 4 vols. 12mo.

The seventh book of the *Mahabarat*, translated into Persian, manuscript, in Howell and Stewart's Catalogue of Oriental Literature, *London*, 1828.

β. *Episodes and Extracts.*

The episodes of the *Mahabharat*, are called *Upakhyânâni*, and the five most esteemed of them are named in India, the five precious stones.

aa. *Bhagavat-Gita.*

The *Bhagavat-Gita*, or, according to Ward, the *Bhuguvu-Dschita*, that is, the divine song, gives, in the form of a discourse between the god *Krishna* and his pupil *Arjuna*, which they hold in the midst of an undecided battle, a full and most curious exposition of the half-mythological, half-philosophical pantheism of the Brahmans, and a general view of the whole mystic theology of the Hindoos. A. W. Schlegel calls this episode the most beautiful, and perhaps the only truly philosophical poem, that the whole range of literature known to us has produced [c]. Mr. Milman observes, that it reads like a noble fragment of Empedocles or Lucretius, introduced into the midst of an Homeric epic [d]. In point of poetical conception, there is some-

[c] Indischen Bibl. ii, 2, p. 219.

[d] See a capital article in the Quarterly Review, vol. xlv, p. 1, ascribed to this gentleman, to which I am indebted for nearly the whole of the above. See also, Catalogue des mss. Sanscrits, p. 19; and Recherches Asiatiques, tom. i, p. 287.

thing singularly striking and magnificent, in the introduction of this solemn discussion on the nature of the godhead and the destiny of man, in the midst of the fury and tumult of the civil war in which it occurs. This episode is said to be an interpolation of later date than the giant epic, of which it forms a part; and if so, it is allied with great address to the main subject of the poem. "On the whole, the *Bhagavat-Gita* is certainly one of the most curious and the most characteristic works we have received from the East. As a record of religious and philosophical opinion it is invaluable; and if the progress of Sanscrit criticism should hereafter be able to fix, with any certainty, the date of this episode, it would throw light on the whole history of Indian civilisation [e]."

An analysis of this poem is given in an interesting article in the Monthly Review, 1787, vol. lxxvi, p. 198 and 205; by Langlois, in his Monumens Littéraires de l'Inde; and another, with metrical specimens, in the article in the Quarterly Review just referred to.

In the library of the Asiatic Society of London, there is a Sanscrit ms. embellished with miniatures, under the title of The *Bhaghavad-Gita* and *Devi Mahatmya.*

The *Bhagavat-Gita* was printed in Sanscrit, *Calcutta,* 1815, 8vo; and 1818, 8vo.

The *Bhagvat-Geeta,* or Dialogues of *Kreeshna* and *Arjoon,* in eighteen lectures, with notes, translated from the original in the Sanskreet, or ancient language of the Brahmans, by Charles Wilkins, *London,* 1785, large 4to. A critique upon this work will be found in the Monthly Review, 1787[f]. In French, Le *Baghvat-*

[e] Quarterly Review, l. c.

[f] This was the first work translated from the Sanscrit into any European language. Adelung states, that the missionary John, in a letter to Rüdiger, writes, that Wilkins, in this version, has introduced many European notions not in the original, and entirely opposed to the Hindoo life and genius. Though I have found no other authority for this opinion, its correctness

Geeta, ou Dialogues de *Kreeshna* et *d'Arjoon*, contenant un précis de la religion et de la morale des Indiens, traduit du Samscrit, langue sacrée des Brames, en Anglais, par Charles Wilkins, et de l'Anglais en Français, par Parraud, *Paris*, 1787, 8vo; German, in the Sammlung Asiat. Original-schriften, *Zürich*, 1801, 8vo; Bd. i, p. 321—330; and by Fr. Majer, in Jul. Klaproth's Asiat. Magazin, Bd. i, p. 406—453. A Russian translation was published at *Moscow*, 1788, 8vo.

A new and improved edition of the English translation appeared in 1809, under the title of *Bhuguvud-geeta*, or dialogues between *Krishna* and *Arjuna*, extracted from the *Mahabarut*, printed at *Khizurpoor* near *Calcutta*, 1809.

Some passages of the English version were turned into German metre, by Fr. Schlegel; and will be found in his work, under the head of "Aus dem *Bhogovot-gita*," Ueber die Sprache und Weisheit der Indier, p. 284—307.

Bhagavadgitæ lectiones, in Othm. Frankii Chrestomathia Sanskrita, vol. i—xvii; ibid. ii, 4. p. 115.

Bhagavadgitæ loca selecta cum versione, ibid. ii, 3, p. 83—115.

Bhagadad-Gita, id est, Θεσπέσιον μέλος, sive almi *Krishnæ* et *Arjunæ* colloquium de rebus divinis, *Bharateæ* episodium. Textum recensuit, annotationes criticas

seems probable, if we consider how little was then known of the people, of their institutions, and their literature. That free intercourse which has had a gradual growth between the learned caste of India and the literati of Europe, was then in its infancy. The priests guarded their sacred books with jealous care from strangers. The translator had to contend with the obscurities of a language, confessedly one of the most difficult to Europeans, and which the Brahmans spend their lives in studying. These circumstances, and many others which might be enumerated, rendered the task of this venerable Sanscrit scholar tenfold more difficult than what it would now be; and will lead us rather to wonder at his eminent success in the Herculean labour he undertook, than to carp at its slight blemishes.

et interpretationem Latinam adjecit, Aug. Guil. a Schlegel, *Bonn,* 1823, 8vo., reviewed by Fr. Bopp in the Götting. gel. Anz. 1824, St. 37, 38. Upon this critic's statements Langlois published some remarks in the Journal Asiatique; and this called forth Observations sur la Critique du *Bhavagad-Gita,* insérée dans le Journal Asiatique, par M. A. W. de Schlegel; Journ. Asiat. tom. ix, p. 3: Lettre à M. le Président du Conseil de la Société Asiatique, et réponse aux observations de M. A. W. de Schlegel, par M. Langlois, in the Journ. Asiat. tom. ix, p. 185. The Latin version is spoken of in the Quarterly Review, vol. i, p. 7, by one of the most elegant Latin scholars of the present day, as composed with singular elegance and dexterity.

Ueber die unter dem Namen *Bhagavad-Gita* bekannte Episode des *Mahabharata,* von Wilh. v. Humboldt, *Berlin,* 1826, 4to. The writer just referred to calls this " a remarkably able and profound disquisition on the philosophy as well as the poetry of the *Bhagavat.*"

Ueber die *Bhagavad-Gita,* Mit Bezug auf die Beurtheilung der Schlegelschen Ausgabe im Pariser Asiatischen Journal, aus einen Briefe von Hrn. Staatsminister von Humboldt.—In Schlegel's Indischer Bibliothek II. 2. p. 218—258. 3. p. 328.

A Persian translation in manuscript, is mentioned in Howell and Stewart's Oriental Catalogue for 1827, Suppl. No. 4439, under the following title: *Shri Bhagvat,* a translation from Shanskrit into Persian of the Discourses of Arjun and Kreeshna.

bb. The History of Nala, King of Nishadha, and his Wife Damajanti.

This is another episode from the *Mahabharat,* of which it forms part of the third book. It is entirely of a different cast from the last, and is said to partake rather of the manner of our own Spenser, than of the philosophic tone of the *Bhagavat-Gita*. A sovereign, named *Yudhisshthira*, the eldest of the five sons of *Pandu*, is an exile in the wilderness, where he and his brothers are doomed to pass twelve years, according to an engagement he had entered into with his opponent *Duryôdhana*, with whom he had lost at dice. The sage Wrihasdasva bears him company; and, to amuse and console him, relates the history of king Nala, who, like himself, had lost his empire and wealth by playing at dice, but in the end became fortunate and happy.

The critic[g] from whom is chiefly borrowed the notice of the *Bhagavat-Gita*, (and who so well able to judge?) calls this a poem full of the most pathetic interest; and adds, that if any portion of Indian song hitherto translated into the European languages is likely to arrest general attention, it is this beautiful tale, which wants only a poet's hand to transplant it, in its living freshness, to our foreign climate. For though, indeed, Indian poetry in general must always lose much of its native interest with us, from its foreign associations and learned character; yet, as the same writer observes, "there are universal feelings, which lie in the very depth of our common nature,—affections and passions of which the language is as universal as the shape and lineaments of man; and when poetry, in however remote a region, speaks this general dialect of the heart, it will command attention, and excite a pleasing or a thrilling interest. Such appears to be the case with the episode of Nala."

The following outline of the subject of this poem, is given word for word from the same article in the Quarterly.

[g] The Rev. H. H. Milman, in Quarterly Review, vol. xlv, p. 13, from whom most of what follows on this poem is copied verbatim.

Nala, the monarch of Nishadha, centred in his person all the noble qualities which could distinguish an Indian monarch. He surpassed all kings in justice, all men in beauty; and he was unrivalled in the management of horses. Bhima, the king of Vidarbha (Berar), possessed an only daughter, the most beautiful and most modest of her sex—the gentle Damajanti. Like the knights and ladies of old, these two perfect beings become mutually enamoured, each from the fame of the other's admirable qualities: but instead of human ambassadors—the faithful squire or the adventurous handmaid,—Indian poetry furnishes the enamoured prince with a very different kind of confidante. Wandering in the woods, Nala beholds a flock of birds with golden wings, who offer to convey the tidings of his passion to the ear of the princess. Nala could not refuse a proposal so courteous, and at the same time so acceptable.

Flew away the swans[h] rejoicing, to Vidarbha straight they flew,
To Vidarbha's stately city; there by Damajanti's feet,
Down with drooping plumes they settled; and she gazed upon the flock,
Wondering at their forms so graceful, where amid her maids she sat.
Sportively began the damsels all around to chase the birds;
Scattering flew the swans before her, all about the lovely grove.
Lightly ran the nimble maidens, every one her bird pursued;
But the swan that through the forest gentle Damajanti followed,
Suddenly in human language spake to Damajanti thus:
" Damajanti, in Vidarbha dwells a noble monarch, Nala,
Fair in form as the Aswinas, peerless among men is he—
Like Kandharba in his beauty, like a god in human form—
Truly if that thou wert wedded to this man, O peerless princess!
Beautiful would be thy children, like to him, thou slender maid.
We have seen gods and gandharvas, men, the serpents, and the Rishis[i];
All we've seen, but ne'er the equal have we seen of noble Nala.
Pearl art thou among all women, Nala is the pride of men."

[h] In the original, according to our translators, this is a far less poetic bird; and we must crave permission for once to turn our 'geese into swans.'

[i] Intermediate beings in Indian mythology.

They receive a favourable answer from the princess, and take flight.

As in ancient Greece, or as in feudal romance, the kings of all the earth, and all the chiefs or warriors who aspire to the hand of this blameless Helen of the East, are summoned to a solemn assemblage, called the *Swayambara*, or self-election, where the princess is to designate the favoured suitor by throwing a wreath of flowers round his neck. The roads to the court of Vidarbha are crowded with rajahs and kings; and groan beneath the weight of steeds, and cars, and elephants. Nala, of course, is among the first; but on his way he encounters four formidable and unexpected rivals, Indra the god of the firmament, Agni the god of fire, Varuna the god of the waters, Yama the god of the infernal regions. They declare that they have descended from heaven to seek the hand of the lovely Damajanti; and they adjure the enamoured Nala, by his piety and dutiful allegiance to the gods, to undertake the ungracious task of bearing their message of love to the fair. Nala remonstrates; but piety triumphs over passion. He is suddenly, by the divine aid, transported into the bower of the princess.

There he saw Vidarbha's maiden, girt with all her virgin bands,
Bright in beauty, full of softness, worthy of her noble blood;
Every limb in round proportion, slender sides and lovely eyes;
Even the moon's soft gleam despising, in her own o'erpowering brightness:
As he gazed, his love grew warmer to the softly smiling maid,
Yet to keep his truth, his duty, all his passion he suppressed.

He delivers the message of the gods; but the maiden, in this delicate situation, permits her candour to prevail over her bashfulness, and declares that, even in the presence of the gods, she shall select the noble Nala. But a new difficulty arises: the assembly is met at the Swayambara, all the royal suitors are in array, and Damajanti discovers, to her dismay, five Nalas; for each of the deities had assumed the form, the features, the dress of the king of Nishadha. She addresses the deities in a supplicating hymn.

With her words and with her spirit uttered she her humble prayer;
Folding both her hands and trembling, to the gods the maiden spake.

The gods are moved with compassion; they stand confessed, pure (literally *sine sudore*), with eyes that do not close, with chaplets of celestial amaranth, their feet not touching the ground, their bodies casting no shadow. The form of the mortal Nala is distinguished by the opposite of all these celestial attributes. He is not free from the dust and heat of earth, his feet press the ground, his body casts a shadow.

Modestly the large-eyed maiden lifted up his garment's hem,
Round his shoulders threw she lightly the bright zone of radiant flowers.

The assembly breaks up amid the applause of the gods, and the jealous lamentations of the unsuccessful suitors.

The nuptials are celebrated: Nala and his bride are blessed with two children: Nala is the model of all virtue; beloved by his subjects, pious to the gods, a diligent reader of the four Vedas, even of the fifth—he at length performs the Aswameda, the celebrated sacrifice of the horse, the height of Indian devotion.

But 'the course of true love never doth run smooth.' The gods, on their return from the Swayambara, had met the fierce and vindictive Kali and another deity, who, enraged to find themselves too late, and jealous of the success of Nala, swore deep and eternal vengeance. But evil spirits have no power over the blameless; offence must be committed before they can possess themselves of the soul of man. In unlucky hour Nala is guilty of a nameless act of impurity in the omission of a certain ablution: the demon Kali at once enters into him; his understanding is perverted, his disposition changed, and one lingering virtue, the love of Damajanti alone remains. He plays at dice with his unnatural brother Pushkara—loses his wealth, palaces, provinces, his kingdom, his very clothes. Damajanti had fortunately seized an opportunity of sending her children, under the care of the chief charioteer (the master of the horse), to her father's court. What stake remains to the ruined gambler? none but Damajanti herself. The brother proposes the hazard; but the demoniac has not yet lost that last holy affection. They are driven together into the wilderness—with but one garment between them; for a bird flew away with the only one Nala had retained, mocking the spendthrift gambler—and proscribed by an edict, which makes it a capital crime to afford them any succour, or to receive them under any roof. Nala persuades his miserable wife to abandon him to his fate, and retire to her father's court. It is our fault if we have entirely marred the exquisite pathos of her reply.

Truly all my heart is breaking, and my sinking members fail,
When, O king, thy desperate counsel once I think on, once again.
Robbed of kingdom, robbed of riches, naked, worn with thirst and hunger,
Shall I leave thee in the forest, shall I wander from thee far?
When thou, sad and famine-stricken, thinkest of thy former bliss
In the wild wood, O my husband, I will soothe thy weariness.
Like a wife is no physician; in a state so sad as thine,
Medicine none is like her kindness—Nala, speak I not the truth?

Nala promises that they shall not part; but the evil spirit within him strives to overpower this last virtue. The frantic man determines to abandon her while she is sleeping; he cuts off part of the single garment they possess, and leaves her half naked, and lying on the hard earth. Once he turns back to take a parting look—

Yet his cruel heart relenting, to the cabin turns he back:
On the slumbering Damajanti gazing, sadly wept the king:

Thou, that sun or wind hath never roughly visited, my lov'd one,
On the hard earth in a cabin sleep'st, with no protecting friend.
When she sees her severed garment, she, that ever smiled so sweetly,
Will not all her senses fail her: loveliest how will 't fare with her?
How will 't fare with Bhima's daughter, lonely, by her lord abandoned,
Wandering in the savage forest, where wild beasts and serpents dwell?

He entreats the protection of all the gods and genii, but rests his chief trust in a still surer safeguard.

Noblest, may they all protect thee, best of all thy virtue guard thee.

The strength of Damajanti, through which she is enabled

To trace huge forests, and unharboured heaths,
Infamous hills, and sandy perilous wilds,

is her deep, and ardent, and self-regardless love for her faithless husband.

Damajanti woke—the beauteous, in the wild wood, full of dread,
When she did not see her husband, overpowered with grief and pain.
Loud she shriek'd in her first anguish—Where art thou, Nishadha's king?
Mighty king! my sole protector! Ah! my lord, desert'st thou me?
Oh! I'm lost, undone for ever; helpless in the wild wood left.
Faithful once to every duty wert thou, king, and true in word;
True in word art thou, to leave me, slumbering in the forest thus?
Couldst thou then depart, forsaking thy weak, faithful, once-loved wife,
Her that never sinned against thee, now, alas! so sinned against?
O, I fear; thou famous conqueror, show thee to me, oh, my lord;
Yes, I see thee—there I see thee—there thou art, Nishadha's king.
In the straw why thus conceal thee? why no answer? speak, my lord,
Wherefore now, like one forsworn, thus sternly stayest thou aloof?
When I come beseeching to thee, wilt thou not console nor cheer me?
For myself I will not sorrow, not for aught to me befalls.
Thou art all alone, my husband; I will only mourn for thee.
How will 't fare with thee, my Nala, thirsting, famished, faint with hunger,
At eve on some hard root reposing, and no more beholding me?

Her adventures are as strange and various as ever happened to errant damsel in romance. She is in danger from a terrible serpent; is saved by a huntsman, only to fall into more peril from his unhallowed desires:

she prays for divine succour, and the lustful huntsman falls dead at her feet.

She then descends into a quiet valley, inhabited by a fraternity of Sanyasis, Gymnosophists or hermits, who are clothed in the bark of trees. In amazement at her beauty they worship her as a divinity.

Fear not thou, oh blessed spirit!
Speak, oh thou! of form so beauteous; who art thou, and what thy purpose?
As thy noble form we gaze on, as we gaze on thy bright eyes,
In amaze we stand and wonder: freely breathe, and wail no more.
Of the wood art thou the goddess? or the mountain-goddess thou?
Or the river-nymph, the beauteous? Blessed spirit, speak the truth.

Her next adventure is more animating and picturesque. She encounters a caravan of travelling merchants, who, in the same manner, are inclined to adore her as a celestial being, and gladly admit her into their cavalcade. The conclusion of this scene is so characteristic that we cannot omit it. At nightfall the tents are pitched by a beautiful stream, covered with the lotus flower.

When the midnight came all noiseless—came in silence deep and still,
Weary slept the band of merchants. Lo! a herd of elephants
Came to drink the mountain river, oozing moisture from their temples.
When the caravan they gazed on, the tame elephants they scented.
Forward ran they, wild and furious, tossing fierce their murtherous trunks.
Irresistible the onset of the rushing ponderous beasts:
As the peak from some high mountain, thundering rolls into the valley,
Strewn was all the way before them with the boughs, the limbs of trees.
On they crash'd to where the travellers slumber'd by the lotus lake.
Trampled down without a struggle, helpless on the earth they lay.
Woe, O woe! shrieked out the merchants; wildly some began to fly,
In the forest thickets plunging; some stood gasping, blind with dread.
With their tusks, their trunks, their feet, beat them down the elephants.
Many saw their camels dying, mingled with the men on foot,
And in frantic tumult rushing, fiercely struck each other dead.
Many, miserably shrieking, cast them down upon the earth;

Many climbed the trees in anguish, or plunged deep beneath the waves.
Such, so fearful was the tumult, the three worlds seemed all appalled.
" 'Tis a fire that burns and blazes; save ye, fly ye for your lives!
Lo! your precious pearls ye trample: take them up;—why fly so fast?
Save them—'tis a common venture: fear ye not I would deceive:"
To each other cried the merchants, and in shrieking anguish scattered.

The calamity is ascribed to the presence of the ill-fated queen. She is forced to fly, and at length reaches a hospitable city, where, though half naked, worn with toil, and withered with sorrow, she is adored for her beauty as she passes through the streets, and is received with the greatest kindness by the mother of the king.

The adventures of Nala are not less strange and stirring. He has an encounter with an enchanted serpent, an incident of which we find, more than once, almost the exact parallel in the Teutonic ballads. His form is entirely changed, and he is received as 'master of the horse' at the court of Ayodhya, or Oude. King Bhima, distressed at the loss of his daughter, traces out her retreat by means of some wandering Brahmans. She returns home; and after some time, in order to discover the retreat of Nala, proclaims her intention of holding another Swayambara, that she may proceed to a second marriage, the worst offence against female propriety[k], especially in a lady of her rank.

Rituparna, the king of Oude, determines to become a candidate for the princess, and sets forth with his charioteer—the disguised Nala. This king was gifted with so wonderful a faculty of calculation, that he could count the fruits upon the tree as he drove rapidly under it. Nala was no less distinguished for his unrivalled management of horses. They mutually communicate their secrets; and Nala thus, already dispos-

[k] Second marriages are prohibited by the laws of Menu; and hence, no doubt, one great motive to the performance of the Suttee.

sessed by the wicked spirit, becomes more than a match for any gamester. As they enter the city of king Bhima, Damajanti recognises the sound of her husband's trampling steeds—his driving could not be mistaken by her ear.

All her heart was thrilled with wonder, as she heard the welcome sound;
On they seemed to come, as Nala drove of yore his trampling steeds;
Damajanti heard and trembled at the old familiar sound.
On the palace roof the peacocks, th' elephants within their stalls,
And the coursers heard the rolling of the mighty monarch's car.
Peacocks, elephants, the trampling of the fiery coursers heard;
Up they raised their necks and clamoured, as at sound of coming rain.

Damajanti employs every artifice to discover her husband. She suspects the charioteer, about whom all is wonderful and miraculous. The gates rise or expand to let him in; self-kindled fire is ever ready at his call; the water flows towards him when he is in want of it. Her suspicions are still further excited by a whimsical incident. She procures some of his food, and recognises the well-known flavour of her husband's cookery. This is Indian, what follows is universal nature. By her handmaid she sends her children to him.

Soon as he young Indrasena and her little brother saw,
Up he sprang, his arms wound round them, to his bosom folding both;
When he gazed upon the children, like the children of the gods,
All his heart o'erflowed with pity, and unwilling tears brake forth.
Yet Nishadha's lord perceiving that she marked his strong emotion,
From his hold released the children, and to Cesina he spake:—
Oh! so like mine own twin children was yon lovely infant pair,
Seeing them thus unexpected, have I broken out in tears.

Damajanti contrives an interview, and questions the mysterious charioteer:—

Hast thou ever seen, Mahaka, an upright and noble man,
Who departed, and abandoned in the wood his wife that slept,—
The beloved wife and blameless,—in the wild wood worn with grief?
Him, who was my chosen husband—him, for whom I scorned the gods;
Could he leave the true, the loving—her that hath his children borne?

Nala can conceal himself no longer; but the jealous thought, that his wife was about to commit the faithless and indecorous offence of taking a second husband, rankles in his heart, and he rebukes her with sternness. Damajanti adjures the wind, the sun, and the moon, to bear witness that she was guiltless of any such design, and only employed the innocent artifice to win back her lord.

He through all the world that wanders, witness the all-seeing Wind,
Let him now of life bereave me, if in this 'gainst thee I've sinned.
And the Sun that ever moveth o'er the bosom of the deep,
Let him now of life bereave me, if in this 'gainst thee I've sinned.
Witness, too, the Moon that travels through the midst of all the world;
Let her, too, of life bereave me, if in this 'gainst thee I've sinned.
These three gods are those that govern the three worlds—so let them speak.
If these gods can say with justice, "Cast her off," so let it be.
Thus adjured, a solemn witness spake the Wind from out the air:—
"She hath done or thought no evil; Nala, it is truth I speak.
King, the treasure of her virtue Damajanti well hath guarded;
We ourselves have seen and watched her, closely for three live-long years."
Even as thus the Wind was speaking, flowers fell showering all around,
And the god's sweet music sounded, floating on the soft west-wind.

Nala re-assumes his form; and the poem ends with his winning back all that he had lost to his unprincipled brother, his re-ascending his ancestral throne, and recommencing a reign of piety, justice, and felicity.

Thus closes a piece which, for interest of story, characteristic variety of incident, purity of moral tone, delicacy of sentiment, and richness of imagery, inspires a very high idea of Indian imagination and feeling, and wants but the aid of a faithful and spirited translator to give the name of Vyasa acknowledged rank among the celebrated poets of antiquity. 'The heroic truth and devotedness of Damajanti,' observes A. Schlegel, at the close of a glowing passage on the general merit of this poem, 'are as celebrated as those of Penelope in the west, and deserve to be as well known in Europe[l].

Besides this, there are many other Indian poems which treat of the adventures of Nala. One of the most celebrated is the *Naishad'hiya*, by *Shri Harscha*, the son of *Shri Kirah*. This is one of the six *Mahakavya*, or capital poems of profane literature. It recites, in twenty-two cantos, the marriage of Nala with Damayanti[m], daughter of Bhima, king of Vidarbha, a very favourite subject of Indian poetry; and though not free from faults, it is by many esteemed the most beautiful composition in the Sanscrit language. Notwithstanding, however, its striking poetical beauties, according to Hindoo taste, it is very barren of incident. The story proceeds no further than the marriage of Nala and Damayanti, and the description of their mutual affection and happiness. Their romantic and interesting adventures subsequent to their marriage are wholly omitted; while the poet, with a degree of licentiousness, but too well accommodated to the taste of his countrymen, indulges in glowing descriptions of sensual love[n].

A copious commentary in Sanscrit upon this poem, with remarks on the various kinds of metre in which it is composed, is in the possession of the Paris Asiatic Society. This manuscript bears the title of *Sâhityavidyâdhari Tika*. See Journ. Asiat. vol. xxxvi, p. 383.

Nala Daya, a poem, with a Commentary, *Calcutta*, 1813, 8vo. This *Nala Daya*, which is ascribed to the celebrated poet *Calidasa*, is a poem in four cantos, comprising two hundred and twenty couplets, or stanzas, on the adventures of Nala and Damayanti.

[l] Indische Bibliothek, i, 98.

[m] In the foregoing extract from the Quarterly their mode of spelling this name is followed, though properly *Damayanti*.

[n] Colebrooke, on Sanscrit poetry, in Asiatic Researches, vol. x, p. 428.

In this singular poem rhyme and alliteration are blended in the termination of the verses: for the three or four last syllables of each hemistich within the stanza are the same in sound, though different in sense. It is a series of puns on a pathetic subject[n].

Nuloduyu, a celebrated romance, formerly translated by Fuezee into Persian verse, under the name *Juldumum*, Khizurpoor, 1814, 4to. The Persian version was made by Scheickh Fizee, Abulfazel's brother. See Götting. gel. Anz. 1813, No. clvi.

A French translation of this episode from the Persian version of the *Mahabharat*, exists among the manuscripts in the Bibliothèque du Roi, presented by professor Schultz of the Société Asiatique of Paris. See Journ. Asiat. Sept. 1825, p. 137.

Srimahâbhârate Nalôpâkhyanam. Nalus, carmen Sanscritum, e *Mahàbàrato*. Edidit, Latine vertit, et adnotationibus illustravit Franciscus Bopp, *Londini, Parisiis*, et *Argentor*. 1819, 8vo. A critique upon this edition and version is given in A. W. v. Schlegel's Indischer Bibl. vol. i, p. 97—128, Götting. gel. Anz. 1820, p. 1; Leipz. Lit. Zeit, 1820, No. clvii—clix; Revue Encycl. 1820, Mars, p. 357[o].

Nala, eine indische Dichtung, von Vyasa, aus dem Sanskrit, im Versmaasse der Urschrift übersetzt und mit Erläuterungen begleitet von J. G. L. Kosegarten, *Jena*, 1820, 8vo.

A German metrical version of detached parts of *Nala* and *Damayanti*, and especially of the ix, x, xi, xii, and xiii cantos, is given by Francis Bopp, in his *Indralokâgamanam*, or Ardscuna's Wanderung zu Indra's Himmel, u. s. w. *Berlin*, 1824.

[n] Colebrooke, in Asiatic Researches, vol. x, p. 402.

[o] This is the second book printed in Europe in the ancient Indian character: the types used for it being the same as those with which Wilkins's Sanscrit Grammar was printed in 1808.

Nal und *Damajanti.* Eine indische Geschichte, von Fr. Rückert, *Frankfort a. M.* 1828, 12mo.

Another attempt of this sort is the *Nala-Champú* of *Trivicrama.* It recounts nearly the same story of the fortunes of King Nala and his wife Damayanti, in prose, with a very frequent mixture of poetry; a style in which numerous works have been composed in Sanscrit, and which is called *Champu* [p].

cc. The History of Dushwanta and Sakuntala.

The Story of *Dooshwanta* and *Sokoontala,* translated from the *Mahabharata,* a poem in the Sanskreet Language, by Ch. Wilkins, esq., originally published in the Oriental Repertory, by Alex. Dalrymple, *London,* 1795, 12mo. Histoire de *Douchmanta* et de *Sakountalâ,* extraite du *Mahâbhârata,* poëme Sanscrit, et traduite sur la version Anglaise de M. Charles Wilkins, Journ. Asiat. 1828, Mai, p. 838—874.

Part of the history of Sakuntala (his birth), from the *Mahabharata,* is translated into German verse by Fr. Schlegel, in his Works: Ueber Weisheit und Sprache der Indier, p. 308—324.

Dushwanta and *Sakuntala,* an episode from *Mahabharata,* in the Asiatic Journal, 1817, May, p. 425; June, p. 548; July, p. 7; August, p. 126.

dd. The Fight with the Giants.

Der Kampf mit dem Riesen, Episode aus *Mahabharat,* in genauer metrischer Uebersetzung, nach einer pariser Handschrift, von Fr. Bopp, in his Conjugationssystem der Sanskrit-Sprache, *Frankf. a. M.* 1816, 8vo. p. 237—269.

[p] Colebrooke, l. c. He mentions the Krishna Champu, the Ganga Champu, Vrindavanna Champu, etc.

ee. The Discourse of Dhritarashtra to his charioteer Sanjaya.

In English in the first number of the Annals of Oriental Literature, *London*, 1820.

Dhritarashtræ sermo ex *Mahabarato* excerptus cum *Nilakànthæ* scholiis et expositione, in Othm. Frankii Chrestomathia Sanskrita, *Monaci*, 1820, 4to. vol i, p. 2. It consists of eighty *slokas*, or distichs, each comprising two lines of sixteen syllables, having a cæsura at the end of the eighth syllable.

ff. The Death of Sisupala.

Sisupâla-Badha, or the death of *Sisupala*, a poem in twenty cantos, ascribed to king Magha; yet, if tradition may be relied on, Magha, though expressly named as the author, was merely the patron, not the poet. As the subject is heroic, and even the unity of action well preserved, and the style of the composition elevated, this poem is entitled to the name of epic[q]. It is taken from the *Mahabharat*, and narrates the war between *Krishna* and the princes who united themselves with *Sisupala* against him. A brief account of it is given by Colebrooke, in the Asiatic Researches, vol. x, p. 401; who observes, that the Indian taste for descriptive poetry, and particularly of the licentious kind, has disfigured this work, which is not otherwise undeserving of its high reputation.

The *Maghu Kavyu*, an epic poem in the original Sungskrit, published by H. H. Wilson, *Calcutta*, 1812, 4to. See W. Ward's View of the Literature, etc. vol. i, p. 511.

The *Sisupala Badha*, or Death of *Sisupala*; also entitled the *Mágha Cávya*, or Epic Poem of *Mágha*,

[q] Colebrooke.

in twenty cantos, with a commentary by Malli Natha. Edited by Vidya Cara Misra and Syama Lada, pundits, *Calcutta*, 1815, 8vo. Printed in the Nagari character.

gg. Arjuna's Journey to Indra's Heaven.

Indralokâgamanam, oder *Arjuna's* Wanderung zu *Indra's* Himmel, nebst andern Episoden des *Maha-Bharata*, in der Ursprache zum erstenmal herausgegeben, metrisch übersetzt und mit kritischen Anmerkungen versehen von Franz. Bopp, *Berlin*, 1824. Reviewed by F. E. Schultz, in the Journ. Asiat. vol. v, p. 164. The ascent of Arjuna, and the palaces of Indra, are described with great splendour of imagery, and in one part with a kind of voluptuous colouring. See Quarterly Review, vol. xlv, p. 30.

hh. Arjuna's Return to Indra's Heaven.

This is a sequel to the above, and is another warlike episode, in which the hero, armed with celestial weapons, assaults and conquers the cities of the Danawi, or demons. It will be found edited and partly translated into German verse, in Fr. Bopp's Die Sündfluth nebst drey andern der wichtigsten Episoden des *Maha-Bharata*, Berlin, 1829.

ii. The Death of Hidimba.

Hidimbabadhah, or *Hidimba's* Death, in the original text, with a German translation by Franz. Bopp, in his *Indralokagâmanam*, etc.

kk. The Brahman's Lament.

Brahmanavilâpah, or the Brahman's Lament, is given in the original text, with a German translation by Bopp, in the same work.

Upon the last two articles the writer in the Quarterly

observes, "The Death of Hidimba is a curious illustration of the universality of the same fictions all over the earth. Hidimba is exactly the blood-lapping, bone-cranching, marrow-sucking giant or ogre, who, having thrilled with terror the bosoms of children of an older growth, in the ballads of our Teutonic ancestors, has sunk into our nursery tales, from whence he is well-nigh exorcised by the more potent spirit of Utilitarianism. But the Brahman's Lament, though grounded on a similar legend, falls again into the softer and more pathetic vein. While the sons of Pandu dwelt in Eketschara, Bhima, sitting alone with his mother, hears the lamentation of a Brahman. A terrible giant infested the neighbourhood of the city, to whom a tribute of human flesh was daily paid. It had now come to the turn of the poorer Brahmans to furnish forth the horrible repast; and in this family either the Brahman himself, the mother, the grown up daughter, or the son, a little child, must be surrendered as the victim. It is a contest of the most affecting self-devotion; and in turn the father, the mother, and the daughter, in what may be fairly called three beautiful elegies, full of curious allusions to the state of Indian society, enforce their claim to the privilege of being made the sacrifice.

At the close they sit down and weep.

Seeing them together weeping, 'gan the little son to speak—
Gazing with both eyes wide open, lisped he thus his broken words:
"Weep not, father, weep not, mother, oh, my sister, weep not thou."
First to one, and then to th' other, went he with a smiling mouth,
Then a spike of spear-grass lifting, spake he thus as though in mirth,
"With this spear point will I kill him, this man-eating giant, dead."
In their bitterness of anguish, as the playful child they heard
Prattling thus, within their bosoms stole unspeakable delight.

ll. The Deluge.

Diluvium cum tribus aliis *Maha Bharati* præstantissimis episodiis. Primus edidit Franciscus Bopp. Fasciculus prior, quo continetur textus Sanscritus. *Berol.* 1824, 4to.

Die Sündfluth, nebst drey andern der wichtigsten Episoden des *Mahà-Bharata.* Aus der Ursprache übersetzt von Franz Bopp, *Berlin,* 1822. *Die Sündfluth* is reprinted in the Berliner Conversations-Blatte für Poësie, Literatur, und Kritik, 1829, No. cix. It had previously been translated by Sir William Jones, in his Works. See Götting. gel. Anz. 1829, St. 137.

Bopp's version of this poem on the Indian Deluge is noticed in the Quarterly Review, vol. xlv, p. 25, where some passages from it will be found elegantly translated into English. It is the Indian tradition of the deluge of Manu, the Noah of the book of Genesis.

mm. Sundas and Upasundas.

Sundopasundopâkhyânam, or *Sundas* and *Upasundas,* in the original text, and a German translation by Fr. Bopp, in his *Indralokâgamanam,* etc.

nn. Bahikavarnana.

An episode from the sixth book of the *Mahabharata,* under the title of *Bahikavarnana,* that is, a description of the *Bahikas,* a people of the Punjab (the country lying about the five rivers flowing from the north-east which fall into the Indus,) is given in the original, together with a Latin translation and notes, in Christiani Lassenii Commentatio geographica atque historica de Pentapotamia Indica, *Bonn,* 1827, 4to. p. 63—91. The reviewer in the Jen. Allg. Lit. Zeit, 1828, No. cxciii, believes that it contains many interpolations of a later date than the original work.

Some extracts from it have also been translated by Wilson, in his paper on the History of Cashmire, in Asiat. Researches, vol. xv, p. 1, etc.

oo. The Rape of Draupadi.

This episode represents the combat of the five husbands of *Draupadi*, in order to revenge the rape of their common wife. A fragment of this will be found in Bopp's grammar, p. 19, etc., and the whole episode in his Sündfluth. This community of husbands is a singular arrangement, and we believe unprecedented in the mythic or heroic age of India. It bears no resemblance to the loose morality said to prevail among some of the tribes at the foot of the Himalaya, and other parts of India. It is a νέμεσις, or a privilege, to which the princes had been predestinated in an earlier state of being. The rescue of the wife from the king of Sind is the subject of a bold and spirited battle-piece. See Quarterly Review, vol. xlv, p. 29. The power of the Indian poets to paint these scenes of tumult and strife, forms the subject of a glowing panegyric by M. Chézy, which will be found translated below, p. 118.

pp. Other Episodes and Extracts.

Die aufopfernde Gattenliebe der *Sawitri*, an episode from the *Mahabharat*. In die Sündfluth, u. s. w. von Franz Bopp, *Berlin*, 1829. The contents and extracts are given in the Berliner Conversations-Blatte, 1829, No. cxlviii.

A Dialogue between *Bhrighu* and *Bharadvadja*, from the twelfth section, containing a philosophical enquiry into the most important points of Indian theology. A French translation of this was presented by professor Schultz to the Asiatic Society of Paris. See Journ. Asiat. Sept. 1825, p. 137.

Story of the Churning of the Ocean to obtain the fourteen Jewels, from the *Mahabharat*, in the Asiatic Journal, 1817, Oct. p. 346—349.

The editor of this translation tells us at its close, that, allowing for the difference of style and habits of thinking, the most unaccountable coincidence of machinery and events is perceptible throughout between the sublimely poetic pieces of Milton and Vyása. The similarity of object in the combatants, the hope of immortal vigour which inflames the etherial beings of Milton, and the thirst of the *Amrita* which causes the quarrel in the *Mahabharat*, will be found to furnish a series of corresponding conceptions in the two poets, more readily perceived than accounted for. The historical connection may indeed be no longer traceable; but for that very reason, we do not recollect to have met with, in all our reading, a more fair opportunity of critically comparing the merits of two bards, than we have here in the specimens of the gigantic imagery of Vyása, and of Milton's 'flood of mind.'

The Hermitage of *Kanwa*, freely translated from the *Mahabharat*, in the Asiatic Journ. 1826, Aug. p. 173.

3. *Harivansa.*

Harivansa, the family of the *Hari*, form a sort of appendix to the *Mahabharat*. They consist of 25,000 verses. *Hari* is a name of *Vishnu* under the shape of *Krishna;* whose adventures, as well as the future fate of his family, are here narrated.

A. Langlois in his Mélanges de Littérature Sanscrite, *Paris*, 1828, 8vo., has given six historical extracts from this work.

1. Histoire de *Câla-Yavana*, p. 49—84. An episode from the war of *Jarâ-Sandha* against *Krishna*. The word *Yavana*, is used by the Hindoos to designate

an inhabitant of the west[r]. An English translation and a critique on the version of Langlois is given in the Asiatic Journal, Feb. 1828. The writer suspects M. L. to have taken great, if not unwarrantable liberties with the original: "The style is florid and redundant, and often appears to us to savour much more of France than Hindoostan."

2. The second story is the Marriage of Rookmini the daughter of Bhishmaka, and, as we have already seen, the favourite mistress of Krishna. The exploits of that god could not disarm her brother Rookmi of his hatred; and he prevailed on his father to promise Rookmini's hand to one of his royal allies in the war so unsuccessfully waged against the incarnate deity. On the day appointed for the marriage, however, Krishna arrived with a few attendants, carried off the princess, and thus secured the happiness of both.

3. The third story, The Entertainments at Dwaraca, are curious from their exhibiting a picture (necessarily concise) of the manner in which the ancient inhabitants of Hindoostan amused themselves on occasions of public festivity.

4. The fourth is The Death of Rookmi. That prince, the successor of Bhishmaka, had a daughter, Soobhangi; and as he had renounced his enmity against Krishna, he consented to bestow her on Radyoomna, the son of that hero and his sister. Balarama is present at the nuptials, and is inveigled into play with Rookmi and other princes. He loses, is ridiculed for his want of skill, becomes so violently enraged that he overturns the table, and afterwards kills Rookmi with the chess-board.

[r] Wilford, and after him Colonel Francklin, are quick-sighted enough to find *Deucalion*, in the Indian words, *Deva Cala Yavana*. This is almost as bad a derivation as we have somewhere seen of *chez* from *apud*.

4. *Ramayana.*

There are many poems bearing this name, and all relating to the same subject. The achievements of Rama, its hero, have been sung by profane as frequently as by sacred poets. His history occupies a considerable place in many of the *Puranas*, and is the sole object of Valmiki's poem, and of another entitled *Ad'hyátma Rámáyana*, which is ascribed to Vyása. There are also others by Bhavabhûti, Murâri-Misra, Paksha-Dhara-Misra, etc. The most complete and valuable of them all, however, is the great epic, the *Ramayana* of Valmiki.

It narrates the banishment of Rama, under the name of Chandra, (resembling the moon,) a prince belonging to the dynasty of the kings of Ayodhyâ; his wandering to the peninsula; the seizure of his wife by the giant ruler of Ceylon; the miraculous conquest of this island; and the restoration of Rama to the empire of his ancestors. It consists of 24,000 distichs, divided into seven books, which are again subdivided into chapters or raphsodies. Some idea of the esteem in which this poem is held by the Hindoos, may be formed from the following passage from the introduction: "He who sings and hears this poem continually, has attained to the highest state of enjoyment, and will finally be equal to the gods."

Analysis of the *Ramayana* in Ward's View of the History, etc. of the Hindoos, ed. 2. tom. ii, p. 187.

Langlès in Catalogue des mss. Sanscr. p. 13, 14.

Craufurd, Researches on India, vol. i, p. 188.

Colebrooke, in Asiatic Researches, vol. x, p. 426.

Polier Mythologie des Hindous, and, after him, Görres in the Heidelb. Jahrb. 1810, vol. vi, p. 245, sqq.

Heeren's Ideen.

Discours prononcé au Collège Royal de France à

l'ouverture du Cours de langue et de littérature Sanskrite, par Mr. de Chézy, *Paris*, 1815, 8vo. where p. 17—26, is given an extract from the *Ramayana*[s].

A very valuable manuscript of the *Ramayana* is mentioned in the Supplement to Howell and Stewart's Oriental Catalogue for 1827, p. 99[t].

A notice on the three Paris mss. of the *Ramayana* in

[s] M. Chézy, in the discourse above quoted, says of this poem, "It is more especially in epic poems that the Sanscrit seems to bear the palm from all other languages; and among the Indian poets, the great Valmiki, in his *Ramayana*, seems to have best understoood the art of displaying all its beauties. Under his magic pencil it becomes pliant, and yields, without effort, to every variety of tone and colour. If he would paint gentle and affecting scenes, this beautiful, sonorous, and copious language, furnishes him with the most harmonious expressions; and, like a winding rivulet creeping softly over banks of moss and flowers, it carries with it, imperceptibly, our ravished imagination, and transports us into an enchanted world. Yet, in subjects requiring energy and strength, as in martial combats, his style becomes rapid and animated as the action itself. Chariots roll and rebound; furious elephants destructively move to and fro their enormous tusks; neighing steeds clash their metalled hoofs on the resounding plain; clubs are violently struck together; arrows hurtle; confusion and death rage on every side: we no longer read, we are in the midst of the terrible conflict." See Le Moniteur, 1815, No. 23, and A. W. v. Schlegel's Ind. Bibl. vol. i, p. 35. This high-flown praise, however, others have endeavoured to lessen: Sainte-Croix in his Observat. prélimin. to the *Ezour-Vedam*, p. 131, and Ward in his Views of the Literature, etc. vol. i, p. 513. Yet it seems sanctioned by one, certainly equally well, and perhaps better, qualified to form a just and enlarged view of the subject than either of these critics, who has cited the whole passage in the Quarterly Review (vol. xlv, p. 3). Even his sanction, however, may be considered as modified by what follows: "If we may presume to judge, from all that is yet before the European public, the excellence of the Indian poets lies rather in softness than energetic action; their battles want the truth, the life, the distinctness of Homer: they seem rather turgid and exaggerated than sublime; though, after all, we must take into the account the vast and unwieldy character of Asiatic warfare. Still, we shall, we conceive, sooner find a parallel in their works to the garden of Alcinoüs, the isle of Circe, or even the parting of Hector and Andromache, than to Achilles standing on the trench and averting the tide of Trojan victory."

[t] It is No. 4414, written in the Bengalee character, and priced 6*l*. 16*s*. 6*d*.

the introduction to J. L. Burnouf's La Mort d' *Yadjnadatta.*

The *Ramayana* was at an early date translated into Bengalee; and from this version Sir William Jones rendered an extract from the last book into English: see his works, vol. vi, p. 399—411. The first portion of a complete translation into English at length appeared, under the following title, but only a very small number of copies were struck off:

The *Ramayana* of *Valmeeki,* in the original Sungskrit, with an English prose translation, and explanatory notes by William Carey and Joshua Marshmann, *Serampoor,* 1806, 4to. vol. i, containing the first book[u]; vol. ii, containing the first part of the second book, *ibid.* 1808; vol. iii, containing the latter part of the second book, *ibid.* 1810. This work, which it was calculated would make ten 4to. volumes, seems to have been interrupted from want of sufficient support. The second part of the three which have appeared is no longer to be procured, as the vessel in which they were embarked for Europe was wrecked. The first part was reprinted at *London* in 1808, and the whole at *Calcutta,* 1813, 3 vols. 4to.

The translation was reprinted without the original text, under the title of The *Ramayuna* of *Valmeeki,* translated from the original Sungskrit, with explanatory notes, by W. Carey and J. Marshmann, *London,* 1808—1814, 8vo[x]. Three parts. An ample review

[u] This portion of the work is priced at 5*l.* 5*s.* in the catalogue of Parbury, Allen, and Co. for 1831: vol. iii, is priced in the same catalogue at 3*l.* 15*s.* These also occur in Howell and Stewart's Catalogue, but in none of them do I find any mention of vol. ii.

[x] I find the following: The *Ramauana* of *Valmeeki,* a poem, translated from the original Sungskrit, by W. Carey and J. Marshmann, vol. 1, containing the "first book," 8vo., *Dunstable,* 1808. See Parbury and Allen's Catalogue of Oriental Literature, 1831.

of this publication, by Doctor Wilkins, will be found in the Heidelb. Jahrb. 1814, April, No. 24.

A Bengalee version of the entire poem was printed at *Calcutta*, in 5 vols. 8vo.

Ramayun, a Prose Translation into Persian, from the Sanscrit of the very interesting History of *Ram*, and his wife *Sita*, and brother *Latchman*, etc., a manuscript in the Supplement to Howell and Stewart's Oriental Catalogue for 1827, p. 100.

A poetical abridgement in Hindostanee appeared with the following title: *Kavita Ramayuna*, in the Devanâgari character, at *Khidirpoor* in *Bengal*, 1815, 8vo. See Catal. de la Biblioth. de M. Langlès, p. 158, No. 1367.

The *Ramayuna*, or the Exploits of *Rama*, abridged and translated in the Tamul language from the celebrated Epic Poem of Valmiki, *Madras*, 1822, 4to.

The opening of the poem, translated into German verse, is found in Fr. Schlegel's Uber die Sprache und Weisch. d. Indier, p. 231—271.

Proeve van Indische Dichtkunde volgens den *Ramayon;* naar het oorspronkelyk Sanskritisch gevolgd door Jacob Haafner, en uit deszelfs nagelatene Papieren in licht gegeven door C. M. Haafner, *Amsterdam*, 1823, 8vo.

A. W. von Schlegel announced a new and complete edition of the *Ramayana* in the original Sanscrit with a Latin version, in a prospectus printed at *London* in 1823. The first part of this edition has made its appearance with the following title: *Ramayana*, id est, Carmen Epicum de *Ramæ* rebus gestis, poëtæ antiquissimi Valmici opus. Textum codd. mss. collatis recensuit, interpretationem Latinam et annotationes criticas adjecit Aug. Guill. a Schlegel, etc. Voluminis primi pars prior, lxxii, and 380, pp. large 8vo. *Bonn*, 1829, typis regiis, sumptibus auctoris. It contains the text of the first and a considerable portion of the second book out of the seven which complete the entire poem.

A portion of the *Ramayana* translated into Tamul, by P. Beschi, exists among the manuscripts at Paris. See Rapport de la Société Asiatique, 1828, p. 43.

The following episodes from the *Ramayana* have been translated separately.

a. The Death of Yadnadatta.

A notice of this extract from the *Ramayana*, which is said to possess "the same simple pathos, the same tenderness of feeling, that charm in the more affecting parts of the Nala," is given, with an outline of the affecting incident which forms the subject of the episode, in the Quarterly Review, vol. xlv, p. 23.

Yadjnadatta-Budha, ou la Mort de *Yadjnadatta*, épisode extrait et traduit du *Ramayanà*, poëme épique Sanscrit, par M. L. Chézy, *Paris*, 1814, 8vo.

This work of M. Chézy's was intended as a specimen of a free translation of the whole poem, which appeared twelve years later under the following title:

Yadjnadattabada, ou la Mort *d' Yadjnadatta*, épisode extrait du *Ramayana*, poëme épique Sanscrit; donné avec le texte gravé et une analyse grammaticale très-détaillée, une traduction Français et des notes, par M. L. A. Chézy, et suivi, par forme d'appendice, d'une traduction Latine littérale, par M. J. L. Burnouf, etc. *Paris*, 1826, 4to. avec planches. Ample reviews of this will be found in the Journal des Savans, *Avril*, 1827, p. 223—230; and by Professor Rosen, in the Berl. Jahrh. für wissensch. Kritik, 1828, No. 17 and 18.

β. The Penances of Visvamitra.

Wiswamitra's Büssungen. Eine Episode aus dem *Ramayana*, aus dem Sanskrit im Versmaasze des Originale getren übersetzt, von Franz. Bopp, in his Conjugationssystem der Sanskritsprache, *Frankf. a M.* 1816, 8vo. p. 159—233.

J. G. Rhode, in his treatise die relig. Bildung, Mythologie und Philosophie der Hindus, considers this episode to have been an early interpolation.

γ. *The Combat of Atikaya.*

Der Kampf des *Atikaya,* ein Fragment aus dem indischen Heldengedichte *Ramayana,* aus dem Englischen übersetzt von C. A. Semler, in the Zeitung für die elegante Welt, 1816, No. clxxix—clxxxi.

Le combat de *Lakshmanas* avec le Géant *Atikayas,* traduit du Sanscrit par M. Chézy, *Paris,* 1818, 8vo.

δ. *The Descent of the Ganges.*

Under this title A. W. von Schlegel has translated into German hexameters the deification of the river Ganges, as found in the first book of the *Ramayana,* sect. 32—35, and illustrated it with annotations. See his Indischen Biblioth. vol. i, p. 50—96.

Mr. Milman has also given an account of this curious mythological poem, with some metrical extracts. He describes it as one of the most singular of the cosmogonical notions of the ancient Indians. Speaking of the above German translation, he calls its author the first of all translators, as well as critics, in the world; and, contrasting his version with the prose translation of Carey and Marshmann, in the *Ramayana,* he says, "The difference between the two is a striking exemplification of the too often forgotten truth, that poetry can only be translated by a poet." Quarterly Review, vol. xlv, p. 34.

The Legend of the Descent of *Gunga;* from the *Ramayana* of Valmiki, in the Asiatic Journal, 1817, Nov. p. 449—451. A prose translation.

ε. *Uttra Candum.*

Estratto del libro detto *Uter Cand*, ultimo tomo del gran libro *Ramaen*, libro dell Incarnazione. Communicato del Msgr. *Münter*, Vescovo di Selanda. In the Fundgruben des Orients, tom. v, p. 80, 188.

Utara Kandam, an extract from the *Ramayana*, was translated by Siddambala Vadyar, professor of the Tamul language at the college of Madras, into Tamul, and printed at Madras in 1817; and again with the following English title prefixed: the *Uttra Candum*, an Episode of the *Ramayana* of Valmiki, translated from the Sanscrit into Tamul by Siddambala Vadyar, professor of the Tamul, *Madras*, 1826, 4to.

An episode of the *Ramayana* translated into the Hindoostanee language, was published at *Calcutta*, 1815, under the title of *Tulasidasa Ramayana*.

4. *Vishnu-Purana.*

Professor Wilson read an account of the *Vishnu Purana*, with an analytical summary of its contents, to the Asiatic Society of Calcutta in 1824. See above, p. 88.

5. *Markandaya Purana.*

Markonday, *Mârkandeya Purana*, or, according to Ward, *Markundeyu Puranu*. Such is the title of a long poem of nearly one hundred thousand verses, containing the victory of the goddess *Bhuvani*, or *Durga*, over the giants and demons *Moisasur*. See the contents at length, in Langlès Catalogue des mss. Sanscrits, p. 54—61.

An extract from this poem, containing the victory of *Durga*, is known in India, under the title of *Chandika*. See Catalogue des mss. Sanscrit, p. 66. This fragment Chandica, or Chandi, is also frequently quoted under the name of *Dévi Mahatmyam*[a], (the great of *Divi*). A description of it, and an extract, are given by M. Eugène Burnouf, in the nineteenth number of the Journal Asiatique, p. 24—32, under the title of Analyse et extrait du *Dévi Mahatmyam*, fragment du *Markandeya Purana*. A complete edition of this episode is expected shortly from professor Bopp.

6. *Brahmá Vaïvartika Purana.*

Respecting this very remarkable work, which describes the origin of the gods, see Catalogue des mss. Sanscrit, p. 36, etc.

L'Ermitage de Kandou, poëme extrait et traduit du Brahmâ-Pourâna, composition Sanskrite de la plus haute antiquité, par M. de Chézy, in the Journal Asiatique, 1822, Juill. p. 1—16. German: Die Einsiedeley des *Kandu*, nach dem *Brahma Purana*, einer epischen Dichtung aus dem höchsten Alterthume. Eine akademische Vorlesung von Hrn. von Chézy. Aus dem noch nicht gedruckten französischen Originale übersetzt von Aug. Wilh. v. Schlegel, in his Indischer Bibliothek. Bd. i, Heft. 3, p. 257—273. To which we may add, Bemerkungen über von Chézy's Einsiedeley des *Kandu*, von Niklas Müller, in his Glauben, Wissen und Kunst der alten Hindus, Bd. i, p. 615.

7. *Agni Purana.*

The *Agni*, or *Agneya Purana*, which *Agni*, the god of fire, is said to have imparted to mankind, is chiefly composed of mystic forms and religious prescriptions, but contains besides a number of treatises on politics, law, medicine, poetry, rhetoric, and grammar. It does

[a] See above, p. 94.

not appear to be very ancient. See Catalogue des mss. Sanscrits par M. M. Hamilton et Langlès, p. 44—48. Asiatic Journal, 1826, Oct. p. 429.

8. *Bhavishyat Purana.*

A description of the territory of Pundra-Desa, part of Bengal, Behar, and Allahabad. Translated in the Oriental Magazine, Dec. 1824; and from that into the Bulletin Univ. 1827, Mai, Géograph. p. 134.

9. *Sheeve Purana.*

Ancient Indian Literature, being a Summary of the *Sheeve Pouran*, the *Brehme Vivertte Pouran*, and the *Arthee Prekash Shastre;* with Extracts and Epitomes, translated from Original mss., *London*, 1807, 4to.

10. *Padma Purana.*

An extract from this *Purana*, containing prescriptions for widows, is found in Description of the Character, etc. of the People of India, by the Abbé J. A. Dubois, *London*, 1817, 4to. p. 224—234.

Bhoûmi-Khandam, section du *Padma Pourâna*, par M. E. Burnouf, Journal Asiatique, vol. vi, p. 3.

11. *Kurma Purana.*

Kurma or *Kaurma Purana*, is included among the eighteen great *Puranas*. It is said to have contained eighteen thousand verses, of which probably not more than eight thousand are now in existence. Professor Wilson, in 1826, read before the Asiatic Society of Calcutta, of which he was then secretary, an abstract of this *Purana*, written by himself. He considers the one now extant of rather doubtful authority; though it is unquestionably received in various parts of India as the genuine *Purana*. On the other hand the copies consulted consist of but about six thousand *slokas*, while the *Kaurma Purana* is said in the *Bhagavat* and *Matsya Puranas* to contain seventeen thousand verses. The *Agni*, however, states eight thousand; and perhaps this difference proves little or nothing either way. A more unanswerable objection is the testimony of the work itself, which very particularly specifies its being one of the four *Sanhitas*, collections, or compendiums, of the *Puranas*. Mr. Wilson seems to think it most likely that the work called the *Kurma Purana* is not the original and genuine *Purana*, but a compendium or summary of its contents, which appears to have supplanted the original, probably lost in consequence, and therefore no comparison can now be made betwixt them.

12. *Upa Purana.*

The *Upa Puranas* belong to the second, subordinate class, and are much less known than the foregoing. They are a sort of supplement to the *Puranas*, containing in eighteen books all those subjects which are omitted in them. See Craufurd's Researches on India, vol. i, p. 187.

13. *Other Writings connected with the Puranas.*

Siva-Sahasra-Nama, or Thousand Epithets of the god *Siva*, enumerating all his attributes, drawn from the *Puranas*, *Mahabharata*, etc. containing twenty-five thousand verses, with a Comment, in two thousand four hundred and ninety-six pages. Sanscrit, in the Devanâgari character. A manuscript in Howell and Stewart's Oriental Catalogue for 1827, Suppl. p. 103.

Rádhácánta Sarman, a pandit of great learning and extensive fame among the Hindoos, composed lately in Sanscrit, a work called *Puránárt'haprecásá*, or the *Puranas* explained. This work contains a genealogy of the kings of *Magada* or *Bahar*. See Sir William Jones's Works, vol. i, p. 288.

Dherma Purana. An extract from this will be found in An Enumeration of Indian Classes, by H. T. Colebrooke, esq., in the Asiatic Journal, 1816, Dec. p. 515—578.

Tartarus, from the *Sarwaswa Purana*, or Compendium of the *Puranas*, in the Asiatic Journal, 1819, June, p. 599.

Vâjoupourână, a Tamul manuscript in the Bibliothèque du Roi at Paris.

Rules for the due observance of the ceremonies on occasion of a widow burning with the corpse of her husband. A fragment translated from the Sanscrit of *Govindapa Raja*, probably an extract from a *Purana*, in the Asiatic Journal, 1817, Oct. p. 349, 350.

Notice sur le manuscrit du *Shrî-Bhâgavata-Purana*, envoyé par M. Duvancel à la Société Asiatique, par Eugène Burnouf, fils, in the Journal Asiatique, vol. vii, p. 46, 193.

In this place also we must mention

Chadda Karinaga Mandanam, an extract from all the *Puranas*.

Raghuwanssa, or the race of *Ragu*, an heroic poem by Kalidasa, and *Kumâra Sambhâwa*, or the birth of *Kumara*, by the same author.

Terurnda-Soren's History; translated from the Sanscrit into Malabaric, by a clergyman, assisted by a Brahman, and out of Malabaric into Danish, by N. S. Fuylsang. Printed in Danish in the Skandinavisk Museum, *Copenhagen*, 1798, 8vo. vol. ii, part ii.

Sanscreet Fragments, or interesting Extracts from the sacred Books of the Brahmans, on subjects important to the British Isles; by the authors of Indian Antiquities (Th. Maurice and K. Vallancey,) *London*, 1798, 8vo.

Account of the Jains, collected from a priest of this sect at Mudgeri: translated by Cavelly Boria, Brahman, for Major C. Mackenzie, in Asiatic Researches, vol. ix, p. 244. Notices of the Jains received from Chárucirti Hcharya, their chief pontiff, at Belligola in Mysore, *ibid.* p. 256. Particulars of the Jains extracted from a Journal by Dr. F. Buchanan, during travels in Canara, *ibid.* p. 279. Observations on the Sect of Jains, by H. T. Colebrooke, esq., *ibid.* p. 287. See also Researches on the Tenets and Doctrines of the Jains and Boodhists, conjectured to be the *Brachmanes* of Ancient India: in which is introduced a Discussion on the *Brachmanes* of Ancient India; and another on the Worship of the Serpent in various Countries of the World, by lieutenant-colonel William Francklin, etc., *London*, 1827, 4to [b].

3. *Sastras.*

Sastra, the book, the interpretation, explanation of the *Vedas*, by *Sasta*, science. Sir W. Jones, in his Works, vol. i, p. 361, explains this word to mean *sacred* ordinance [c].

At present our information extends to seven of these *Sastras*, of which some account, with extracts, will be found in A Discovery of the Sect of the Banians, containing their History, Law, Liturgy, Castes, Customs and Ceremonies, gathered from their Brahmans, teachers of that sect, as the particulars were comprised in the book of their law, called the *Saster;* together with

[b] Some account of the Jains will also be found in Asiatic Journal, January, 1824, p. 22; and December, 1824, p. 573.

[c] Craufurd's Researches on India, vol. i, p. 188. Halhed, in the preface to his Code of Gentoo Laws, attempts to determine the age of some of these *Sastras*, and gives to one 7,204,990, and to another 4,004,905 years.

a display of their manners, by Henry Lord, *London*, 1630, 4to. Again in Wilkins's *Bhagvat-Geeta*. And in French, Histoire de la Religion des *Banians*, contenant leurs Loix, leurs Liturgie, leurs Coûtumes, et leurs Cérémonies, tant anciennes que modernes; recueillie de leurs Bramanes, et tirée de leur Loy, qu'ils appellent *Schaster*, Paris, 1667, 12mo.

Bedang-Schaster, or *Vedanga-Schastra*, book of the principal verses of the *Veda*.

Neardirsen or *Neaderzen-Schaster*, *Ni-a-der-szena Schastra*, book of the explanation of the law.

Schastra-Bhade.

Extracts from this *Sastra* will be found in the work of Holwell and Dow already quoted, and these are translated into German in the Asiat. Originalschriften, *Zurich*, 1801, 8vo. Bd. i.

A Summary of the *Arthe Prekash Sastre*, in the Sanscrit Fragments quoted at page 78.

Metamorphoses of Sona, a Hindoo tale; with a glossary descriptive of the mythology of the *Sastras*, *London*, 1811, 8vo.

The collection of prayers called *Néaeschs* and *Jeschts*, Sanscrit and Zend, 214 leaves, 8vo. Manuscript in the library of the East India Company at London. See Nouv. Journ. Asiat. 1828, Février, p. 124.

To this place also seem to belong the twenty-four books *Yagamon*, which treat of prayers and offerings.

JURISPRUDENCE.

OF ANCIENT HINDOO LEGISLATION IN GENERAL.

THE legislative system of India was the first branch of Sanscrit literature that attracted the attention of the English; not so much as an object of learning as of policy; for it evidently must have been to them a matter of first rate importance to become acquainted with the jurisprudence of a people whom they had to govern[d].

The first step taken by the English in the study of Hindoo legislation was made by governor Hastings: as a commentary upon it, *Vivadarnava-Setu*, compiled under his directions, was printed at the cost of the East India Company in 1776, 4to.

A Code of Gentoo[e] Laws, or Ordinations of the Pundits, from a Persian translation made from the original, written in the Shanscrit language, published by Nathaniel Brassey Halhed[f], *London*, 1776, 4to., 1777, 8vo., with plates. French: Code des Loix des Gentoux ou Réglement des Brames, trad. de l'Anglais, *Paris*, 1778, 4to. German: Gesetzbuch der Gentoos oder Sammlung der Gesetze der Pundits, nach einer persianischen Uebersetzung des in der Shanskritsprache geschriebenen Originals. Aus dem Engl. von Rud. Erich Raspe, *Hamburg*, 1778, 8vo. The East India Company printed an elegant edition of this work in 4to. at Bengal[g].

The high antiquity ascribed to the Indian laws by Halhed, was controverted in A Letter to Nathaniel Brassey Halhed, esq., containing some remarks on his Preface to the Code of Gentoo Laws, lately published, by George Costard, *Oxford*, 1778, 8vo.

Respecting the Sanscrit original of this collection of laws, see Catalogue des mss. Sanscrit, p. 89.

[d] Heeren's Ideen—Inder.

[e] Gentoos is the Portuguese appellation of the Hindoos.

[f] Halhed may be regarded as the first European who learned the Sanscrit.

[g] Watts's Bibliotheca Britannica.

LAWS OF MENU [h].

THE Institutes of Menu contain, in twelve books, the institutes of criminal and private jurisprudence. They are composed in a kind of measured prose, called *Pungtee Chund;* their language evincing their high antiquity. They describe the occupations of men, and the religious exercises of the four castes; and, as colonel Haughton observes [i], whether regarded for their great antiquity and classic beauty, or for their importance, as being considered a divine revelation by nearly a hundred millions of people, they must ever claim the attention of those who devote themselves to the study of the Sanscrit language. Though inferior to the *Vedas* in antiquity, they are held to be equally sacred; and owing to their being more closely connected with the business of life, have tended so much to mould the opinions of the Hindoos, that it would be impossible to comprehend the literature or local usages of India, without being master of their contents.

Sir William Jones, in the preface to his translation, tells us, that it is the general opinion of Pandits, that Brahma taught his laws to Menu in a hundred thousand verses, which Menu explained to the primitive world in the very words of the *Mánava Dherma-Sastra,* or Institutes of Menu; but, in a short preface to the law tract of Náred, it is asserted that Menu, having written the laws of Brahma in a hundred thousand *slocas* or couplets, arranged under twenty-four heads, in a thousand chapters, delivered the work to Háred, the sage among gods, who abridged it, for the use of mankind, in twelve thousand verses, and gave them to a son of Bhrigu, named Sumati, who, for

[h] Jones, vol. i, p. 58, 59.

[i] Preface to the *Mánava Dherma-Sastra.*

greater ease to the human race, reduced them to four thousand: that mortals read only the second abridgement by Sumati, while the gods of the lower heaven, and the band of celestial musicians, are engaged in studying the primary code, beginning with the fifth verse, a little varied, of the work now extant on earth; but that nothing remains of Háred's abridgement except an elegant epitome of the ninth original article on the administration of justice. Now, since these institutes consist only of two thousand six hundred and eighty-five verses, they cannot be the whole work ascribed to Sumati, which is probably distinguished by the name of *Vriddha*, or ancient, *Mánava*, and cannot be found entire; though several passages from it, which have been preserved by tradition, are occasionally cited in the new digest[i].

The ordinances of Menu belong to the second period of Indian literature, the work containing them being placed by Sir William Jones between the publication of the *Vedas* and that of the *Puranas* and *Itihasas*, about 880 B. C. Fr. Schlegel ascribes to it a still higher antiquity, and calls it a monument to which no sound criticism can assign a later date than that given to the most ancient one known in western Europe. Ritter questions the opinion both of Jones and Schlegel; and enters upon the discussion of the age and merits of the Institutes of Menu, from the internal evidence they afford, and from a comparison of them with other Sanscrit works[k]. From this he concludes, what in itself seems very reasonable, that the work attributed to

[i] Sir William Jones's Preface, p. 59, etc. Fried. Mayer's Brahma, p. 125, etc.

[k] Ritter exposes the defiance contained in the assertion of Schlegel; and quotes as authorities, of equal weight with his, the criticisms of Schlosser, in his View of General History; and Rhode, ueber religiose Bildung, etc. i Th. p. 124, 125.

Menu is a collection made from various materials, but not according to one plan, and scarcely from the laws delivered by one individual. This may be fairly presumed from the beginning and conclusion of the work, and proved from its containing various laws for one and the same offence; hence also the probability of their having been made at different periods. This seems established; as in many of the ordinances the simplicity of antiquity is visible, while some evince a degree of civilisation incompatible with the first rise of a nation, and others a deep state of national corruption and decline. That poison and poinards, eunuchs, extreme jealousy of the chiefs towards one another, towards their ministers, and even towards the people, may have been primeval in the East, may indeed be conceived; but that the refined system of espionage, the shameless plans of avowedly selfish policy, and the general communities of atheists, that are mentioned in the institutions of Menu, could belong to the infancy of civilisation cannot for a moment be believed. Traces, moreover, are found in this work that the ancient institutions of Indian life, such as the division into castes, had ceased to be strictly observed; and that various opinions had been formed respecting religious dogmas; both proving that it could not form part of the early literature of the nation: besides which, the authors of these laws were not only acquainted with the Brahmanas and Upanishads of the *Vedas*, but cite also the *Puranas*, the *Vedangas*, and *Sastras* —that is, the treatises on grammar, metre, mathematics, as well as a glossary to the *Veda*[1]. What should we say (asks M. Ritter) if a high antiquity was assigned to a Greek writer, who quoted such learned treatises?

[1] Geschichte der Phil. vol. i, p. 78. The glossary, as he observes, seems a decided proof that the language of the *Vedas* was then ancient. See

The Institutes of Menu contain abundance of matter extremely interesting to all who study the history of mankind, and the progress of civilisation. It contains much to be admired, and much to be condemned. It is a system of despotism and priestcraft, both limited by law, but artfully conspiring to give mutual support, though with mutual checks. The punishments will not always be found proportionable to European notions of crime; but a spirit of sublime devotion and amiable benevolence pervades the whole work, sufficient "to prove the author to have adored, not the visible sun, but *that divine* and incomparably *greater light*," to use the words of the most venerable text in the Indian Scripture, "*which illumines all, delights all, from which all proceed, to which all must return, and which alone can irradiate* (not our visual organs merely, but our souls, etc.) *our intellects* [m].

Sir W. Jones forced upon the attention of the government the necessity of bringing together a complete body of the Hindoo laws; and, as preparatory to this great undertaking, was published the following work:

Institutes of Hindoo Law, or the Ordinances of *Menu*, according to the gloss of *Culluca*, comprising the Indian System of Duties, religious and civil, verbally translated from the original Sanscrit, with a preface by Sir William Jones. Printed by the order of government, *Calcutta*, 1794, 4to., reprinted at *London*, 1796; and in Jones's Works, vol. iii. Again,

the Institutes of Menu, vol. ii, p. 105; vol. iii, p. 183; vol. iv, p. 98, 99, 100; vol. xi, p. 263; vol. xii, p. 109, 1011. It is also to be remarked, that among the foreign nations of which mention is made in the Laws of Menu, vol. x, 44, the Chinese and Persians cannot well be mistaken; and even the *Yavanas* are introduced, which, according to the genius of oriental language, must signify the Greeks.

[m] Sir William Jones's Preface, p. 62.

a new edition, collated with the Sanscrit text, and elucidated with notes, by G. C. Haughton, *London*, 1825, 4to. German: Hindu's Gesetzgebung, oder *Menu's* Verordnungen nach *Culluca's* Erläuterung, ein Inbegriff des indischen Systems religiöser und bürgerlicher Pflichten. Aus der Sanskritsprache wörtlich ins Englische übersetzt von W. Jones, und verdeutscht nach der Calcuttischen Ausgabe, und mit einem Glossar und Anmerkungen begleitet von Joh. Christ. Hüttner, *Weimar*, 1797, 8vo.

The original has since been printed in Sanscrit, with the following title: *Manu-Sang-Hitâ*, or the Institutes of *Manu*, in the original text, with the gloss of *Culluca Bhatta*, (Nagari character). *Printed at the Sanscrit Press*, 1813, 4to. (*Calcutta*, published by Bäbu Rám, pundit).

The several glosses and commentaries, that have been composed by the Munis or ancient philosophers, on the code of Menu, are termed collectively *Dherma-Sástra*, or body of law. The most excellent of these commentators is Culluca, of whose treatise Sir W. Jones observes [n], that it is perhaps the shortest, yet the most luminous; the least ostentatious, yet the most learned; the deepest, yet the most agreeable commentary ever composed on any author ancient or modern, European or Asiatic.

Dharma Sástra Mánava, Sanscrit, *Calcutta*, 1818, large 4to.

Mánava Dherma-Sástra; or, the Institutes of *Menu*, according to the Gloss of *Culluca*, with a verbal translation and preface, by Sir William Jones, edited by Graves Chamney Haughton, M. A. F. R. S. *Calcutta*, 1824, 4to., 2 volumes, the first containing the Sanscrit text, and the other the English translation, *London*,

[n] Preface to his translation, p. 60.

1825, 2 vols 4to. See Journ. des Savans, Oct. 1826, p. 586, Article by M. Rémusat. Journ. Asiatique, Oct. 1826, p. 243, by M. E. Burnouf, which has been translated into English, and published with notes in the Asiatic Journal, 1827, Feb. p. 237. Perhaps it will not be too much to say of this work, that it has been printed with the greatest elegance, and edited with the greatest care of any Sanscrit book that has yet issued from the press. With regard to that portion of the work which is exclusively Mr. Haughton's own, it will be esteemed, by impartial judges, as one of the finest monuments which have been raised to the knowledge of Indian Antiquities[o].

Mitakshara Dharma Sastra, Sanscrit, published by H. T. Colebrooke, esq., *Calcutta*, 1813, oblong royal 8vo.

Mitakshara Darpana, translated from the Sanscrit into the Bengalee language, by Lukshmi Narayan Nyayal Ankar, *Calcutta*, 1824, 8vo.

Extracts from the Institutes of Menu.

Partes codicis legum quem *Manus* edidit, cum versione. Select passages from the first and twelfth book, in Othm. Frankii Chrestomathia Sanscrita, vol. ii, p. 1.

Kullúkabhattæ animadversiones ad codicem legum *Manu*, cum versione, ibid. ii, 2. p. 13—83.

The Laws and Institutes of *Menu*, by Q. Craufurd, esq., in his Researches concerning India, *London*, 1817, 8vo. vol. i, p. 27—90.

Aphorisms from *Menu* (extracts from the *Mánava Sastra*), in the Asiatic Journal, 1825, p. 513—518.

[o] See the article in the Asiatic Journal cited in the text, in which it is stated, that it was Mr. Haughton's intention to add to these two elegant and learned volumes a third, containing the Commentary of *Calluca Bhatta*. His want of health, unfortunately, has not permitted him to carry this laudable design into execution.

Extract from the Readings of Hindoo Law, by Mr. Ellis, in the Asiatic Journal, 1819, July, p. 17—23.

The Law of Inheritance.

Dataka-Mimansa, on the Order of Succession, in Sanscrit, *Serampoor*, large 4to.

Mohammedan Law of Succession to the Property of Intestates, Arabic, on copper plates, with a verbal translation and explanatory notes, by Sir William Jones, *London*, 1782, 4to.

Al Sirajiyyah, or the Mohammedan Law of Inheritance, Arabic and English, with a commentary by Sir William Jones, *Calcutta*, 1792, fol.[p].

A Digest of Hindoo Law on Contracts and Successions, with a commentary by Jogannatha Tercapanchanàna; translated from the original Sanscrit by H. T. Colebrooke, esq., judge of Mirzapore, resident at the court of Berar, and M. A. S. vol. i, *Calcutta*, 1797; vol. ii, iii, and iv, 1798, fol. and afterwards printed at *London*, 1801, 8vo., 3 vols. Also separately. A Disquisition on Regal Succession, etc., in the Asiatic Annual Register, 1800, p. 245—250.

Two Treatises on the Hindoo Law of Inheritance, from the *Dáya Bhága* and the *Mitakshara*, translated from the Sanscrit by H. T. Colebrooke, esq., *Calcutta*, 1810, 4to.; *London*, 1813, 4to; *College of Fort St. George, near Madras*, 1825, 4to.; translated into Persian, under the title of *Furaiz-i-irtazeeah*, by Moulavi Mohamed-Irtaza-Adi-Khan-Bahadur, *Madras*, 1825, fol.; again into Arabic, *Madras*, 1827, fol. This work in Sanscrit is called *Dayabhaga*, and forms part of a greater, entitled, *Vivahara Khandam De-Ritâ-Nitakehara*, containing a commentary upon the text of the

[p] The two foregoing works are both printed with the Arabic texts, in Sir William Jones's Works, vol. iii, 4to. I do not see any reason for their being mentioned here.

Yagnyavalkia. The whole, being a general view of Hindoo Laws, was translated into Tamulic, by Purur Vadyar, and was put to press by his brother Sidambala Vadyar, professor of the Tamulic language at the college of Madras, in *Madras*, 1817.

The *Dayubhagu*, or Law of Inheritance of *Jeemootu Vahunu*, Nagree character, *Calcutta*, 1813, 4to.

Dáya Bhága, a Sanscrit Treatise on Inheritance, by Yîmúta Vahana, with a Commentary, by Krishna Bhatta, published by H. T. Colebrooke, *Calcutta*, 1814, 4to. A new edition of this work, with a commentary by Krishna Terkalankara, *Calcutta, Education Press*, 1829, 8vo., is mentioned in Parbury, Allen, and Co.'s Catalogue for 1831.

Dáya Bhága, a Treatise upon Inheritance and Division of Property, in verse, Sanscrit and Bengalee, published by the Pundit Lukshmi Narayan Nyayal Ankar, *Calcutta*, 1822.

Daya Tatwa, a Treatise on the Law of Inheritance, by Raghunandana Bhattáchárya, edited by Lakshmi Nárâyan Serma, *Calcutta, Education Press*, 1828, 8vo.

Daya-Crama-Sangraha, or an Abstract of the Hindoo Law of Inheritance: an original treatise in Sanscrit, by Sri Krishna Tarkalankara, with an English translation by P. M. Wynch, esq., *Calcutta*, 1818, 4to. Of this work there is another edition, by Krishna Terkalankara Bhattáchárya, edited by Lakshmi Nárâyan Serma, *Calcutta, Education Press*, 1828, 8vo.

Brief Remarks regarding modern Encroachments on the ancient Rights of Females, according to the Hindoo Law of Inheritance, by Rammohun Roy, *Calcutta*, 1822, 8vo. See Asiat. Journ. 1823, Sept. p. 446—451.

Adoption.

The *Dattaka Mimansa* and *Dattaka Chandrika*, two original Treatises on the Law of Adoption, by Nanda

Pundita and Devanda Bhatta; translated from the Sanscrit, by J. C. C. Sutherland, esq., *Calcutta*, 1814, 4to.; 1817, 8vo.; reprinted at the *College of Fort St. George near Madras*, 1825, 8vo.

The *Duttak Meemansa* and the *Duttuk Chund*, two esteemed Treatises in the original Sanscrit on the Hindoo Law of Adoption, *Calcutta*, 1818, 4to.

Other Treatises on Jurisprudence.

Législation Orientale, par Anquetil Duperron, *Amsterdam*, 1778, 8vo.

Digest of Mohummudun Law, by col. J. Baillie, esq., *Calcutta*, 1801, 4to.

A Dictionary of Mohammedan Law, Bengal Revenue Terms, Shanscrit, Hindoo, and other words, *London*, 1802, 8vo., by S. Rousseau.

Veeru-Mitroduyu, a complete Digest of Hindoo Law, on the Administration of Justice, edited by Babooram, pundit, *Calcutta*, 1814, 4to.

Vîra-Mitrôdaya, the legal Work of Mitra-Mishra, in Sanscrit, published by H. T. Colebrooke, esq., printed at the *Sanscrit Press*, at *Kizurpoor*, near *Calcutta*, 1815, 4to.

Elements of Hindoo Law, published by Thomas Strange, *London*, 1825, 2 vols. 8vo.

A Treatise on Obligations and Contracts, translated by H. T. Colebrooke, esq., *Calcutta*, 1810, 4to.

Karma-Lotchana, translated from the Sanscrit into Bengali, and printed at *Serampoor*, 1821. This work contains prescriptions respecting domestic duties and the various grades of impurity, as determined by the law. Extracts from this are given in Essays relative to the Habits, Character, and Moral Improvement of the Hindoos, *London*, 1823, 8vo. See Journ. des Savans, 1823, Août, p. 459.

PROFANE LITERATURE.

PHILOSOPHY[a].

Literature.

Mr. Adelung, under this head, refers the reader to the following works:

Colebrooke's Essays on the Philosophy of the Hindoos, in the Transactions of the Royal Asiatic Society, vol. i, p. 92, 439, 549.

Sur la Philosophie des Hindous, d'apres les Mémoires de M. Colebrooke, in the Nouv. Mélanges Asiat. par M. Abel-Rémusat, *Paris*, 1829, 2 vols. 8vo. vol. ii, p. 331 (p. 348)—424.

Litteratur der Philosophie der Hindoo, in *Vjasa*, von Othm. Frank, 1 Bandes, i, ii, und iii Heft.

Philosophie et Religion des Indiens, ou Relation du Voyage d'un Grec dans l'Inde mille ans avant J. C. in Mélanges de Littérature Sanscrite, par A. Langlois, p. 235—268.

To these may be added, 1st, The fifth and sixth lectures of Victor Cousin's Cours de l'Histoire, de la Philosophie du xviiieme Siècle, *Paris*, 1829; where the reader will find a lucid and highly interesting exposition of Hindoo philosophy, compiled chiefly from the papers of Mr. Colebrooke above mentioned, and an Analysis of A. G. Schegel's Latin version of the *Bhagavat-Gita*[b], which M. Cousin, following the learned G. Humboldt, holds to be a monument of the *Sánc'hya* philosophy.

2nd, The second chapter of Ritter's History of Philosophy, which is devoted to an enquiry into the chronology and genuineness of the sacred books and legis-

[a] This article is entirely new. [b] See above, p. 95.

lation of the Hindoos, as forming the groundwork of their philosophic systems. It seems to be the leading object of this author, to expose the absurd and extravagant notions which some writers have been inclined to adopt respecting the antiquity of Hindoo history and learning. The style in which this work is written, and the information it contains, will make its perusal agreeable to all who have mastered the German language[c].

3rd, Some account of Hindoo philosophy will also be found, together with a copious list of authorities, in Tennemann's Manual of the History of Philosophy, translated by the Rev. Arthur Johnson, *Oxford*, 1832[d].

Various Schools of Hindoo Philosophy.

It is the professed design of all the schools of Indian philosophy, to teach the method by which eternal beatitude (the supreme good) may be attained, either after death or before it.

The path by which the soul is to arrive at this supreme felicity, is science or knowledge. The discovery, and the setting forth of the means by which this knowledge may be obtained is the object of the various treatises and commentaries which Hindoo philosophy has produced. A brilliant summary of them will be found in the work of Victor Cousin already referred to; in which he endeavours to trace among the Hindoo philosophers, the *Sensualism*, the *Idealism*, the *Scepticism*, the *Fatalism*, and the *Mysticism*, of the ancient Grecian and modern European Schools.

[c] Von der indischen Philosophie in Ritter's Geschichte der Philosophie, tom. i, *Hamb*. 1829, 8vo. p. 58—136.

[d] The two following works, which did not come in my way till this article was in print, must also be mentioned here. Rhode, uëber religiose Bildung Mythologie und Philosophie der Hindoos, 1827, 2 vols. 8vo.; and Schlegel on the Philosophy of the Indians, in his Uëber die Sprache und Weisheit der Indier.

The Hindoos possess various ancient systems of philosophy, some of which they consider orthodox, as consistent with the *Vedas;* others they regard as heretical, from their being incompatible with the doctrines of their holy books.

In all there are enumerated six principal schools of Hindoo philosophy: 1st, The *Mimansa* founded by Jaimini; 2nd, The *Vedanta,* by Vyasa; 3rd, The *Nyaya,* founded by Gotama; 4th, The *Vaiseshica,* by Canade; 5th and 6th, The two *Sánc'hyáya,* founded by Capila and Pantanjala.

The Prior Mimansa, founded by Jaimini.

The two *Mimansas* (for there are two schools of metaphysics under this title) are strictly orthodox.

The prior one (*Púrva*), founded by Jaimini, teaches the art of reasoning with the express view of aiding the interpretation of the *Vedas.* The latter (*Uttara*), commonly called the *Vedanta,* deduces from the text of the Indian scriptures, a refined psychology, which goes to a denial of the material world.

It may here be remarked, that as religion, during the early stages of civilisation, was generally of a gross and mystical character, men, as they became more enlightened, made it their study to understand and explain the obscurities of their faith, and to accommodate the rude superstitions of the early popular belief to their own more refined conceptions of the being and attributes of God. This was more particularly the case in India. Philosophy undertook to reconcile the written precepts of Brahma with the new state of moral feeling, and to give them a meaning which should not contradict the more enlightened views of wisdom and science. Thus the obscurities of the *Vedas* gave the first impulse to Hindoo philosophy; since the most perfect faith could not seize their divine precepts without the aid of reflection. Hence, too, became almost imperceptibly formed the school of *Mimansa*, which, professing the most perfect obedience to the sacred commands of the *Vedas*, undertook to render them clear and intelligible. The aim of the Mimansa school was to determine the sense of the *Vedas*, and to collect from them a perfect system of religion and morality; for so nearly allied are these in Hindoo philosophy, that Ethics seem no more than a form of religious duties: the same word (*Dharma*) signifying, in the masculine gender, virtue or moral merit, and in the feminine, devotion, or merit acquired by acts of piety.

The prior (*Púrva*) *Mimansa*, therefore, is practical, relating to works (*Carma*), or religious observances undertaken for specific ends. It is not directly a system of philosophy; but, in delivering canons of scriptural interpretation, it was natural that philosophical topics should be introduced; and scholastic disputants have elicited from its dogmas, principles of reasoning applicable to the prevailing points of controversy agitated in the Hindoo schools of philosophy.

The business of the *Mimansa* is to investigate what it is incumbent to perform as a duty. A subject or case (*adhicarania*) is given for investigation. One of these in full consists of five parts:

1st, The subject or matter to be explained.

2nd, The doubt or question arising upon the matter.

3rd, The first side (*púrva-pacsha*), or *prima facie* argument concerning it.

4th, The answer (*uttara*), or demonstrated conclusion (*siddhanta*).

5th, The pertinence or relevancy.

The whole of these five members are not always set forth in Jaimini's text; the subject, and the question concerning it, are frequently merely hinted or left to be surmised[d]. These are supplied by the commentators.

Five sources of knowledge, or modes of proof, are admitted by all Mimansacas; namely, perception[e], inference, verbal communication, comparison, presumption. Privation is sometimes added to these as a sixth source of knowledge.

This school of philosophy rests entirely upon the authority of the *Vedas*, the words of which it regards as decisive. Mr. Colebrooke has given a copious analysis of the lectures of Jaimini in the paper already referred to.

The *sootras* or *aphorisms* attributed to Jaimini, are arranged in twelve lectures, divided into sixty chapters, which are again subdivided into sections, cases, or topics. These *sootras*, like the *aphorisms* of other

[d] Mr. Colebrooke elsewhere observes, that Jaimini's arrangement is not philosophical; but that the logic of the *Mimansa* is the logic of the Hindoo law, the rule of determination of civil and religious ordinances. Each case is examined and determined upon general principles.

[e] *Simple apprehension* is defined in these words: When the organs of man are in contiguity with an object, that source of knowledge is perception. *Inference* in these: On sight of one member of a known association, the consequent apprehension of the other part, which is not actually proximate, is (*anumana*) inference; but the association must be such as had been before directly perceived, or had become known by analogy. *Presumption* is deduction of a matter which could not else be. It is assumption of a thing which is not itself perceived, but necessarily implied by another which is seen, heard, or proven. *Knowledge* of a thing which is not proximate (or subject to perception), derived through understood sound, that is, through words the acceptation whereof is known, is (*sastra*) ordinance or revelation; or it is (*sábda*) verbal communication.—I have introduced this long note from Colebrooke, to give the reader some idea of the definitions of the Sanscrit philosophy. It may be added, that the Chavacas recognise but one source of knowledge, viz. perception: the followers of Canade, and those of Sugata (Buddha) two, perception and inference. To these two the Sánc'hya schools add affirmation. They also give the following explanation: An external sense perceives; the internal one examines; consciousness makes the selfish application; and intellect resolves: an external organ executes. Trans. Asiat. Soc. vol. i, p. 31.

Indian sciences, are extremely obscure and unintelligible; and from their first promulgation, must have been accompanied by an oral or written exposition. An ancient scholiast (Vritticara) is quoted by the herd of commentators for subsidiary aphorisms, supplying the defect of the text, as well as for his commentary. Besides this work, the *sootras* have been elucidated by a perpetual commentary by Sabara Swámi Bhatta, after whom it is called *Sabara Bháshya;* and by corrective annotations upon this commentary, by Bhatta Cumarila Swámí, the great authority of the Mimansa school[f].

Among the numerous expounders of the *Mimansa*, the next in eminence is Párthasarat'hi Misra, upon whose commentary, entitled *Sastra-Dipica*, there is an ample exposition by Sómanátha, called *Mayúc'hamálá*. The *Mimánsá-nyaya-viveca* is another commentary by a distinguished author, Bhavanát'ha Mísra. The two foregoing are spoken of as commentaries, because they follow the order of the text, recite one or more of the aphorisms from every section, and explain its subject.

Among numerous other commentaries on Jaimini's text, the *Nyáyá valididhiti* of Rághavánanda is not to be omitted. It contains an excellent interpretation of the *sootras*, which it expounds word by word: it is brief, but clear; leaving nothing unexplained, and wandering into no digressions.

A summary or paraphrase of Jaimini's doctrine was put into verse by an ancient author, whose work is cited by the name of *Sangraha*. Another metrical

[f] Another esteemed commentary, by Guru, sometimes called *Prabhacara*, is mentioned by Colebrooke. Cumarila Bhatta is celebrated in the traditionary religious history of India. He is considered to have been the chief antagonist of the Buddha heresy; and to have instigated an exterminating prosecution against its disciples.

paraphrase is employed in the *Vartica*, or forms a part of the work itself.

The most approved introduction to the study of the *Mimansa* is Mádhava Acharya's *Náya-mala-vistara*. It is in verse, accompanied by a commentary in prose by the same author, forming a summary of Jaimini's text, and of approved deductions from it.

The Aphorisms of Jaimini are extremely ancient; but they have been reconstructed at various epochs, and illustrated in so many various commentaries, that the cases assume a very diversified aspect in the hands of the different interpreters.

2. *The Vedanta.*

The other Mimansa (the *Vedanta*) though strictly within the pale of orthodoxy, carried human knowledge a step forward. Although it appealed to revelation for its principles, it ventured upon a bolder interpretation of the sacred text, and penetrated into the metaphysical precepts of the *Vedas*. To this it owes its name *Vedanta*, which signifies a philosophy resting upon the *Vedas;* though in fact it formed thus early a metaphysical system, a true school of philosophy.

This system Mr. Colebrooke has reserved for a future essay. Among the literature of the *Vedanta* philosophy are reckoned the works of Sancara; particularly a highly esteemed commentary on the *Vedas*, about A. D. 790—825; the works of Madhava, of the thirteenth century; *Vedanta-Sara*, the essence of the *Vedas*, by Sadanandana[g].

3. *The Nyaya, or System of Logic.*

The *Nyaya*, founded by Gotama, furnishes a philosophical arrangement, with strict rules of reasoning, not unaptly compared to the Dialectics of Aristotle.

[g] See Vjasa, von Othm. Frank, tom. i, p. 38.

Nyaya philosophy is strictly a system of logic[h]. The text of Gotama is a collection of *sootras*, or succinct aphorisms, in five books, or lectures, each divided into two *days*, or diurnal lessons.

In a logical arrangement the predicaments or objects of proof are six: substance, quality, action, community, particularity, and aggregation, or intimate relation.

A regular argument, or complete syllogism (*Nyaya*) consists of five members: 1st, the proposition; 2nd, the reason; 3rd, the instance; 4th, the application; 5th, the conclusion. Ex.:

1. This hill is fiery:
2. For it smokes.
3. What smokes is fiery: as a culinary hearth.
4. Accordingly, the hill is smoking.
5. Therefore it is fiery.

Some confine the syllogism to three members; either the three first or the three last. In this latter form it is quite regular. The recital, joined with the instance, is the major; the application is the minor; the conclusion follows.

Of the logic of the Hindoos we have the *sootras* of Gotama, in Ward's Work on India, and some others in the Annals of the Asiatic Society of London, as well as the following:

Nyaya Sootra Vritti, the Logical Aphorisms of Gotama, with a commentary by Viswanath Bhattacharya, *Calcutta, Education Press*, 1828, 8vo.

Bhasha Paricheda, and *Siddhanta Muktavali*, an Elementary Treatise on the Terms of Logic, with its commentary, by Viswanatha Panchanana Bhatta, *Calcutta, Education Press*, 1827, 8vo.

4. *The Vaiséshica.*

The *Vaiséshica*, of which Canade is the reputed

[h] See a curious anecdote respecting Aristotle's Dialectics below, p. 161.

author, is a system of philosophy connected with the last. Its founder, like Democritus, maintained the atomic theory. This system has so bad a reputation in India, that it is regarded as opposed to the truth of their scriptures. It may well be so, for it is purely physical, and professes to account for all things, like the Epicurians, by primary molecules, simple and indecomposable; which, by their own nature, and by certain inherent principles, were continually in motion, congregated, formed various bodies, and the universe. Canade's collection of *sootras* is comprised in ten lectures, subdivided into lessons for two days each.

5. *The Sanc'hyà.*

The *Sánc'hya* is another philosophical system, partly heterodox, and partly conformable to the established Hindoo creed. It embraces at once physics, psychology, dialectics, and metaphysics, and is, in short, a complete philosophical system. Its followers are divided into two schools; one usually known by the general name of *Sánc'hya* [i], the other called *Yóga*. Capila [k], an ancient sage, whose origin and adventures are variously recounted, is the reputed founder of the Sánc'hya; and

[i] A commentator (Capila-Bhaish) expounds *Sánc'hya* as here signifying the discovery of the soul by means of right discrimination. Mr. Colebrooke says, a system of philosophy in which precision of reckoning is observed in the enumeration of its principles, is denominated *Sánc'hya*, a term which has been understood to signify numeral, agreeably to the usual acceptation of *Sánc'hya*, number; and hence its analogy to the Pythagorean philosophy has been presumed. But the name may be taken to imply, that its doctrine is founded in the exercise of judgment; for the word from which it is derived signifies reasoning or deliberation.

[k] He is represented as a son of Brahma; as an incarnation of the deity; as the holy first and wise one, entering a mind by himself framed, and becoming the mighty sage (*Capila*) who compassionately revealed this science to Asuri. Mr. Colebrooke doubts whether Capila might not have been altogether a mythological personage, to whom the true author of the system thought fit to ascribe it.

Pantanjali of the Yoga school of metaphysical philosophy.

The tenets of the two schools of the *Sánc'hyáya*, are on many points the same; but they differ upon the most important of all—the proof of the existence of a supreme God. The school of Pantanjali, therefore, which recognises God, is called theistical; and that of Capila atheistical; the latter, like the sects of Jina and Buddha, acknowledge no Creator, nor supreme ruling Providence. The gods of Capila are beings superior to man; but, like him, subject to change and transmigration. A third school may likewise be mentioned called *Paurânica Sánc'hya*, which conforms in most points to the doctrine of Pantanjali, except in holding nature as an illusion.

A collection of *sootras*, or succinct aphorisms, in six lectures, attributed to Capila himself, is extant under the title of *Sánc'hya-pravacana*[1]. As an ancient work this must have been expounded by early scholiasts; but the only commentary which can at present be referred to by name, is the *Capila-Bháshya;* or as the author himself cites it in his other books, *Sánc'hya-Bháshya.* The title at full length, in the epigraph of the book, is *Capila-Sánc'hya-Pravachana-Sastra-Bháshya.* It is by Vijnyana-Bhicshu, a mendicant ascetic, who wrote a separate treatise on the attainment of beatitude in this life, entitled *Sánc'hya-sara*, as well as several other books.

Of the six lectures or chapters into which the *sootras* are distributed, the first three comprise an exposition of the whole *Sánc'hya* doctrine. The fourth contains illustrative comparisons. The fifth is contro-

[1] In the preface to the *Capila-Bháshy*, a more compendious tract is mentioned, in the same form of *sootras* or aphorisms, bearing the title of *Tatwa Samása*, which is also ascribed to Capila. The scholiast intimates that both are of equal authority, and in no respect discordant. Colebrooke.

versial, confuting other opinions. The sixth and last treats of the most important part of the doctrines, and enlarges upon topics before touched.

The best text of the *Sánc'hya* is a sort of treatise in verse, which is denominated *Cáricá*. The acknowledged author is Iswara-Crishna, described, in the concluding lines, as having received the doctrine through a succession of intermediate instructors, from Panchaisèc'ha, by whom it was first promulgated; and who was himself instructed by Asuri, the disciple of Capila. On this brief tract, containing seventy-two stanzas in *áryá* metre, there are numerous commentaries. One of these is the *Sánc'hya-Bhashya* of Gaudapáda; a second is the *Sánc'hya-Chandrica*, of Náráyana, who seems to have been an ascetic: there is a third, under the title of *Sánc'hya-tatwa-caumudi*, by Váchespati Misra, a native of Tirhut, author of similar works on various other philosophical systems. One more commentary, bearing the simple title of *Sánc'hya Caumudi*, is by Ramachrishna Bhattacharya, a learned and not ancient writer of Bengal.

The foregoing are the principal works in which this system of philosophy may be now studied: there are some others cited by the scholiasts; but they are scarce, and no satisfactory account of them can be given upon the strength of a few scattered quotations. Among them, however, the *Rája-vartica* seems to be referred to as a work held in much esteem.

Sanchia, one of the principal philosophical systems of the Brahmans, translated from the Sanscrit, under the direction of M. Carey, *Calcutta*, 1811, 4to.

Sankya Sara, a metaphysical work, translated by Ward, in his Researches on India.

Sánc'hya Cárica, by Is'wara-Chandra, with a commentary by Vachespati, contains seventy-two stanzas in the metre called *Ariá*.

The *Sánc'hya Cárica*, translated by Henry Thomas Colebrooke, esq. Printed in London under the directions of the Royal Asiatic Society.

De la Doctrine appellée Sankia, in Nouv. Mélanges Asiat. par M. Abel-Rémusat, vol. ii, p. 348.

The following sketch of the *Sánc'hya* system of Capila will, it is hoped, convey to the reader some notion of Hindoo philosophy. It is mostly drawn from the papers of Colebrooke, in the Transactions of the Asiatic Society of London, and the lectures of Cousin already referred to.

It is the aim of all the philosophical systems of India, as I have before said, to attain the sovereign good—eternal felicity. Such is especially the aim of the Sánc'hya system. This *summum bonum* is to be sought for, not in religious exercises, or in the schemes and calculations of ordinary prudence for avoiding pain and securing happiness; but it is, according to Capila and his followers, true knowledge alone that can secure entire and permanent deliverance from evil. The question then is, how this knowledge is to be obtained?

According to Capila, there are two philosophical means of acquiring true knowledge, perception, and inference or induction. In addition to these his school admitted a third, legitimate affirmation, that is, human testimony, tradition, true revelation[m], and the authority

[m] True revelation, according to the Carika, the great Sánc'hya authority to whom Colebrooke refers, is that of the *Vedas*, to the exclusion of pretended inspirations and impostures. It may here be remarked, that the Vaiséshica, the School of Canada, rejects tradition; and that a branch of the Sankhya, the Charvakas, only admits of sensation as a source of knowledge. Capila admits three, but apparently makes but little use of the third; and adopts conclusions so widely different from those of the *Vedas*, that it is clear he did not consider their authority as very sacred. His school, however, managed to escape the fate of the Buddhists. See Cousin, l. c. p. 192.

of the *Vedas*. From these three sources, by the right exercise of judgment, and due application of reasoning, the disciples of Capila are instructed that true knowledge is to be derived; consisting in a right discrimination of the principles, perceptible and imperceptible, of the material world, from the sensitive and cognitive principle, which is the immaterial soul.

Twenty-five of these principles are enumerated. The first of them, from which all the others are derived, is *Prakriti*, or *Moula-Prakrita*, nature: termed *Prad'hána*, the chief one, the universal material cause[n]. It is eternal matter, indiscrete; undistinguishable as destitute of parts; inferrible, from its effects: being productive, but no production.

The second principle is intelligence, called *Budd'hi* and *Mahat*, or the great one: the first production of nature, increate, prolific; being itself productive of other principles. It is identified by the mythological Sánc'hya with the Hindoo triad of gods. The great principle is said to be produced from modified nature; and becomes distinctly known, as three gods, through the influence of the three qualities of goodness, foulness, darkness; being one person and three gods: namely—Brahmá, Vishnóu, and Mahesnara.

After these, passing over the physics and cosmogony of Capila, we come to the twenty-fifth and last principle, *Purusha*, the soul, which is neither produced nor productive. It is multitudinous, individual, sensitive, eternal, unalterable, immaterial.

These twenty-five principles are thus summarily contrasted in the *Carica*. Nature, root of all, is no production. Seven principles; the GREAT or intellectual

[n] Identified by the cosmogony of the *Puranas* with *Máyá* illusion; and by mythologists with *Bráhmi* the power or energy of Brahma.

one, etc., are productions and productive. Sixteen are productions (unproductive). Soul is neither a production nor productive.

Besides this, the *Sánc'hya* of Capila contains many excellent observations upon method, on the causes of our errors, upon the obstructions of the intellect, and the same host of wise precepts which everywhere recommend the writings of the Epicurean school. Capila also analyses, with much acuteness and address, the various physical and moral obstructions which oppose the perfection of the human soul. He enumerates forty-eight physical and sixty-two moral obstacles; numbers nine things which satisfy the mind, and in which it may repose; and adds eight more which raise it to perfection. He exhorts us to follow with docility the instructions of nature, who by sensation furnishes us with the materials of all our thoughts. But he enjoins us, at the same time, not to be her idle passive scholars, but to interrogate her freely; and, instead of being satisfied with her first reply, to draw from her, with all our skill and address, her most hidden secrets, her most lucid and extensive commentary upon her own works. It is by resting upon nature and experiment, that man, with the power of induction which belongs to him, may arrive at true knowledge. Capila says, it is from the contemplation of nature, and abstraction, that the union of the soul with nature takes place. He compares this union to the mutual want which the lame and the blind have of one another, who become companions, one to be borne, and directing; the other to be guided, and carrying. The spectacle of nature is always instructive, but many of her secrets can be torn from her only by penetrating into her profoundest sanctuaries, and by finding picklocks that will open her most hidden treasures.

Nature, says Capila, is like a dancing girl exhibiting

herself to the soul as to an audience; she at first makes many scruples; but, when once overcome, gives herself up without shame to the gaze of the soul, and has no reserve till she has been sufficiently examined [o].

The system of Capila leads directly to fatalism, and mediately to atheism. For, since he denies the relation of cause and effect, human action, which we believe an independent cause, is in fact no more than a necessary effect. The application of this to exterior nature is atheism. Capila denies the existence of a God who governs the world. He argues, that there is no proof of one by simple perception; nor to be deduced from sensation, by inference or induction; the only means he admits of obtaining true knowledge. He acknowledges an intelligence; but it is an intelligence derived from nature, an attribute of matter, a sort of soul of the world.

Besides the *Sánc'hya* of Capila and his disciples, another system, bearing the same denomination, but more usually termed the *Yóga-Sastra*, or *Yóga-Sutra*, is ascribed to a mythological being, Pantanjali, the supposed author of the great grammatical commentary emphatically named the *Mahábashya*, along with a medical treatise, and other distinguished performances.

The collection of *Yóga-Sutras*, bearing the common title of *Sánc'hya Pravachana*, is distributed into four chapters *(pada)*: the first on contemplation *(samád'hi)*; the second on the means of its attainment; the third on the exercise of transcendent power *(vibhuti)*; the fourth on abstraction or spiritual insulation *(caiwalya)*.

An ancient commentary on this fanatical work is

[o] See Cousin, p. 179, who asks if, under the simplicity and freedom of this language, we do not discover something of the grandeur of Bacon. Capila is also considered by the same author to have preceded Ænesidemus and Hume in his notions respecting cause and effect.

the *Pántánjala Bháshya;* attributed to Veda-vyasa, the compiler of the Indian scriptures, and founder of the *Vedanti* school of philosophy. Vachespati has furnished scholia on both text and gloss; and the number of copies found of his work evince how much it is esteemed. There are also the *Yoga-vartica* of Vijnyana-Bhicshu; the *Raja-martanda* of Rana-Ranga-Malla, surnamed Bhoja-Raja, sovereign of *Dhara,* a lucid exposition; and a more ample commentary by a modern Brahman, named Nágógí-Bhatta-Upád'hyáya, called *Pantanjali-Sutra-Vritti,* which is both clear and copious [p].

But perhaps the most complete exposition of this scheme of philosophy is the *Bhagavat-Gita*[q]*;* now almost universally considered as a development of Pantanjali's system. It is a half mythological, half philosocal episode of the great *Mahabharatta,* leading to fatalism and absolute quietism. The subject is skilfully interwoven by the poet into the greater epic. Two rival armies are drawn up, ready to join battle, and decide a civil contest for the throne of India. Arjuna, one of the competitors, is favoured by the deity Crishna, who, in disguise, accompanies him in his chariot, and under the name of Madhuis becomes his Mentor. At the moment the combatants are about to make the onset, Arjuna feels a melancholy compunc-

[p] Adelung mentions *Joya Vasishtha,* a great philosophical poem, which however was not composed by Vasishtha, an ancient sage and tutor to the son of Rama Chandra, although the instruction contained therein was addressed to him. A manuscript of it is in the library of the Royal Asiatic Society of London.

[q] See above, p. 95, and the works there referred to, particularly Schlegel Uëber die Sprache und Weisheit der Indier, and Humboldt, uëber die *Bhagavat-Gita:* add to these the sixth lecture of Cousin; Cours de l'Hist. de la Philos.; and the *Vjasa* of Oth. Frank. See also Milman in Quarterly Review, vol. xlv, p. 6. In the work of Cousin, Schlegel's Latin Version of the *Bhagavat-Gita* has been made use of, with the criticism of Chézy in the Journal des Savans, 1825, Jan. p. 37, and others.

tion at the idea of wading to the throne through the blood of his brothers, kinsmen, and friends, whom he recognises in the ranks of his enemy. He opens his mind to his companion; who, chiding him for his tameness of spirit, tells him that he belongs to the caste of warriors, that war is his element and his duty, and that for him now to recede, will be to lose both empire and honour. These reasons, not appearing to make a sufficient impression upon Arjuna, his mysterious companion reveals to him the system of metaphysics, which forms the subject of the *Bhagavat-Gita*. Upon Arjuna's still testifying his reluctance to begin the work of death, he replies to him in a strain 'that breathes the terrible sublime' of the *Sánc'hya* doctrine of fatalism.

"What canst thou urge of brothers, of kinsmen, and friends; or of men, of beasts, and of stones? for they are all as one. A perpetual, irresistible force has made all thou seest, and unceasingly renews it. What is to-day a man, was yesterday a plant, and will perhaps to-morrow be a stone. This principle is eternal. As a warrior thou art doomed to fight. A dreadful slaughter will be the result. Be it so. Next day the sun will shine upon the world, upon new scenes, and still the eternal principle will exist. Except this principle, all is illusion[r]."

The eternity of the soul is made an awful argument to Arjuna, for him to work the work of fate without regard to the sufferings of his fellow-creatures in their

[r] "The presumptuous," says the *Bhagavat-Gita*, "believe themselves the authors of their own actions; while they are all the result of the irresistible decrees of fate." A good or evil destiny is expressly attributed to the good or evil spirit; and under the influence of one or the other of these principles, every man is destined, not merely to good or ill, but to walk in the ways of error or truth, that is, to adopt a false or true system of philosophy. Cousin.

present state of existence. It is thus beautifully rendered by Mr. Milman:

Ne'er was the time when I was not, nor thou, nor yonder kings of earth:
Hereafter, ne'er shall be the time, when one of us shall cease to be.
The soul, within its mortal frame, glides on through childhood, youth, and age;
Then in another form renew'd, renews its stated course again.
All indestructible is He that spread the living universe;
And who is he that shall destroy the work of the Indestructible?
Corruptible these bodies are that wrap the everlasting soul—
The eternal unimaginable soul. Whence on to battle, Bharata!
For he that thinks to slay the soul, or he that thinks the soul is slain,
Are fondly both alike deceived: it is not slain—it slayeth not;
It is not born—it doth not die; past, present, future, knows it not;
Ancient, eternal, and unchang'd, it dies not with the dying frame.
Who knows it incorruptible, and everlasting and unborn,
What heeds he whether he may slay, or fall himself in battle slain?
As their old garments men cast off, anon new raiment to assume,
So casts the soul its worn-out frame, and takes at once another form.
The weapon cannot pierce it through, nor wastes it the consuming fire;
The liquid waters melt it not, nor dries it up the parching wind;
Impenetrable and unburn'd; impermeable and undried;
Perpetual, ever-wandering, firm, indissoluble, permanent,
Invisible, unspeakable.

Arjuna is further instructed, that the root of all error consists in the taking for reality what is only apparent—that is, all things except the eternal principle; and that supreme wisdom is action without passion. "If thou attachest," he continues, "value to these appearances, thou deceivest thyself; if thou attachest value to action thou deceivest thyself still more; for as all is but a great illusion, action, when seriously considered, is no more. The beauty, the merit of the action consists in its being performed with a perfect indifference to the effects it may produce. We are doomed to act; but let it be as though we were not acting."

The mysterious preceptor of Arjuna speaks with

disdain of the knowledge to be gained from books; and even slightingly of the sacred books of the *Vedas*. He ridicules the religion which exacts a thousand ceremonies, and promises rewards in a future state. He attacks the theological dogmas to which its interpretation gives birth; and regards as silly those who hold strictly to the letter of the *Vedas*, and believe that certainty is not to be found elsewhere. The scriptures are of no service but to him who is capable of true contemplation, and to him they are altogether useless. "As a well or cistern is useless to him who has a running spring at hand, so are the sacred books to the true divine"—that is, to him who is inspired, and has delivered himself up to contemplation.

Having set aside books, theology, science, and the employment of a regular and methodical manner of reasoning, and prescribed a life of contemplation and abstraction, the nature of the soul is next expounded. It is represented as above perception; but inferior to intelligence, which is again inferior to *being*. Contemplation, in the intellectual scale, is regarded as superior to the common employment of reason, and existence as superior to thought; hence it follows that in the moral, that which bears most analogy to pure contemplation and the simple state of being, that is, inaction, absolute inaction, will be superior to action.

This is only a further development of the same spirit of mysticism. Arjuna is first taught to act with indifference, and to attune his soul to a state of passionless tranquillity; but Hindoo mysticism does not stop here. The highest perfection of the human soul is to withdraw all its senses from external objects, 'as the tortoise draws its limbs within its shell.'

In this state of unbroken quietude, the soul 'floats like the lotus on the lake, unmoved, unruffled by the tide,' with its senses bent continually on the absolute eternal principle, which alone has a real existence. The truly pious is taught to despise all action, good or bad, and to give himself up to faith without works. The words of Crishna are, " He who has faith has science, and he who has science and faith by that may attain supreme tranquillity. He who has deposited the burden of action in the bosom of devotion, and who has overcome all doubt by science, is no longer held in the bond of works."

Such is the wisdom and devotion of the *Sánc'hya* of Pantanjali. Among its highest attributes is the perfect detachment of all affection from wife, children, and country. " To the wise, the Brahman full of wisdom and virtue, the ox, the elephant, dogs, and men, are all equal." His only exercise is the contemplation of his God; and this God is the abstraction of being, which exists as much in one part of nature as the other—in the dog as in the man. Into this abstract being he aspires to annihilate himself.

Crishna, after these instructions, throws off his disguise, and continues no longer the Mentor of Arjuna, but gradually reveals himself as the supreme Deity, as God himself, from whom all things proceed, and into whom all things are re-absorbed.

Arjuna is favoured with the sacred privilege of beholding the godhead in its proper form. The god shows himself to him as creator, as preserver, as destroyer, as spirit, and as matter.

" In an agony of terror, his hair uplift, his head on high, his hands clasped in supplication, Arjuna addresses the awful being:—

" All beings, God, in thee I see, and every animated tribe, and Brahma on his lotus throne, and all the wise and heavenly host. I see thee with thy countless arms, and sides, and visages, and eyes; infinite on every side, without beginning, middle, or end[s]."

In the enumeration of his attributes and perfections he is tedious, for he is all things. Behold a few.

"I am the author of the creation and of the dissolution of the universe. There is nothing greater than I; and all depends upon me, as the pearls upon the thread on which they are strung[t]. I am the light in the sun and the moon, the invocation in the *Vedas,* the masculine energy in man, the soft perfume in the earth, the brightness in flame, the life in animals, the eternal seed of all nature. I am the wisdom of the wise, the power of the powerful, the glory of the glorious.—I am the father of this world, and its mother and tutor,—I am the source of heat and of rain,—I bear in my hand immortality and death,—I am what is and what is not,—I am the beginning, the middle, and end of all things.—I am Vishnou among the gods; the sun among the stars.—In the body I am the soul, and in the soul intelligence.—In the orator I am eloquence,—in the secret, silence,—in the learned, science. I am the essence of all things, and nothing animate or inanimate can exist without me. My divine virtues are inexhaustible: there is nothing great, or happy, or good, but forms a part of my glory. In short, Arjuna, what more is wanting to fill up the examples of my power? A single atom emanating from me produced the universe, and still I remain entire."

"I may be seen such as thou hast seen by the help of the *Vedas,* by mortifications, by sacrifices, and by alms."

"Put thy confidence in me; be poor in spirit, and

[s] Mr. Milman in Quarterly Review, vol. xlv, p. 12.

[t] Mr. Milman compares this with a passage in Homer, Iliad viii, 25.

renounce the fruit of works. Science is superior to practice, and contemplation is superior to science."

"Among my disciples he is especially dear to me, whose heart is friendly to all nature; whom men fear not, and who fears not men. I love him still more who is without hope, and trusts not in human strength. He is equally worthy of my love, who neither rejoices. nor sorrows, who desires nothing, who is content with all, and, because he is my servant, endureth all things. Finally, he is my best beloved disciple who is the same towards his enemy as towards his friend, in glory and in disgrace, in cold and in heat, in pain and in pleasure, who cares not for the things of this world, to whom praise and blame are indifferent, who speaks little, who rejoices in all things, and serves me with a love immoveable."

The third chapter of Pantanjali's *Yóga-sastra* relates almost exclusively to the powers which may be attained by man in this life. It is full of directions for bodily and mental exercises, consisting of intensely profound meditation on particular topics, accompanied by suppression of the breath, and restraint of the senses, while steadily maintaining prescribed postures. By such exercises the adept may acquire the knowledge of every thing past and future, remote or hidden: he divines the thoughts of others, gains the strength of an elephant, the courage of a lion, and the swiftness of the wind; flies in the air, floats on the water, dives into the earth (as though it were fluid), contemplates all worlds at one glance, and performs other wonders. See Colebrooke in Trans. of the Royal Asiatic Society, vol. i, p. 36; who adds, that the notion that this transcendent power is attainable by man in this life is not peculiar to the Sánc'hya sect; but prevails generally among the Hindoos; and amounts to a belief in magic. It will not fail, however, to strike the philosophic reader, that it is little more than an amplification of Lord Bacon's apophthegm, that KNOWLEDGE IS POWER, coupled with an exaggerated picture of the intense application and study required to obtain it.

The Jainas and Bauddhas.

Several other sects, eminently heterodox, are considered as related to the Sánc'hya school of philosophy: the Jaina and Buddha are the principal[u]. The Buddhists rejected so avowedly the authority of the *Vedas*, that they were not only opposed by moral force, but were so violently persecuted with fire and sword by the orthodox Mimansa school, that they were constrained to flee beyond the Ganges, and take refuge in the Indo-Chinese peninsula, and even in China itself; where their doctrine has taken deep root, and now exhibits itself among a philosophic class in a shape which it would at present be difficult to describe, and among the vulgar as an extravagant superstition, the religion and philosophy of Fo.

Many observations are made by Mr. Colebrooke on the similarities of the Greek and Indian philosophy. They are interesting and numerous, but cannot be entered upon here. I shall only add his last remark, namely—that a greater degree of similarity exists between the Indian doctrine and that of the earlier than of the later Greeks; and, as it is scarcely probable that the communications should have taken place, and the knowledge have been imparted, at the precise interval of time which intervened between the earlier and later schools of Greek philosophy, and especially between the Pythagoreans and Platonists; he feels

[u] An account of them forms the subject of Mr. Colebrooke's fourth paper in the Trans. of the Royal Asiat. Society, vol. i, p. 549.

disposed to conclude that the Indians were in this instance teachers rather than learners [x].

The Karm Bibak may still be added to these. It teaches that every disease and every infirmity is a consequence of our conduct in an earlier state of existence, and shows that beneficence and penance are sufficient to atone for them.

ETHICS.

Poorooshu Pureckshya, (*Purusha Parikshya*,) or the Test of Man, a work containing the moral doctrines of the Hindoos, translated into the Bengalee language, from the Sunskrit, by Huruprusad, a pundit attached to the college of Fort William, *Calcutta*, 1814, 4to.

Bhartrihari's Sentences, in Carey's Sanscrit Grammar.

The Sanscrit Original of the Moral Sentences of the

[x] Colebrooke, in Trans. of Royal Asiatic Society, vol. i, p. 579. The following curious fact, respecting a Sanscrit translation of the Dialectics of Aristotle, is related in the Asiatic Journal, June 1827, p. 814.

After the introduction of juries into Ceylon, a wealthy Brahman, whose unpopular character had rendered him obnoxious to many, was accused of murdering his nephew, and put upon trial. He chose a jury of his own caste; but so strong was the evidence against him, that twelve (out of thirteen) of the jury were thoroughly convinced of his guilt. The dissentient juror, a young Brahman of Rumiserum, stood up, declared his persuasion that the prisoner was the victim of conspiracy, and desired that all the witnesses might be recalled. He examined them with astonishing dexterity and acuteness, and succeeded in extorting from them such proofs of their perjury, that the jury, instead of consigning the accused to an ignominious death, pronounced him innocent. The affair made much noise in the island; and the chief justice (Sir A. Johnston himself) sent for the juror who had so distinguished himself, and complimented him upon the talents he had displayed. The Brahman attributed his skill to the study of a book, which he called " Strengthener of the mind." He had procured it, he said, from some pilgrims at Rumiserum, who obtained it from Persia; and he had translated it from the Sanscrit, into which it had been rendered from the Persian. Sir A. Johnston expressing curiosity to see this work, the Brahman brought him a Talmul ms. on palm leaves, which Sir Alexander found, to his infinite surprise, to be the Dialectics of Aristotle.

Indian Philosopher Sanakea or Schanakei, were presented, in the year 1825, by a Greek, Nicolo Kiephala of Zante, to the library of the Vatican. He had brought it himself from Benares. A Greek and Italian translation of it likewise appeared under the following title:

Συνοψις γνωμῶν ηθικῶν τοῦ 'Ινδοῦ φιλοσοφου Σανακέα ἐκ τῆς Σανκρίτης ἤτοι Βραχμανικῆς τῶν 'Ινδῶν διαλεκτοῦ ἐις τὴν 'Ελληνίδα καὶ 'Ιταλιδα μετενεχθεῖσα φωνὴν ὑπο τοῦ 'Ελληνος περιηγητοῦ Κ. Νικολᾶ Καιφαλα τοῦ ἐκ Ζακῦνθου. 'Αφιερώνεται ἐις ὅλους Γενικῶς τους πατέρας τῶν φαμιλιῶν. Το κειμενον 'Ινδικὸν 'αφηερώθη ἀπο τον μεταφραστὴν ἐις τὴν 'Αγίαν Παπικὴν Βιβλιοθήκην τοῦ Βατικάνου ἐις γενικὴν θεωρίαν. Ρωμη ϙωκε[z].

An original Sanscrit manuscript of these moral sentences of Chanakya, with a Nevari translation by H. B. Hodgson, esq., was presented to the Asiatic Society of Calcutta in 1826. See Asiatic Journal, 1826, May, p. 618.

Môhadmudgara, (properly, the mallet of the ignorant,) composed by the holy, devout, and prosperous Sancar Acharya. Some fragments of this were translated from the Sanscrit, under the title of The Ignorant Instructed, by Sir William Jones: see his Works, vol. vi, p. 428-30. A French version was made from this translation by Langlès, in the Catal. des mss. Sanscr. p. 71. The correctness of Sir William Jones's translation is questioned by Lebedeff, in his Grammar cited above: see p. 39.

To this place belongs a kind of Encyclopædia, which was published at Calcutta in 1818, under the title of *Vidyâ Darpan*, or the Mirror of Science.

[z] The Italian title is: Sommario di Sentenze Morali del Filosofo Indiano Sanekea, del dialetto Sanscrite ossia Bracmanico Indiano nella lingua Greca e Italiano tradotto dal Viaggiatore Greco Cap. Nicola Chiefala di Zante, dedicato a tutti li Padri di famiglia. Il testo indiano è stato depositato del translatore nella sacra Papale Bibliotheca di Vaticano a generale osservazione. In Roma, 1825.

MATHEMATICS.

a. Astronomy.

THE history of Hindoo astronomy, like almost every other part of their literature, is involved in much mystery and doubt. Respecting its antiquity, a very wide difference of opinion prevails. M. Bailly[a], founding his belief upon a series of calculations made from various astronomical tables brought from the East, was of opinion that it reached back to a very remote period, farther than any other record of profane history, and to upwards of three thousand years before our present era. This opinion was very generally adopted by the learned of Europe previous to the publication of the papers of Mr. Bentley in the sixth and eighth vols. of the Asiatic Researches, in which that gentleman attempts to prove that the *Surya Siddhanta*, the most ancient Sanscrit treatise on astronomy, is of no higher antiquity than the year 1068 of the Christian era. These papers were examined, at some length, in several numbers of the Edinburgh Review, in which, not only the results of Mr. Bentley's calculations are disputed, but likewise the principles on which they rest. Since this, Mr. Bentley has published a History of Astronomy, in which he has treated the subject with much learning and ability. In this work, speaking of the ancient astronomy, he carries back the era of its foundation to somewhere between the fourteenth and sixteenth centuries before Christ; and finally seems inclined to fix its commencement at about the year B. C. 1425. This is said by a critic in the Westminster Review to be so well established in Mr. Bentley's work, that no remoter age can ever again be attributed to it. In this work, too, the birth of Rama, the most famous epoch in Hindoo history, is computed to have fallen on the sixth of April,

[a] Bailly, Histoire de l'Astronomie Indienne, *Paris*, 1787, 4to.

B. C. 961. Other epochs also are calculated, the last of which is the year of our Lord 538, from which modern Hindoo astronomy is dated.

The reader will find ample information on this subject, in the papers of Mr. Bentley in the sixth and eighth numbers of the Asiatic Researches; in vol. i, x, and xii, of the Edinburgh Review: in the Westminster Review, vol. ii: and in.

An Historical View of the Hindoo Astronomy, from the earliest dawn of that science in India to the present time, by the late J. Bentley, *Calcutta*, 1824, 8vo; again, *London*, 1825, 8vo. plates.

Astronomie der Inder, in the Blättern für literar. *Unterhalt*, 1829, Juli, No. clxxv.

Rapport sur le *Kala Sankalita*, recueil de mémoires du lieutenant-colonel John Warren, publié à *Madras*, en 1825, 1 vol. in 4to.; Lu à la Société Asiat. dans sa séance du 3 Déc. 1827, par M. Stahl, in the Journ. Asiat. 1827, lxvi, p. 356.

Sir William Jones states, that he had seen a catalogue of seventy-nine astronomical works in the Sanscrit language. See Craufurd's Researches on India, vol. i, p. 243.

The principal and most ancient astronomical work of the Hindoos is the *Surya Siddhanta*, which forms one of the six supplementary works, *Vedangas*, to the *Vedas*, (see above, p. 84,) and whose author is said to have lived in the fifth century of the Christian era[a].

Part of the first chapter of the *Surya Siddhanta*, in the Asiatic Journal, 1817, May, p. 429, 430; June, p. 546, 547.

An English translation of the whole of the *Surya*

[a] See Asiatic Researches, tom. vi, p. 540. According to the notion of the Hindoos, this work was a divine revelation made at the close of the *Satya-yug*, of the twenty-eighth *Maha-yug*, of the seventh *Manwantara*: that is, about 2,164,899 years ago. See l. c.

Siddhanta was printed at Madras in the treatises of Captain Warren, upon the chronology of the Hindoos.

This was succeeded by *Vishnu Chandra* and *Brahmagupta* in the early part of the seventh, and *Munjâla*, towards the middle of the tenth century.

Siromani, an astronomical work, by Bháscara, surnamed Acharya, (the teacher,) dates from the middle of the twelfth century: it is translated by Taylor in the *Lilavati*, which will presently come under notice. It is divided into two sections; the *Gola Adhyaya*, or lectures on the earth, and the *Ganita Adhyaya*, or lectures on numbers as applied to astronomy.

Opinions of Bháscara, respecting the globe and the attraction of the earth, in the Asiatic Journal, 1817, Feb. p. 110: see also Millin's Annales Encyclop. 1818, Sept. p. 108. This is nothing more than an extract from Dr. Taylor's translation of the *Lilavati*.

A translation by Colebrooke, mentioned in this place by Adelung, is placed under Arithmetic, to which it properly belongs.

Tithi Tatua and *Jyatisha Tatua*, two treatises on Astronomy and Astrology. Manuscripts in the Royal Library at Copenhagen.

Bârah Másá, a poetical description of the year in Hindoostan, by Mirza Cázim Ali Tawun, *Calcutta*, 1812, 4to.

The Asiatic Society of London possesses a manuscript treatise in Sanscrit upon the Eclipses of the Sun.

β. *Arithmetic.*

Short Account of the present mode of teaching Arithmetic in Hindoo schools, from Taylor's translation of the *Lilavati*, in the Asiatic Journal, 1817, March, p. 213—217.

The principal work upon Arithmetic is the *Lilavati*,

which is reckoned one of the six supplements (*Vedangas*) to the *Vedas*. The author, Bháscara Acharya, gave his work the name of his daughter, in order to console her for the want of a husband[h].

The original Sanscrit was printed for the first time at Calcutta, with the English title, The *Lilavati*, or System of Hindoo Arithmetic.

Lilavati, or a Treatise on Arithmetic and Geometry, by Bháscara Acharya, translated from the original Sanscrit, by John Taylor, *Bombay*, 1816, 4to. A copious extract from it is given in the Journal des Savans, 1817, Sept. p. 535—545.

Translation of the *Lilavati* and *Vidyaganita*, Treatises of Arithmetic and Algebra, by Bháscara, and an Extract from the Course of Astronomy of Brahmágupta, comprising his Arithmetic and Algebra, translated from the Sanscrit by H. T. Colebrooke, esq., and published with a preliminary Dissertation on the Origin of Algebra, *Calcutta*, 1818, 4to. This had already been printed under the title of, Algebra, with Arithmetic and Mensuration, from the Sanscrit of Brahmágupta and Bháscara, by H. T. Colebrooke, esq., *London*, Murray, 1817.

This work is considered of much importance in the Edinburgh Review, where it is made the subject of an article, vol. xviii, p. 141. It contains four different treatises in Sanscrit verse. Two of these, the *Lilavati* and *Vidyaganita* are the works of Bháscara Acharya; the first on Arithmetic, the second on Algebra. The others are still more ancient, and were composed by a mathematician named Brahmágupta, who is supposed to have lived in the sixth or seventh century. These, like most of the mathematical

[h] Respecting another Sanscrit work bearing the title of *Lilavati*, see Catalogue des mss. Sanscrits, p. 65, 66.

writings of the Hindoos, form systems of astronomy; the first two being the introduction to the *Siddhanta Siromani*, and the other two forming the twelfth and eighteenth chapters of the *Brahma Siddhanta* of Brahmágupta.

Mr. Taylor possesses another manuscript under the title *Udaharna*, which contains the proofs of rules given in the *Lilavati*.

γ. *Algebra.*

A Dissertation, by Mr. Colebrooke, on the Early History of Algebra in India, Arabia, Greece, etc. will be found prefixed to his translation of the *Lilavati* and *Vidyaganita*, just mentioned under the preceding head. It is full of learned and judicious research[1].

Bija Ganita, or the Algebra of the Hindoos, by Edward Strachey, of the East India Company's Bengal Civil Service, with notes, by Davis, *London*, 1813, 4to.

The *Bija Ganita*, or System of Hindoo Algebra, translated into the English, *Calcutta*, 1827.

Algebra of the Hindoos, with Arithmetic and Mensuration, from the Sanscrit of Brahmágupta and Bháscara, translated by H. T. Colebrooke, esq., *London*, 1817, 4to. See notice of this work under Arithmetic.

Kala Sankalita, a complete System of Algebra, of Arithmetic, and Geometry of the Hindoos, translated from the Sanscrit, by J. Warren, *Madras*, 1827. See Journal Asiatique, vol. xi, p. 356.

Some account of a Sanscrit work on a game resembling Chess will be found in the Asiatic Journal, 1818, February, p. 121, by Sir William Jones. This was first printed in vol. ii of the Asiatic Researches, and will also be found in Sir William Jones's Works, vol. i,

[1] There is a notice of it in the Edinb. Review, Nov. 1817. It is also made the subject of an appendix to Mr. Mill's History of India, vol. i, Appendix, No. ii, and again Asiatic Journal, Dec. 1818.

4to. Some particular positions at Chess from the Sanscrit, are given in the Asiatic Journal, Oct. 1819, p. 347. Sir W. Jones believed that this game was invented by the Hindoos, and the Persians are of the same opinion.

HISTORY.

Professor Wilson informs us, that the only Sanscrit composition yet discovered to which the title of historical can with any propriety be applied, is the *Rája Taringíni*, a history of Cashmire. This work was first introduced to the knowledge of the Mahommedans by the learned minister of Acber Abufazl; but the summary which he has given of its contents was taken, as he informs us, from a Persian translation; the Hindoo original being so scarce as not to be procured. Sir William Jones sought for it without success; and it escaped the search of all Europeans, until Mr. Colebrooke fortunately procured a copy in 1805, from the heirs of a Brahman, who died in Calcutta. Since that time the late Mr. Speke procured another transcript from Lucknow; and professor Wilson procured a third, which was brought for sale to Calcutta. The latter gentleman states, that he was unable to meet with another copy either in that city or at Benares.

The *Rája Taringíni*, as we are informed by professor Wilson, is not one entire composition, but a series of compositions written by different authors at different periods: a circumstance that gives a greater value to its contents; as, with the exception of the early periods of the history, the several authors may be regarded almost as the chroniclers of their own times.

The first of the series is *Rája Taringini* of Calhana Pundit, who begins with the fabulous ages, and comes down to the reign of Sangrama-Deva (A. D. 1027). He states his having made use of earlier authorities, and gives an interesting enumeration of several that he had consulted.

The next work is the *Rájavalí*, of Jona Raja, which professor Wilson was unable to meet with. It probably begins where Calhana ends, and comes down to the 815th year of the Hijra.

The third work is the *Sri Jaina Rájá Taringíni*, by Srí Vara Pandita, the pupil of Jona Rája, whose work it professes to continue, and which it brings down to the 882 of the Hijra, A. D. 1477.

The fourth, which completes the series, and was written to bring down the history to the time when Cashmire became a province of Acber's empire, is called *Rája vali Pataca*, and is the production of Punya, or Prájnya Bhatta.

From such of the foregoing works as he could obtain, and the addition of various Persian authorities, professor Wilson has composed a valuable and learned essay on the Hindoo History of Cashmire. A slight glance at its contents will convince the reader of the industry, research, and learning of its author. A short introduction gives an account of the authorities made use of; and the work is followed by eight appendices, some of which will be found highly interesting to classical scholars. The whole is embodied in the fifteenth volume of the Asiatic Researches; and at page 81 will be found a chronological table, carrying back the history, according to one account, to B. C. 3714; but, according to the more accurate adjustment of the author, to B. C. 2666[k].

[k] The account of this work, given by Adelung, is a tissue of errors, as may be seen by comparing it with the above which I have taken from an

Râghava-Pândaviya, a poem, by Caviraja (the prince of poets). A poetical foppery, in which every word may be taken in a variety of meanings, so that the history of Rama, as well as that of Crishna, is entirely related by the same expressions.

The *Raghu Vansa*, a Sanscrit historical poem, *Calcutta*, 1827.

Mr. Adelung mentions under this head, the extravagant tales of *Beital Pachisi*, and *Vicrama Charitra*, which will be found noticed under Works of Fiction.

Kiratyooneeyu, a celebrated historical work in the original Sanscrit, with the commentary of Mullee Nath, *Calcutta*, 1814, 4to. See Colebrooke on Sunskrit and Prakrit Poetry, in Asiatic Researches, vol. x, p. 431[1].

Cumara-Palacharitra, and *Bodcha Charitra*, two historical works clothed in allegories.

History of *Ram* and *Sectah* his Wife, Sanscrit, Devanâgari character. Manuscript in Howell and Stewart's Catalogue of Oriental Literature, *London*, 1828.

The *Goroo Mooka*, or from the month of the *Goroo Nanick*, the founder of the *Sikhs*, commonly called the *Garsunti*, in Sanscrit. A manuscript in the Catalogue of Ogle, Duncan, and Co. of London.

Vansavali (d. i. Familienverzeichniss) ein Sanskritwerk über die Geschichte von Orissa, vor 300 Jahren

inspection of Professor Wilson's work in the Asiatic Researches. It may be sufficient to mention, that the original Sanscrit work, and a translation by Mr. Wilson, are spoken of as to be found in the volume referred to, neither of which will be there discovered. He also refers to an extract from Wilson's translation, by Klaproth, in the Journal Asiatic, 1825, Juillet, p. i, etc.; and the Bulletin Univ. 1826, Dec. Philologie. p. 394, which I suppose to be extracts from the Professor's original essay.

[1] The following is the title as given in the Catalogue of Parbury and Allen: *Kiráta Arjuníya*, a poem by Bharvi, with the comment of Mallinátha, named Ghantapatha, *Calcutta*, 1814, 4to.

geschrieben. See an Account, etc., of *Orissa Proper*, or *Cuttack*, by A. Stirling, esq., in the Asiatic Researches, vol. xv, p. 163—338[m].

GEOGRAPHY.

Col. Wilford[n] is of opinion that the ancients, in the times of Pliny and Ptolemy, had a better geographical account of India than we had forty years ago. The geographical treatises in Sanscrit do not appear to be numerous or instructive; and relate rather to local than general geography. In some of the *Puranas* there is a section called the *Bhuvana-cosa*, a magazine, or collection of mansions; but these are entirely mythological, and of no value. Besides these there are other geographical tracts, to several of which is given the title of *Cshétra-samása*, or collection of countries: one is entirely mythological, and is highly esteemed by the Jainas; another is entirely geographical, and a very valuable work. There is also the *Trai-locya-derpana*, or mirror of three worlds, (which again is entirely mythological,) as well as lists of countries, rivers, and

[m] I have let this work stand in the text as given by Mr. Adelung. At page 256 of the volume of the Asiatic Researches, to which he refers, Mr. Stirling says: "The sources from which my information has been chiefly derived, are 1st. A work in Sanscrit called the *Vansavali*, belonging to a learned Brahman of Puri, said to have been originally composed by some of his ancestors three or four centuries back, and continued down in the family to the present date, etc." He also mentions in the following page, as his third authority, another *Vansavali*, or genealogy, written in Sanscrit on palm leaves, procured from another Brahman. The full title of Mr. Stirling's paper is, An Account, Geographical, Statistical, and Historical, of *Orissa Proper*, or *Cuttack*.

[n] On the Ancient Geography of India, in Asiatic Researches, vol. xiv, p. 373—470.

mountains, in several *Puranas* and other books; but they are of little or no use, being mere lists of names without any explanation whatever. Col. Wilford thinks these were known to Megasthenes and Pliny °.

The same author tells us that real geographical treatises do exist; but that they are very scarce, and the owners unwilling to part with them, or to allow them to be copied, as they consider it highly improper to impart any knowledge of the state of the country to foreigners, and they regard these works on geography as copies of the archives of the government of their country.

Col. Wilford, though he spared neither trouble nor money, could only procure information respecting seven of these treatises, namely:

1. *Munja-prati-désá-vyavast'há*, or An Account of various Countries, written by Rája Munja, in the latter end of the ninth century: it was revised and improved by Rája Bhoja his nephew; and republished in the tenth, under the title of,—

2. *Bhoja-prati-désá-vyavast'ha*. Neither of these treatises could be obtained by Col. W. nor did he ever see any account of them in any Sanscrit book he had seen; though he was assured of their existence, and was informed they might be procured in Guzerat. They are both voluminous.

3. The next is one written by command of Buccaraya or Bucca-Sinha towards the end of the thirteenth century. It is mentioned in the commentary on the geography of the *Máhabhárata*, and it is said he wrote an account of the three hundred and ten Rája-ships of India. Col. Wilford thinks this to be the geographical work called (in the *Dekhin*) *Bhuvana Ságara*, or sea of mansions.

° He refers the reader to lib. vi, ch. 17 and 20, and says the account of so many countries scattered over India, cannot be the result of the travels of several individuals, but must have been extracted from such lists, p. 374.

4. The fourth is a commentary on the Geography of the *Mahábhárata*, written by order of the Rája Paulastya in the peninsula by a pandit, who lived in 1485. This was in the possession of Col. Wilford, who describes it as very voluminous, curious, and interesting.

5. The fifth is the *Vicrama-Ságara*, author unknown, said to exist in the peninsula, as it did in Bengal, in 1648. It is considered very valuable: Col. W. possesses seventeen leaves of it, and says they are certainly very interesting.

6. The sixth is *Bhuvana-cosá*, which is declared to be a section of the *Bhavishya Purana;* if so it has been revised, and many additions made to it: very properly, for in its original state, it was a most contemptible performance. It is a valuable work and dates later than 1552.

7. The seventh is the *Cshétra-samása*, already mentioned, written by Bijjala, the last Raja of Patna, who died 1648. Though modern, it is a valuable and interesting performance [p].

Besides these, Wilford mentions the following geographical treatises: *Dacsha-C'hand'aca; Désá-vali Crita-dhará-vará-vali*, by Rámés'wara; *Ch'hpana-désá*, or the fifty-six provinces; and *Gálava-tantra.*

The titles of the following geographical treatises are taken from Professor Wilson's Catalogue of the Mackenzie manuscripts. See above, p. 61.

1. *Trailokya Dipika*, a Description of the three Worlds according to the doctrine of the Jainas: this work however is chiefly confined to the geography of the earth. Ms. on paper, Devanâgari character.

2. *Bhugola Sangraha*, ms. on paper, Telugu character. A collection of the geographical portions of

p This author reminds one of the simple manner of Herodotus. He says, I have written this work after the *Vicrama-Sagara* and from enquiries made of respectable well-informed people, and from what I have seen myself.

various *Puranas*, as the *Matsya, Kudma, Markandeya, Vishnu, Varáha, Narasinha*, the *Bhágavat* and *Rámáyana.*

3. *Desanirnaya*, ms. on palm leaves, Grandham character, incomplete. This is a description of the fifty-six countries into which India is divided; said to be a portion of the *Brahmanda Purana.*

MEDICINE.

Some account of the medical and surgical sciences among the Hindoos will be found in the following paper, from which it appears that they were at one time highly esteemed and extensively cultivated in India: On the Medical and Surgical Sciences of the Hindoos, Oriental Magazine, Feb. 1823; also in the Asiat. Journ. 1823, Sept. p. 241—243; translated into German under the following title: Ueber die medizinischen und chirurgischen Kenntnisse der Hindus im Allgemeinen, im Morgenblatte, 1823, No. 292, 293.

The *Ayur-Veda*, is a collection of the medical treatises of the highest antiquity and authority, and is considered to form a part of the *Atharva Veda.* It is consequently the work of Brahma, by whom it was communicated to Dascha the *Prajapati*, who instructed the two Aswins, the sons of Surya, the sun, who became the medical attendants of the gods. This genealogy cannot but recal to our minds the two sons of Esculapius, and their descent from Apollo. The *Ayur Veda*, which originally consisted of one hundred sections of a thousand stanzas each, was adapted to the limited faculties and life of man, by its distribution into eight subdivisions, the enumeration of which conveys to us an accurate idea of the objects of the *Ars Medendi* amongst the Hindoos. The divisions are thus enumerated—

1. *Salgu* is the art of extracting extraneous sub-

stances, whether of grass, wood, earth, metal, bone, etc. violently or accidentally introduced into the human body; with the treatment of the inflammation and suppuration thereby induced; and by analogy, the cure of all phlegmonoid tumours and abscesses.

2. *Salakya* is the treatment of external organic affections or diseases of the eyes, ears, nose, etc.

3. *Kaya Chikitsa* is, as the name implies, the application of the *Ars Medendi* (*Chikitsa*) to the body in general (*Kaya*), and forms what we mean by the science of medicine. The two preceding divisions constitute the surgery of modern schools.

4. *Bhatavidya* is the restoration of the faculties from a disorganised state, induced by demoniacal possession. This art has vanished before the diffusion of knowledge; but it formed a very important part of medical practice through all the schools, Greek, Arabic, or European.

5. *Kaumarabhritya* means the cure of infancy, comprehending not only the management of children from their birth, but the treatment of irregular lactic secretion, and puerperal disorders in mothers and nurses.

6. *Agada* is the administration of antidotes.

7. *Rasayana* is chemistry, or, more correctly speaking, alchemy, as the chief end of the chemical combinations it describes, and which are mostly metallurgic, is the discovery of the universal medicine; the elixir that was to render health permanent and life perpetual.

8. The last branch, *Bajikarana*, professes to promote the increase of the human race.

An abstract of this work, in the Devanâgari character, is contained in the Royal Library at Copenhagen.

According to some authorities, the Aswins instructed Indra, who became the preceptor of Dhanwantari;

while others make Atreya, Bharadwaja, and Charaka prior to the latter. Charaka's work, which goes by his name, is still extant. The disciple of Dhanwantari was Suruta, the son of Viswamitra, and consequently contemporary of Rama: his work *Sausruta* is still extant, and is the great authority of Hindoostan practice. It is unquestionably of great antiquity, though not of the prodigious age assigned to it by Indian fable. We must therefore be satisfied with knowing that it is the oldest work on the subject, except that of Caraka. A commentary on the text, by Ubhatta, a Cashmirian, is probably as old as the twelfth or thirteenth century; and his commentary, it is believed, was preceded by others. The work is divided into six portions, namely:

1. *Sutra-St'hana*, surgical definitions.
2. *Nidana St'hana*, on the diagnosis.
3. *Sarira St'hana*, anatomy.
4. *Chikitsa St'hana*, internal application of medicine.
5. *Kalpa St'hana*, doctrine of antidotes.
6. *Uttara St'hana*, a supplementary section upon various local diseases of the eyes, ears, etc. In all these divisions, however, surgery, and not general medicine, is the object of the *Sausruta*. See Asiat. Journ. 1823, Sept. p. 242.

The six following medical works are copied from Professor Wilson's Catalogue of the Mackenzie mss. See above, p. 61.

1. *Vaidyajivana*, ms. on palm leaves, Nandinágari character. A work in three sections, on the practice of medicine, by Rolamba Raja.

2. *Vaidya grantha*, ms. on palm leaves, Telugu character. A section of a medical work, author unknown: it includes the description of the body, or anatomy, the treatment of women in childbirth, and the symptoms and treatment of various diseases.

3. *Shadrasa Nighanta*, on the properties of drugs, Telugu character.

4. *Chikitsá Sata Sloka*, on the cure of sundry diseases.

5. *Hara pradipiká*, a work on alchemy and mercury, and its combinations.

6. *Vaidya Sangraha*, a collection of medical formulæ.

Besides these, another medical manuscript exists in the Royal Library of Copenhagen. It is quoted in the Litter. Tidende for 1819, p. 124, under the following title: *Pathyapathya*, sive tractatus de Materia Medica et Diætetica; auctore Baidyakeya, fol.

Account of the Spasmodic Cholera, from Hindoo writers, by Calvi Virumbon, in Asiatic Journal, 1819, Sept. p. 232—235.

Rogantaka Sara, Materia Indica, auct. Whitelaw Ainslie, *Londini*, 1827, 8vo. See Asiatic Journal, vol. i, p. 126.

FINE ARTS.

POETRY.

On Sanscrit Poetry in general.

A HISTORY of Sanscrit poetry would be a general history of Sanscrit literature. Not only the *Vedas*, the most ancient sacred books of the Hindoos, but even treatises on science, apparently the most awkward to reduce to a metrical form, are composed in verse; as examples of which we may mention the vocabularies of *Amara Sinha*, and Menu's Code of Laws: and although, in the extensive range of Sanscrit learning, there are some few compositions which may be called prose, yet, even the style of most of these bears so great a resemblance to the language of poetry, from their being written in a kind of modulated prose, as scarcely to form an exception[a]. The age of Sanscrit poetry, therefore, like that of all other nations, is coeval with the earliest vestiges of the language; and its antiquity, after deducting every fair demand that can be made upon it, will still be sufficient to render it venerable, and give it a high claim to our attention. But Sanscrit poetry,—confining the term to its stricter sense, as designating such compositions as from their nature and form come within our ideas of the term,—has much loftier claims than this to our regard. Nor has it been neglected; though, perhaps, of all the countries of Europe it has been treated with most indifference in England, where, from the political connection of the people with the land of its birth, it might have been expected to excite the most general and lively interest.

The classical poets of ancient India are divided into three periods. The first is that of the *Vedas;* the second, that of the great *Epics;* the third, that of the *Drama*. A fourth is mentioned; but as it is of a later date, (since the birth of Christ,) it is not considered as belonging to the classic age. These three periods are assigned to Sanscrit poetry, not only from historical testimony, but from the language and style of the compositions themselves[b]. One of the first Sanscrit scholars of the present day observes, that the specimens we have of the *Vedas* are sufficient to enable us to trace a difference of style between them and the other specimens of early Sanscrit literature, so great, as

[a] Sir William Jones, vol. v; Colebrooke, Asiatic Researches, vol. x, p. 447, 8vo, mentions several kinds of prose, but scarcely one used in any reputable work which can be strictly called by that name.

[b] Heeren's Researches: Indians, ch. i.

to prove that many centuries must have elapsed between the *Vedas* and the *Ramayana*. The language of the former is visibly softened and polished in the epic, nearly as much as that of the Iliad in the hands of the Grecian dramatists [c].

The scholar who would estimate the character of the ancient poetry of India, and see what has been done by various critics and poets towards making its beauties and deformities familiar to the nations of Europe, will find an article in the Quarterly Review [d], already frequently referred to, which will fully satisfy him on this point, while to the general reader it will afford a literary treat of great interest and amusement. What the learned author there says of the Schlegels, may with perfect truth and justice be applied to himself; and in referring to him, "I appeal to a poetical critic, whose boundless acquaintance with ancient and modern literature, whose high and philosophic principles of taste, if they do not command universal deference, have at least a right to universal respect and attention." It is meet, therefore, that I should acknowledge the use I have made in the following hurried sketch of the paper just referred to, written by one who has so well known how to mould into the most pleasing forms, and to set in the splendid adornments of language and eloquence, the rich ore which has been dug from the productive mines of Indian poetry.

The bards of India have given to poetry nearly every form which it has assumed in the western world; and in each, and in all, they have excelled. Its heroic poets have been likened to Homer, and their epics dignified with the appellations of Iliad and Odyssey [e].

[c] Professor Ewald, in the Götting. gelehrte Anzeigen.

[d] No. lxxxix, ascribed to the late professor of Poetry, Mr. Milman.

[e] See Heeren's Researches: Indians, chap. i; Quarterly Review, vol. xlv, p. 6.

In the drama, Ca'lida'sa has been designated as the Indian Shakspeare[f]; Vyása is not unworthy of comparison with Milton[g]; the adventures of Nala and Damayanti, with the Faerie Queene of Spenser[h]; the philosophic *Bhagavat-Gita* reads like a noble fragment of Empedocles or Lucretius[i]; their didactic, their lyric, their writers of fables, and of the lighter kinds of poetry, have all carried their art to the same high point of perfection[k]; and so nicely are their respective merits balanced, that it seems rather a matter of individual taste than of critical acumen, to which class the palm should be conceded. M. Chézy, with the Hindoos themselves, gives it decidedly to the epic; Milman to the softer and less energetic; A. W. Schlegel appears inclined to bestow it upon the didactic, while, if the praise of one of the first and earliest judges of Sanscrit poetry be not lavish, it will be difficult to say how any thing can excel their descriptive[l]. Indeed among no people of the world has poetry exhibited more magnificent appearances, or been accompanied by a more bland and fascinating imagery.

There exist, for instance, in our European literature, few pieces to be compared with the *Megha Duta* (The Cloud Messenger) in sentiment and beauty; and in erotic poetry the voluptuous Jayadéva, in his little poem on the loves of Madhava and Radha, far sur-

[f] Sir William Jones's preface to Sacontala.

[g] See above, p. 115.

[h] Quarterly Review, vol. xlv, p. 13.

[i] Ibid. vol. xlv, p. 7. A. W. Schlegel calls it the most beautiful, and perhaps the only truly philosophical poem in any language Indischen Bibl. vol. ii, p. 219. See above, p. 93.

[k] Heeren's Researches: Indians, sect. i.

[l] Sir William Jones, in his preface to the Seasons (Works, vol. vi, p. 432), says of the season of Calidas, "Every line is exquisitely polished; every couplet exhibits an Indian landscape, always beautiful, sometimes highly coloured, but never beyond nature."

passes all elegiac poets known. Never were the fires of love and its soft languors depicted in colours so lively and enchanting as in the *Gitagovinda*. Yet, according to the pandits, this entirely mystical work expresses nothing but the aspirations of the soul, seeking to unite itself to the Deity; and in this point of view it affords a striking resemblance to the delightful allegory of Psyche and Cupid [m].

In the development of the higher powers of poetry, the sublime and the pathetic, the Indian bards have been eminently successful. Instances of the former will be found in the extracts from the *Bhagavat-Gita*, translated by Mr. Milman. See one specimen above, p. 157, on the immortality of the soul. The *Mahabharat*, indeed, altogether, must be regarded as one of the most splendid efforts of the genius of epic poetry.

But the power of the Indian bards in awakening the more tender sympathies of our nature, in describing the soft touches of domestic feeling, and in breathing, with simple pathos, the passionate sorrow of parental affliction, is still more manifest. See for example the beautiful story of Nala and Damayanti [n], the pathetic episode from the Ramayana, of the death of Yajnadatta, and the affecting yet beautifully simple tale of the Brahman's Lament. The former of these, so wonderful in invention, and still more wonderful in its style, contains many passages that would do honour even to Homer.

It has been an almost universal complaint against the poetry of the East, that it is overcharged with glitter and ornament; that it is too lavish of fantastic metaphor and unapt similitude; that it offends by a

[m] Chézy, Discours sur la Littérature Sanscrit. See above, p. 118, for his descriptive panegyric on their epic poetry. A notice of the *Gitagovinda* will be found under the Drama.

[n] See above, p. 96, sqq.

florid and redundant diction; in short, that it is more fitted to dazzle than to please, to excite admiration than delight; and that its effect is rather to fatigue the attention by a rapid succession of glaring and startling images, than to maintain a rising interest, or win a growing sympathy by a more moderate and less confused display of attractions.

This exuberance of ornament in oriental poetry is denied by two excellent judges, the late bishop Heber and Mr. Milman. The latter goes so far as to pronounce, what his own versions of Sanscrit poetry seem to prove, "that the diction of the Indian poets is peculiarly simple, and that their luxuriance is not in language but in the subject matter of their poetry—in the infinite variety, vastness, and exuberance of their mythological fables."

The mythology of the Hindoos is the great obstacle which must ever prevent their poetry from becoming popular in Europe. If the pantheon of the heathen deities of our own classic world requires a guide to Parnassus, or a Lempriere to enable us to understand the poets of Greece and Italy; how much more shall we be at a loss, where every thing is not only new and strange, but frightful and shocking?—where the great personifications of nature and mind have not been softened down by the *beau ideal* of the Greeks to the perfection of human symmetry; but are still exhibited in their original, barbarous, and unwieldy forms; majesty by enormous stature, power by multitudinous hands, providence by countless eyes, wisdom by the trunk of the elephant, omnipresence by innumerable bodies [o].

In addition to this, and besides the ordinary loss which all poetry must undergo by being translated

[o] Heeren's Researches: Indians, chap. i; Quarterly Review, vol. xlv, p. 31. The number of Hindoo deities is said to be not less than *three hundred and thirty millions.*

into a foreign language, that of India must suffer from causes which seem almost to prevent the possibility of its ever being familiar with us. "These causes," observes Mr. Milman, "are obvious. Poetry, which departs from what may be called the vernacular idiom of thought and feeling, must content itself with being the treasured delight of the few. If it speak a dialect the least foreign or learned, or require a more than ordinarily vivid imagination to transport us into the new world which it opens before us; if it not only should awake no old delightful associations, but depend upon others which are altogether alien to our habits and usual tone of thinking; it must win its way, even if successful, very slowly; nor is it likely at any time to become completely naturalized among the mass of readers." Many of our own great bards are far from popular; and perhaps it may be said of these, as well as of those of modern Europe, and of the ancient classics of Greece and Italy, that they are more or less so, nearly in exact proportion to the degree of effort required to transfuse the spirit and feelings of the poet into our own bosom. If this be an obstacle in the case of our own Chaucer and Spenser, and increasingly so in that of Dante, Lycophron, etc.; to what an immeasurable degree must it operate upon the poets of a people whose political and religious institutions, as well as their moral habits in general, are so much at variance with our own; and who dwell in a region where nature altogether is clothed in so different a garb, that it is not too much to say, no labour or skill could render its associations familiar by translation into any European language.

Sanscrit Works on Poetry and Rhetoric.

The following list of books on this subject are mostly taken from professor Wilson, On the Dramatic System of the Hindoos, prefixed to his Hindoo Theatre. The works relating exclusively to the drama, and Sanscrit prosody, will be found below under their respective heads.

The first treatise on poetical and rhetorical composition in general, is the *Saraswatí Kanthábharana,* ascribed to Bhoja Raja. There is a commentary upon it by Retneswara Mahopádhyáya.

The next work to be mentioned is the *Kávya Prakása,* by Mammatta Bhatta, a Cashmirian, written about five centuries ago. It is on rhetorical composition in general, and of great repute.

The *Sáhitya Derpana,* by Viswanáth Kavirája, a Bengali pundit, is described as a work of great merit on poetical writing, and comparatively modern; perhaps four or five hundred years old.

The works which treat of the poetic art in general are exceedingly numerous; some of the principal are the *Kávyádersa,* by Dandi; the *Kávyátankára Vritti,* by Vámana Acharya; the *Kuvaláyamanda,* by Apyáya Dikshita; the *Alankára Suvaswa* of Bháma; the *Rasá Gangádhara* of Jagannath Pandit Raj, and the *Alankára Kaustubha,* by Kavi Kernapúraka, who illustrates all his rules by verses of his own, relating to the loves of Crishna and Rádhá, and the pastimes of the deity with the Gopis of Vrindávan.

Besides these, there are several treatises on the passions and emotions which poetry is intended to depicture or excite; as the *Sringáva Tilaka* of Rúdra Bhatta; and the *Rasa Manjarí,* and the *Rasa Taringiní* of Bhánu Datta: the latter comprises a number of rules which are quoted as those of Bharata.

a. On Metre and Prosody.

The capital essay on Sanscrit and Pracrit Poetry, by H. T. Colebrooke, in the Asiatic Researches, vol. x, p. 399, etc., is the great authority on this subject. It discusses the laws of metre, the rules for which are contained in Sootras, or brief aphorisms, attributed to Pingalanaga, a fabulous being, represented by mythologists in the shape of a serpent. The aphorisms of Pingala are collected into eight books, of which the first allots names, or rather signs, for feet consisting of one, two, or three syllables. The second book teaches the manner in which passages of the *Vedas* are measured. The third explains the variations in the subdivision of the couplet and stanza. The fourth treats of profane poetry, and especially of verses in which the number of syllables, or their quantity, is not uniform. The fifth, sixth, and seventh exhibit metres of that sort which has been called monoschemastic, or uniform, because the same feet recur invariably in the same places. The eighth and last book serves as an appendix to the whole, and contains rules for computing all the possible combinations of long and short syllables in verses of any length.

Pingala cites earlier writers on prosody, whose works appear to have been lost: such as Saitava, Craushtica, Tándin, and other ancient sages, Ya'sca Cas'yapa, etc.

"Pingala's text," says Mr. Colebrooke, "has been interpreted by various commentators; and, among others, by Hela'yud' habhal'l'a, author of an excellent gloss, entitled *Mrita Sanjívini.* It is the work on which I have chiefly relied. A more modern commentary, or rather a paraphrase in verse, by Na'ra'yan'a-bhat't'a-lará', under the title of *Urtilócti-ratna,* presents the singularity of being interpreted throughout in a double sense, by the author himself, in a further gloss entitled *Parieshâ.*

"The *Agnipurána* is quoted for a complete system of prosody, founded apparently on Pingala's Aphorisms; but which serves to correct or to supply the text in many places; and which is accordingly used for that purpose by commentators. Original treatises likewise have been composed by various authors, and among others by the celebrated poet Cálidása. In a short treatise entitled *Sruta bód'ha,* this poet teaches the laws of versification in the very metre to which they relate; and has thus united the example with the precept. The same mode has been also practised by many other writers on prosody; and in particular, by Pingala's commentator Nara'yan'a-bhat't'a; and by the author of the *Vritta Retnacara* and *Vritta Dupan'a.*

"Cálidása's *Sruta bód'ha* exhibits only the most common sorts of metre, and is founded on Pingala's Pracrit rules of Prosody; as has been remarked by one of the commentators on the *Vritta Retnacara.*"

Colebrooke's Essay gives an account of the various metres, with specimens from the most esteemed poets, and engraved plates of the original text. Sanscrit prosody has two sorts of metre; one governed by the number of syllables, and the other measured by feet, like the hexameters of the Greek, and both are arranged into a great variety of stanzas. Their poetry also admits both of rhime and alliteration.

Sâhityavidyâdhari Tikâ, ou Traité sur les mètres Sanscrits, Journ. Asíat. vi, p. 383.

The Prosody of Pingala forms part of the six *Vedangas,* or supplements to the *Vedas.* See above, p. 86. Sir William Jones quotes the poem upon Sanscrit Prosody, by Cálidása, called *Sruta Bodha,* and in the Royal Library at Paris is a manuscript of an analysis of rhimes by him, under the title of *Chandasâng Mandjarî.*

Principles of Sanscrit metre and prosody, in the preface to A. W. v. Schlegel's *Baghavad-Gita, Bonn,* 1823, 8vo.

Some account of Sanscrit metre will also be found in the preface to Halhed's Translation of the Code of Gentoo Laws.

Von dem epischen Sylbenmasse der Indier, von A. W. v. Schlegel, in s. Indischen Bibl. vol. i, p. 36—40.

On the metre of the *Mahabharata,* by M. Chézy, in the Journ. des Savans, 1825, p. 44.

Ueber einige ältere Sanskrit-Metra, ein Versuch von Geo. Heinr. Ewald, *Göttingen,* 1827, 8vo.

Slokaratchanavidi. Théorie du *Sloka,* ou mètre héroïque Sanskrit, par M. Chézy, *Paris,* 1828, 8vo.

β. *Epic Poetry*[p].

Considerations upon the Indian Epos, in Schlegel's preface to his edition of the *Ramayana.*

Vrihatcatha, by Somadeva. Sir William Jones compares this work with the poems of Ariosto, and even gives it the preference in point of eloquence.

Raga Bansa, or *Raghu-Vansa.* A poem by Cálidása[q], in nineteen cantos. This work is among the most admired compositions in the Sanscrit tongue. It contains the history of Rama and of his predecessors and successors from Dilipa, father of Raghu, to Agnivebna; with a genealogical table of twenty-nine princes. See Asiatic Researches, tom. x, p. 426. There is a

[p] The greatest and most important of the Epic poems have already been noticed among the sacred writings.

[q] The poets *Cálidása, Bhâravi, Sri-Harcha,* and *Magha,* are dignified with the surname of *Mahacavya* the great.

manuscript of it in the library of the Asiatic Society of London. Captain Fell presented this society with an abridgement of it, see Asiatic Journal, 1821, Nov. p. 487, which was afterwards printed at *Calcutta*, 1826.

Cumâra-Sambhava, or The Birth of *Cârtikeya*, the god of war, a long poem by Cálidása. It has the appearance of being incomplete; and a tradition reports that it originally consisted of twenty-two books.

Cirata-Arjuniya; a poem, by Bharavi; with the comment of Mallinátha, named *Ghantapatha*, published by H. T. Colebrooke, *Calcutta*, 1814, 4to. It contains an account of the wars which Arjuna carried on against savage nations. Colebrooke gives us the contents of this poem in the Asiatic Researches, tom. x, p. 410; which are copied into Ward's View, etc., vol. i, p. 514. Colebrooke, also, p. 410, 411, etc., gives specimens of the original. There is a manuscript of this poem in the library of the Asiatic Society of London.

Uttara-Rama-Charitram, The Later Fortunes of Rama, by Bhavabhutis, who is placed in the eighth century of our era. See A. W. v. Schlegel's Ind. Bibl. vol. ii, 2, p. 150.

Nêschadîya, by Sriharcha, in twenty-two cantos, is one of the six great poems which the Hindoos regard as the masterpieces of their profane literature. A manuscript of this poem, containing only the last six books, was presented to the Asiatic Society of Paris. See Journ. Asiat. tom. vi, p. 383.

A poem by Somadéva upon the death of Nauda and the accession of Chandragupta to the throne.

Vivahara Caudam, of *Ritumitacshara*, translated from the Sanscrit into Tamul, by the late Porur Vadiar, completed and revised by his brother Sidumbala Vadiar, late head Tamul master at the College of Fort St. George, *Madras*, 1826.

The *Butteesee Sing Hasunu*, from the Sunskrit,

translated in the Mahratta language, *Calcutta*, 1814, 4to.

Vètala-Pantschavimsati, by Sivadasa.

The *Bhoga Prahbendha;* The *Bhoga Charitra;* and The *Vikrama Charitra*, manuscripts in the library of the Asiatic Society of London.

γ. Erotic Poetry.

The *Migha Duta* (*Meghudovta*), or Cloud Messenger, a poem in the Sanscrit language, by Cálidása: translated into English verses, with notes and illustrations by Horace Hayman Wilson, esq., assistant-surgeon in the service of the honourable East India Company, and secretary of the Asiatic Society, published under the sanction of the College of Fort William, *Calcutta*, 1813, 4to; reprinted *London*, 1815, 8vo. Cálidása, one of the celebrated poets of India, was called by his enraptured countrymen, the Bridegroom of Poetry.

The contents of the Cloud Messenger are given by Colebrooke, in the Asiat. Res. vol. x, p. 435, and by Ward in his View, etc. vol. i, p. 516.

Analyse du *Mégha-Doûtah*, poème Sanscrit de Kâlidâsa, par M. A. L. Chézy, *Paris*, 1817, 8vo.

The National Library at Paris possesses three copies of this delicious poem, which consists of only one hundred and sixteen *strophees;* one under No. 44, in Devanâgari, and two, Nos. 115 and 172, in Bengali character.

A few strophees of the original, with a Latin translation, had already been presented to the world by Paulinus a S. Bartholomæo, in his *Sidharubam*, p. 66—68.

The Message, from the *Mégha Dûta*, or Cloud Messenger, a poetical translation of a fragment, in the Asiatic Journal, 1816, Sept. p. 253—256.

Chora-Panchâsicâ, a short poem of fifty stanzas, in which the poet Sundara, son of the king of Kantchipoor, sings his early fate. He had the misfortune, in a mighty adventure, while going to visit Vidya, the daughter of the king of Burdvan, Verâ-Singha, to be taken and condemned to death.

Bhámanî-Vilâsa, erotic poems by Jagannátha.

Sapta-Satî, erotic poems by Govarddhana.

The erotic poem of Amaru, in a collection of a hundred stanzas, compiled by Sâncarâtschâryya.

δ. *Lyric Poems.*

Lyric Poems by Cálidása, as *Sringara Tilaka*, *Prasnottara Mala*, *Aasjanorwa*, or *Lachmeer*, and some others.

Song of *Jaya Deva*, from the Sanscrit, in the Asiat. Journ. 1828, June, p. 741.

Paddhati, a Collection of Poems by S'arngadhara, a manuscript in the library of the Asiatic Society of London.

Chunda Stotra, Hymns to Chandi, *Calcutta*, 1817, 8vo.

Chandi, Hymns to Durga, Sanscrit, *Calcutta*, 1818, 8vo.

Chandana, an elegant Sanscrit stanza, in the Asiatic Journal, 1825, April, p. 423.

ε. *Elegy.*

Elegy on the Death of a Wife, from the Sanscrit of Jagannátha Bandita Raja, in the Asiatic Journal, April, p. 363.

ζ. *Idyls.*

G'atakarparam,[r], or the Broken Vase, printed in the original with Indian scholia, *Calcutta,* 1812.

Ghata-Karparam, ou l'Absence, Idylle dialoguée, traduite du Samskrit, par M. de Chézy, in the Journal Asiatique, 1823, vol. vii, p. 39—45.

G'atakarparum, oder das zerbrochene Gefäss, ein Sanskritisches Gedicht, herausgegeben, übersetzt, nachgeahmt und erläutert von G. M. Dursch, *Berlin,* 1828, kl. 4. See Allgem. Liter. Zeit, 1829, No. lxxi, lxxii; and Jahrb. für wissensch. Kritik, 1829, No. lxv, lxvii, lxxiii, lxxvi, by Wilh. von Humboldt.

Das Wiedersehn Elegie aus dem Sanskrit übersetzt von P. von Bohlen, in the Berliner Conversations-Blatt, 1829, No. lix.

η. *Didactic Poetry.*

Ritu Sanhara, the Seasons, a descriptive poem by Cálidása, printed in the original Sanscrit, at Calcutta. A short account is given of it by Sir William Jones, in an advertisement to this edition. See his Works, vol. vi, p. 432[s]. Wilson gives sixteen verses of it in his edition of the *Migha Duta,* p. 63.

[r] This little poem consists of thirty-two stanzas of various metres. Its title, *Ghata-Karparam* (Broken Vase), is merely the last word of the singular epilogue with which the poet, whose name is unknown, has thought proper so pleasantly and cheerfully to close this graceful composition. M. Chézy has given it the title of Absence, a name which suits it very well, as its subject matter is the plaints of a young wife, separated from an indifferent husband, whom the rainy season, the happy epoch in which the distant travellers return to the bosom of their families, brings not back to her embraces.

[s] It is as follows: This book is the first ever printed in Sanscrit; and as it is by the press alone that the ancient literature of India can long be preserved, a learner of that most interesting language, who had carefully perused one of the popular grammars, could hardly begin his course of study with an easier or more elegant work, than the *Ritusa'nhara,* or

Vana-Bhatta is the author of an incomplete descriptive poem, bearing the title of *Câdambarî*, full of double allusions.

FABLES.

See concerning the Hindoo fables from books and oral traditions, the Abbé Dubois Description of the Character, etc. of the People of India, p. 502, etc.

Gilchrist's Oriental Fabulist, or Polyglot translations of Æsop's and other Ancient Fables, into Hindostanee, Persian, Arabic, Sanscrit, etc., *Calcutta*, 1802, 8vo.

α. *Pancha Tantra.*

Though it be impossible to trace the channel by which they came into Europe, it is universally admitted that the old tales which first roused the inventive faculties of our ancestors are of oriental origin. It is too late to enquire whether Persia was their birthplace; for if so, they must have been clad in the Pahlvi language; and both body and dress are irrecoverably lost. It is to the Hindoos, then, that we must look for the source of nearly all that has interested and amused our forefathers and ourselves in this department of literature.

The *Pancha Tantra* is the parent stock of the *Hitópadésa*[1], Pilpay's Fables, and several other similar col-

Assemblage of Seasons. Every line composed by Cálidása is exquisitely polished; and every couplet in the poem exhibits an Indian landscape, always beautiful, sometimes highly coloured, but never beyond nature. Four copies of it have been diligently collated; and, where they differed, the clearest and most natural reading has constantly had the preference.

[1] The *Hitópadésa* is not the only Sanscrit epitome of the *Pancha Tantra*. Another abridgement of it, following the original much more closely, both in matter and arrangement, is the *Cat'hámrita-nichte* (Treasure of the Nectar of Tales), by Ananta Bhatta. Note of Mr. Colebrooke, Transactions of Asiatic Society, vol. i. p. 200.

lections. Mr. Colebrooke gave a sketch of the contents of this ancient work, in the preface to his edition of the *Hitópadésa;* and professor Wilson a full and interesting analysis of it in his Analytical Account of the *Pancha Tantra*, illustrated with occasional Translations, in the Transactions of the Royal Asiatic Society, vol. i, part ii, *London*, 1826, p. 155—200. From this the following brief account is taken.

The *Pancha Tantra* is so called from its being divided into five *tantras*, or sections; it is better known, however, in common speech, by the denomination *Panchópákhyána*, which may be rendered the Five (collections of) Stories. And under this appellation the work may be met with in most parts of India. It is attributed to *Vishnu Sarmá*, who is said to have extracted the essence of all the most celebrated works of this class, and to have composed the *Niti Sastra*, in five *tantras* or chapters. Its origin is thus narrated.

Amara Sucti, a learned and munificent prince, had three sons, without capacity or diligence. Observing their aversion to study, the king called his counsellors, and said to them, "You are aware that my sons are disinclined to application, and are incapable of reflection. When I contemplate their conduct, my kingdom is full of thorns, and yields me no pleasure. Better is a dead son than one who is a fool. Better that a family should become extinct, than that a son, endowed with their form, wealth, and family credit, should want understanding! If, therefore, their minds can be aroused to a due sense of their situation, do you declare it." On this, one of his counsellors answered him, "As life is short, and to acquire a knowledge of sciences demands much time, some means should be found of shortening the path of learning, and of communicating the substance of each science in a compendious form; for it is said, the *Sabda Sastra* alone (philology) is a boundless ocean, its difficulties are many, and the end of life soon arrives. The essence, therefore, is to be taken, as the swan extracts milk from the water. There is a Brahman named Vishnu Sarma, celebrated for his perfect knowledge of the sciences; to him intrust your sons, and he will render them well-informed." Vishnu Sarma was accordingly sent for. "Venerable Brahman," said the king, "confer a favour upon me, by instructing these princes, and rendering them superior to their companions; in recompense of which I promise you lands of large extent." Vishnu Sarma replied, "Hear, O king, my words. I am not a retailer of knowledge for lands and wealth; but if I do not instruct your sons in the *Nítí Sastra*[u] I will forego my own name." The king delivered his sons to him, and retired. Vishnu Sarma took the princes with him, and composed for their instruction these five chapters: *Mitra Bheda*, dissension of friends; *Mitra Prapte*, acquisition of friends; *Kákólukiya*, inveterate enmity; *Labdha Prasamana*, loss of advantage; *Aparîkshita Cáritwa*, inconsiderateness. Reading these, the princes became, in six months, highly accomplished; and the five *Tantras* were henceforward famous throughout the world. Whoever reads this work acquires the whole *Nítí Sastra*, and will never be overthrown by Indra himself.

A complete translation of this work into French appeared under the following title, Le *Pantcha-Tantra*, ou les cinq Ruses, fables du Brahma *Vichnou-Sarma*; aventures de *Paramatra* et autres contes: le tout traduit pour la première fois sur les originaux Indiens,

[u] *Niti Sastra* is translated Ethics by Sir William Jones, in his works; but I have seen it somewhere stated to mean the whole course of learning necessary for a prince.

par M. l'Abbé J. B. Dubois, *Paris*, 1826, 8vo. An ample review of this translation appeared in the Journ. des Savans, 1826, Août, p. 468—479.

This work, from the earliest times, has been exceedingly popular in India, and translated into almost every language of Asia. It was rendered into French by Petit le Crox, from a Persian version said to have been made in the seventh century of the Christian era. It was translated into Tamul under the title of *Pancha Tantra Katha*, Stories translated into the Tamul language, by Tandavigia Mudaliyar, *Madras*, 1826, small folio.

β. *Hitópadésa, or the Friendly Instructor.*

The oldest collection of fables and tales which has been introduced among us, is the one that goes under the name of *Bidpai* or *Pilpay*. The history of this work is too well known to require any elucidation. Mr. Wilkins and Sir William Jones first brought to light the original text from among the hidden stores of Sanscrit literature, and Mr. Colebrooke has published it in its proper language: finally, the learning and industry of the Baron de Sacy have traced the work through all its stages; and few subjects of investigation have been better illustrated than the bibliographical adventures of the Salutary Instructions of *Vishnúsarma*, or the Fables of Pilpay. Its Sanscrit name is *Hitópadésa*, or Friendly Instructor; but, properly, it is a collection of the political and moral apologues of Pilpay, written half in prose and half in verse.

A detailed account of *Hitópadésa* is given by Langlès, in his Contes Indiens, *Paris*, 1790, 12mo., and by Silvestre de Sacy in his Extraits et Notices de la Bibliothèque du Roi, vol. x, p. 257; and, especially, a very circumstantial history of it in his edition of Calila and Dimna, mentioned below. These fables have spread in two different branches over nearly the whole civilised world. The one under the original name of *Hitópadésa* remains nearly proper to India, while the other, under the title of *Calila* and *Dimna*, is famous over all Western Asia, and in all the countries of Europe.

EDITIONS OF THE ORIGINAL.

The original Sanscrit was first printed at Serampoor under the superintendence of Mr. Colebrooke, bearing the title of *Hitópadésa*, or Salutary Instruction, in the original Sanscrit, with Introductory Remarks in the English Language, by H. T. Colebrooke, esq. The real editor was Carey, but the introduction was written by the learned Mr. Colebrooke. The *Hitópadésa*, p. 1—60, is followed by *Dasa Cumâra Charita*, or Adventures of the Ten Youths, abridged by Apayga, in twenty-two pages. Three *Satacas*, or Centuries of Verses, by Bhartri Hari, p. 23—iii. This edition was reprinted under the management of Charles Wilkins, esq., *London, Library of the East India House*, 1810, 4to.

Analysis (without further title) seventy-two pages in 4to. An Analysis of the first eleven pages of the London edition of the *Hitópadésa*, with continual reference to Wilkins's Sanscrit Grammar, by Alexander Hamilton, 1818, printed for the scholars of Hertford College.

Hitopadesi particula. Edidit et glossarium Sanscrito-Latinum adjecit G. H. Bernstein. Accedunt V Tabulæ. *Vratislaviæ*, 1823, 4to. See Götting. gel. Anz. 1823, St. 76.

TRANSLATIONS.

Perhaps there is no book, except the Bible, which has been translated into so many languages as the Fables of Pilpay. We can only mention here the most esteemed, and must refer the reader for an account of the remainder, to Silvestre de Sacy's Calila et Dimna.

αα. Pahlvi.

The physician Barzuyeh brought this work from India into Persia in the reign of Nushirwan, where he translated it into Pahlvi, with a preface by Buzurjmihr.

ββ. Persian.

The *Hitópadésa* was translated into Persian at the beginning of the tenth century of the Hegira, by Hosain ben Ali, surnamed Vaez, under the title of *Musarrihu-l-kulub,* or *Mufarrihu-l-kulub,* that is, Heart's Balsam.

In the year 1805 Mulli Hussein, in conjunction with Charles Stewart, published this translation, under the title of *Anvari Sohaili,* or *Unvar-i-Soohuelee, Calcutta,* folio. Under this head also must be mentioned, An introduction to the *Anvari Sohaili* of Hussein Vaiz Kashify, by Charles Stewart, *London,* 1821, 4to. See Catalogue de la Bibliothèque de M. Langlès, p. 162, No. 1407.

In the Notices et Extraits des mss. de la Bibliothèque du Roi, tom. x. Silvestre de Sacy describes two other translations; one by Abulfazel, under the title of *Eyari danish,* the other by *Taj-Eddin.*

γγ. Hindoostanee.

Ukhlaqui Hindee, or Indian Ethics, translated from a Persian version of the celebrated *Hitoopades,* or Salutary Counsel, by Meer Buhadoor Ulee, head Moonshee in the Hindoostanee department of the New College at Fort William, for the use of the students, under the superintendence of John Gilchrist, *Calcutta*, 1803, 4to.

Mufarrihu-l-Kulub, the Expander of Hearts, being a Hindoostanee translation of the *Hitópadésa*, a celebrated Sanscrit work on friendship, etc. translated by Mir Bahadur Ali Husaini, from a Persian version, in Arabic characters, manuscript, 4to., purchased at London, price 1*l.* 4*s.* Ogle, Duncan, and Co.

The *Khirud Ufroz*, originally translated into the Hindostanee Language, by Muolovee Hufeez Ood-Deen Uhmud from the *Eyarï Danish*, written by the celebrated Shueckh Ubool Fuzl, prime minister to the illustrious Ukbur, emperor of Hindoostan, revised and compared with the original Persian, and prepared for the press, by Capt. Thomas Roebuck, acting secretary and examiner in the College of Fort William, *Calcutta*, 1815, 2 vols. 4to.

A passage of the *Hitópadésa* was translated by Sri Lalkab, of Guzurate, out of the Sanscrit into Hindoostanee, and printed in Devanâgari character, at Fort William in 1814, under the title of *Raj-Nitî*.

Ukhlaqui Hindee, or Indian Ethics, in Hindoostanee, translated from a Persian version of the celebrated *Hitoopudes*, or Salutary Counsel. Engraved under the direction of Sandford Arnot and Duncan Forbes, A. M. *London*, 1828, 4to.

δδ. *Bengalee.*

Hitópadésa, or Salutary Instruction, translated in the Bengalee from the original Sanscrit, *Serampoor*, 1801, 8vo., 1808, 1814.

εε. *Mahratta.*

Hitopudeshu, from the Sanscrit, translated in the Mahratta language, printed under the superintendence of Dr. Carey, at Serampoor, 1805, 8vo; and again, 1814, 4to.

Hitopades Mahárâshtri Bháshent tarjama Vaijanáth panditane Kélé, Serampoor, 1815, 8vo.

ζζ. *Arabic.*

The *Hitópadésa* was first translated from the Pahlvi into Arabic in the reign of Mansur, by Ibn Mokaffaa, under the title of *Kelila ve Dimné* (the proper name of two jackalls). An elegant and learned edition of this translation, or rather compilation, appeared at Paris with the following title: *Calila et Dimna*, ou Fables de Bidpai, en Arabe; précédés d'un Mémoire sur l'origine de ce livre, et sur les diverses traductions qui en ont été faits dans l'Orient, et suivies de la *Moallaka de Lebid*, en Arabe et en Français, par M. Silvestre de Sacy, *Paris*, 1816, 4to. Reviewed at length by Chézy in the Journal des Savans, 1817, Mai.

From this translation two metrical versions were attempted; one by Sehl, the son of Neobacht: another, entitled *Durro-l-hikam-fi amthali-l-hindi-wa-l-ajami* (pearls of wisdom from Hindoo and Persian discourses), by Abdolmumin ben Hassan, is in the Imperial Library at Vienna.

Silvestre de Sacy describes another Arabic translation made from the Persian, by Abou'lmaali Nasr-Allah, about the year 1140. See Notices et Extr. des mss. de la Bibl. du Roi, tom. x.

Pars versionis Arabicæ libri *Colailah wa Dimnah*, sive fabularum Bidpai philosophi indi, in usum auditorum edita ab Henr. Alb. Schultens, *Lugd. Batav.* 1786, kl. 4.

Silvestre de Sacy quotes, altogether, twenty oriental translations; that is, seven Indian, three Turkish, five Arabic, three in prose and two in verse, and five

Persian, of which two are metrical and three in prose.

A Syriac and a Malayan version are mentioned in Nyerup's Catalogus librorum Sanskritanorum, *Hafniæ*, 1821, p. 27.

Homain Nameh, the celebrated Turkish Version of the Fables of Bidpai, from the Persian of Anvary Sohahyly, manuscript. See Howell and Stewart's Catalogue of Oriental Literature, *London,* 1828.

ηη. *English.*

Hitópadésa of *Vishnusarman,* translated by Sir William Jones, in the sixth vol. of his works, p. 1—176.

The Heetopades of *Veeshnov-Sarma;* in a series of connected fables, interspersed with moral, prudential, and political maxims, translated from an ancient manuscript in the Sanscrit language, with explanatory notes, by Charles Wilkins, *Bath,* 1787, 8vo. This translation is highly esteemed. See Langlès' notice of it in the Revue Encyclop. 1819, vol. vi, p. 517, and Schlegel in his Ind. Bibliothek. vol. i, p. 17. The appended remarks contain a treasure of important information respecting Hindoo religion and Sanscrit literature.

Kalila and *Dimna,* or the Fables of Bidpai, translated from the Arabic, by the Rev. Wyndham Knatchbull, *Oxford,* 1819, 8vo. A free translation.

The Serpent and the Frogs, a fable freely translated from the *Heetópadésa,* in the Asiatic Journal, 1824, Sept. p. 253—255.

θθ. *French.*

Les Conseils et les Maximes de Pilpay, philosophe Indien, sur les divers états de la vie, *Paris,* 1709, 12mo.

Contes et fables Indiens de Bidpai et de Lokman, traduction du Turc d'Ali-Tchélebi-Ben-Saleh, commencée, par M. Galland et finie par M. Gardonne, *Paris*, 1778, 2 vols. 12mo.

The above quoted elegant version of Wilkins, was translated into French by Parraud, *Paris*, 1787, 8vo.

Fables et Contes Indiens, avec un discours préliminaire sur la religion, etc. des Hindous, par M. Langlès, *Paris*, 1790, 8vo. and 18mo.

Dévouement de *Vîravare*. Tiré de l'Hitópadésa, Liv. iii; in Mélanges de la Littér. Sanscr. de A. Langlois, p. 215—224; Journ. Asiat. vol. i, p. 239.

Le Jeune Prince et le Marchand Ambitieux. Tiré de l'Hitópadésa, Liv. i.; in Mél. de la Lit. Sanscr. de A. Langlois, p. 225—234.

Traduction d'une fable indienne, intitulée le Serpent et les Grenouilles, par Eugène Burnouf, fils, in the Journ. Asiat. vol. ii, p. 150.

ιι. *German.*

Respecting the German translation, by Eberhardt im Bart, Count of Würtemberg, or which he caused to be made, see D. Chr. Frid. Schnurrer Orationes Academicæ, ex edit. O. Henr. Eberh. Gottl. Pauli, *Tübingen*, 1828, p. 205—222.

Die Fabeln des Pilpai, übersetzt, von Lucian Werber, *Nürnberg*, 1802, 8vo.

Die Fabeln des Indischen Weltweisen Pilpai. Uebersetzt von Volgraf, *Eisenach*, 1803, 8vo.

κκ. *Danish.*

De gamle Vises Exempler og Hofsprog, etc. *Kiob.* 1618. See Nyerup's Almindelig Morskabslasning i Danmark og Norge, *Koibenhavn*, 1816.

λλ. *Latin.*

Liber de Dina et Kalila, translated from the Spanish into Latin, about 1313, by Raimond de Bezières. See Notices et Extr. de la Bibl. du Roi, tom. x.

Hitopadæsi particula. Edidit et Glossarium Sanscrito-Latinum adjecit G. H. Bernstein, *Vratisl.* 1823, 4to.

Hr. von Hammer, in the Fundgruben des Orients, vol. ii, p. 271, mentions thirty-six translations of the *Hitópadésa;* and Eichhorn in his History of Literature, vol. i, p. 588, cites a Greek, six German, one Dutch, and two Swedish.

THE DRAMA.

ON THE DRAMATIC POETRY OF THE HINDOOS.

For information respecting the dramatic poetry of the Hindoos, see the preface to Halhed's Grammar of the Bengal Language, p. iv; and Q. Craufurd's Researches on Ancient and Modern India, vol. ii, p. 183; but the most satisfactory and interesting account of the Indian drama will be found in Professor Wilson's preface to his Theatre of the Hindus, and his preliminary discourse On the Dramatic System of the Hindus [x]. Some information also upon this subject, but mostly taken from Mr. Wilson's work, will be found in the Asiatic Journal, 1827, January, March, April, and May; and likewise in the Quarterly Review, vol. xlv, p. 39 [y].

[x] The learned professor read a paper on this subject to the Calcutta Asiatic Society, of which he was then secretary, as early as the year 1822. See Asiatic Journal, June, 1823, p. 581. A notice of this was translated into French, by M. Dondey Duprey, and published in the Journal Asiat. vol. x, p. 174—193.

[y] In the Asiatic Journal for May 1828, p. 612, there is a description of a kind of dramatic representation of the history of Rama, called the Rama Leela. This seems to bear no relation to the regular drama, but is quite modern. It constitutes one of the principal festivals of the Hindoo calendar; at which it seems that the sacred legend of the Ramayana is chanted by a band of priests from day to day, occupying altogether twenty or thirty days, and that whatever incidents are capable of being acted are simultaneously performed in dumb show.

Sur la littérature dramatique des Hindous. Mémoire lu à la Société Asiatique de Calcutta le 26 Dec. 1823, in the Bulletin Univ. Août, 1826; Philologie, p. 90—92; from the Orient. Magazine, Févr. 1823, p. 250. German: Ueber die dramatische Literatur der Hindu, in the Blättern zur literar. *Unterhalt*, 1827, No. 86.

No branch of Sanscrit literature has been placed so fully, so pleasingly, and so familiarly before the English public as that of the drama in the Hindu Theatre of Professor Wilson; a work which is not confined to the mere translation of two or three Sanscrit plays, but gives the reader full information respecting the history and antiquity, the laws and language, the authors and actors,—in short, respecting the whole way and manner of scenic representation in India. It is a matter truly surprising, that the publication of this work, which has been rapidly translated into German and French, and is now, as I am told, reprinting in America, should not have awakened a more lively interest among the literary countrymen of the author; and the more so, because the Indian drama, independently of its importance as throwing a considerable light upon the manners and habits of Hindoo society before it had been sophisticated by foreign invasion and influence, has high claims to our regard as abounding in rich and forcible delineation of character; in pure and graceful descriptions; and in plots full of life and bustle, arranged with sufficient ingenuity and skill to arouse the attention, and keep alive a continual interest in the business of the stage.

The Hindoo drama, moreover, possesses, in its originality, one striking peculiarity which it might be supposed would alone ensure it general favour. Professor Wilson says, it is impossible the dramatic compositions of India should have been borrowed from any other people either of ancient or modern times; besides which, they present characteristic features in their conduct and construction which plainly evince their original design and national development.

The Hindoo drama, too, is said to bear, in most respects, a closer resemblance to the romantic than to the classical school. Yet the *Nátaka*, the highest kind of composition in this department of literature, possesses many characteristics bearing a striking analogy to the tragedy of the Greeks: these are pointed out by Professor Wilson, as well as many particulars in which they disagree. Like the Greek tragedy, the *Nátaka* is to represent none but worthy or exalted personages; the action, or more properly the passion, should be but one, as love or heroism; the plot should be simple, the incidents consistent, the business should spring direct from the story, as a plant from its seed, and should be free from episodical and prolix interruptions. The time should not be protracted, and the duration of an act, according to strict rule, should not exceed one day, though some allowances are made on this score. Besides this, the Hindoo drama was derived from, and formed a part of their religious ceremonies; many of their pieces contain a mixture of pantomime, music, and dancing; and were seldom or never performed except upon solemn or public festivals. On the other hand, in the whole range of Indian scenic representation there is nothing that can be properly called tragedy; prose and verse, the serious and the comic, are intermingled in their compositions, with all the licence, as Mr. Milman informs us, of the English and Spanish scene. Yet, according to the aphorism of Bharata, " the poet is to employ choice and harmonious terms, and an elevated and polished style, embellished with the ornaments of rhetoric and rhythm." The injunction, adds Professor Wilson, has not been disregarded; and in no department of Hindoo literature are the powers of the Sanscrit language more lavishly developed. One very extraordinary fact connected with this part of the dramatic art in India, is the employment of different dialects for different characters, according to their respective grades in society. Thus, the more lofty personages speak pure Sanscrit, while women and the less dignified classes of men make use of the Pracrit, more or less refined, according to the rank of the speaker.

According to Heeren, the Hindoo drama must be considered as the latest offspring of the classical literature of India. Professor Ewald also remarks, that as great a difference of style is observable between the dramatic writings and the *Ramayana,* as between the *Epics* and the *Vedas:* Professor Wilson likewise admits, that none of the plays at present extant can boast a very high antiquity. Hindoo traditions, however, carry the scenic art back to the age of fable, and ascribe its invention to an inspired sage, named Bharata; while some assert that it was gathered from the *Vedas* by the god of Brahma, and by him communicated to Muni. Three different kinds of dramatic representations are spoken of: first, *Natya,* which is properly the dramatic, being defined to be gesticulation with language; the second is *Nritya,* or pantomime; and the third is *Uritta,* which is simple dancing.

The general term for all dramatic compositions is *Rúpaka,* from *rupa,* form; it being the chief object to embody character and feelings, and to exhibit the natural indications of passion. They are divided, however, into two classes, the *Rúpakas,* properly so called, which are again subdivided into ten different species; and the *Uparúpakas,* or minor theatre, subdivided into eighteen. But all these varieties, as Professor Wilson informs us, may be clearly reduced to two, " differing according to the loftier or lowlier tone of the composition, the more serious or comic tenor of the subject, and the regularity or irregularity of the construction." It would be of no service here to enumerate the minor distinctions; they prove, however, the great extent to which dramatic literature was once cultivated by the Hindoos.

Professor Wilson believes that the invention of dramatic performances is attributed to Bharata, from his having been one of the earliest writers who reduced the art to a system. His sootras, or aphorisms, are constantly cited by commentators on different plays, and suggest the rules which are taught by later authors; but his work is not supposed to be extant in an entire form. One of the best and earliest treatises on dramatic literature, among those still in existence, is the *Dasa Rúpaka*, or description of the ten kinds of theatrical composition. It is exclusively devoted to dramatic criticism. It consists of a text and a gloss, with examples. The text was written in the eleventh century, (at which time the dramatic art of the Hindoos must have been complete, or rather in its decline,) by Dhananjaya: the date of the gloss is not known; though, from its rarity, it is supposed to be ancient.

The *Sangíta Retnakara*, by Sárngi Deva, a Cashmirian pundit, treats rather of singing and dancing than of dramatic literature. It furnishes, however, some curious notices of theatrical representation and gesture. It was written between the twelfth and fifteenth centuries. There is a commentary upon it by Kallinath.

Besides these, Professor Wilson enumerates various other Sanscrit authorities, which he consulted in compiling his interesting view of the Hindoo stage. See above, p. 186.

COLLECTIONS OF INDIAN PLAYS.

Select Specimens of the Theatre of the Hindus, translated from the original Sanscrit, containing the Dramas of *Mrichchakati, Vikrama* and *Urvasi, Malati* and *Madhava, Uttara Rama Cheritra, Mudra Rakshasa*, and *Retnavali;* together with an Account of the Dramatic System of the Hindus, Notices of their different Dramas, etc., by H. H. Wilson, esq., *Calcutta*, 1825—1827, 3 vols. 8vo. This work was published in six parts in the following order:

No. I. The *Mrichchakati*, or the Toy Cart, a drama translated from the original Sanscrit, by H. H. Wilson, esq., *Calcutta*, 1825.

No. II. The Drama of *Vikrama* and *Urvasi*, or the Hero and the Nymph, translated by H. H. Wilson, esq., *Calcutta*, 1826.

No. III. *Malati* and *Madhava*, or the Stolen Marriage, *Calcutta*, 1826.

No. IV. *Uttara Rama Cheritra*, or continuation of the History of *Rama*, *Calcutta*, 1826.

No. V. *Mudra Rakshasa*, or the Signet of the Minister, *Calcutta*, 1826.

No. VI. *Retnavali*, or the Necklace; and an appendix, containing short accounts of different dramas, *Calcutta*, 1827[z].

Chefs d'œuvre du Théatre Indien, traduits de l'original Sanskrit en Anglais, par M. H. H. Wilson, etc., et de l'Anglais en Français, par M. A. Langlois, etc., accompagnés de notes et d'éclaircissemens, suivis d'une table alphabétique des noms propres et des termes relatifs à la mythologie et aux usages de l'Inde, avec leur explication, *Paris*, 1828, 2 vols. 8vo. German: Klassisches Theater der Hindus. Aus der Englischen

[z] The original texts of four of these dramas were presented by Professor Wilson to the Royal Asiatic Society, May, 1832.

Uebertragung des Sanskrit-Originals, von H. H. Wilson metrisch übersetzt, von K. H. Hermes, erster Theil., *Weimar*, 1828, 8vo.

Separate Plays.

MYTHOLOGICAL DRAMA.

aa. Sakontala.

Sakontala, or the Fatal Ring. The plot of this play is taken from an episode in the *Mahâ Bhârata.* It was written by Cálidása, who lived in the court of Raja Vicramaditya, and died in the year 56 B.C.

Sakontala, or the Fatal Ring, an Indian drama, by Cálidása, translated from the original Sanscrit and Pracrit, by Sir Will. Jones, in the Asiatic Researches; and in his Works, vol. vi, p. 200—312. Printed also separately at *Calcutta*, 1789, 8vo; *London*, 1790, 4to. It was translated into French, by A. Bruguière, *Paris*, 1804, 8vo.; into German, by G. Forster, *Frankf. a. M.* 1791, 8vo; and a second edition, revised by J. G. v. Herder, *ibid.* 1803, 8vo.

Sakontala, oder der verhängnissvolle Ring; indisches Drama des Kalidas in sechs Aufzügen. Metrisch für die Bühne bearbeitet von Wilhelm Gerhard, *Leipzig*, 1820, 8vo.

Sakontala, ou l'Anneau Fatal, drame Indien, en sept actes, imprimé pour la première fois en France, en caractères Samscrits, d'après les meilleurs textes, suivi d'une version Française et de notes explicatives; par M. de Chézy, *Paris*, 1826, 4to.

Sukoontula-Natuk; being an Appendix to the English and Hindoostanee Dialogues, in a separate form and as a dramatic performance, translated long ago from the original Sunskrit, into elegant Hindoostanee, but now first exhibited in the universal character, by Dr. J. B. Gilchrist, *London*, 1827, 8vo.

An analysis of the *Sakontala* will be found in Crawford's Researches on India, vol. ii, 186—188; Neue Bibliothek d. schönen Wissensch. vol. xlvi, p. 64; Herder's Werke, zur schönen Liter. und Kunst, Th. ix, p. 207—248; F. Schlegel's Gesch. der Literatur, Th. i, p. 177; Heeren's Ideen, Th. i, p. 531—538.

Of the Dramatic Art among the Indians, and of the play of Sakontala, translated from the Polish, in the Asiat. Boten (a Russian Journal) 1825, Nos. vii and viii.

Sir William Jones, in the preface to his translation of this piece, says it must have been very popular when it was first represented; for the Indian empire was then in full vigour, and the national vanity must have been highly flattered by the magnificent introduction of those kings and heroes in whom the Hindoos gloried[a].

ββ. Gitagovinda, or the Songs of Jayadéva[b].

The subject of this little pastoral drama, like the loves of Crishna and Radha, as related in the tenth book of the *Bhágavat*, is the reciprocal attraction between the divine goodness and the human soul. It derives its name from *Gita*, a song, and *Govinda*, an appellation of Crishna as a pastoral deity. Jayadéva, its

[a] See, however, above, p. 206. Mr. Adelung, in his note on this article, has fallen into several mistakes. I may notice, that he applies what Sir W. Jones says respecting the language and style of *all* the Sanscrit plays, as though it were said of this *one in particular*. He also makes Mr. Crawford attribute the translation of a modern Indian epigram to Halhed, which was made by Sir W. Jones. See his preface, where he says, "A modern epigram was lately repeated to me, which does so much honour to the author of *Sakontala* that I cannot forbear exhibiting a literal version of it." "Poetry was the sportful daughter of Valmic, and, having been educated by Vyása, she chose Cálidása for her bridegroom, after the manner of Viderbha: she was the mother of Amara, Sundar, Sanc'ha, Dhanic; but now, old and decrepit, her beauty faded, and her unadorned feet slipping as she walks, in whose cottage does she disdain to take shelter?"

[b] This article altogether seems to me to be improperly inserted under the head of the Drama. There is a piece founded on it described by Professor Wilson. See below, p. 212.

author, is said to have flourished before Cálidása, and Calinga and Berdwan dispute the honour of being his birthplace. The inhabitants of the latter celebrate an annual jubilee to his honour, passing a whole night in representing his drama, and singing his beautiful songs[c].

Gitagovinda, or the Songs of *Jayadéva*, literally translated from the Sanscrit, by Sir William Jones, in the Asiatic Researches, tom. i, p. 262, 4to; tom. iii, p. 185—207, 8vo; and in his Works, vol. i, p. 463. This has been translated into German by the Baron F. H. v. Dalberg, under the title of *Gitagovinda*, oder die Gesänge *Jayadévas*, eines altindischen Dichters, aus dem Sanscrit ins Englische und aus diesem in Deutsche mit Anmerkungen übersetzt, *Erfurt*, 1802, 8vo. See Allgem. Deutsches Bibl. Th. lxxxi, p. 74—76, and Fr. Majer in Klaproth's Asiat. Magazine, Bd. i. An entirely new German translation has since appeared with a long preliminary discourse, under the following title: *Gitagovinda* oder *Krischna* der Hirt, ein idyllisches Drama des indischen Dichters *Yayadéva;* metrisch bearbeitet, von A. W. Reimschneider, *Halle*, 1818, 12mo.

The Sanscrit original was printed by itself in 1808 with the following English title: The *Geetu-Gôvinda*, or Songs of *Juyudéva*, in Devanâgari character.

Fragmenta *Gitagovindæ*, in Othm. Frank's Chrestomathia Sanscrita, *Monaci*, 1819.

METAPHYSICAL DRAMA.

Prabod'h Chandro'daya, or Rise of the Moon of Intellect, an allegorical Drama, and *Atma Bod'h*, or Knowledge of Spirit, translated from the Sanscrit, by

[c] See Sir William Jones on the Mystical Poetry of the Persians and Hindoos, in his Works, vol. i, p. 462, or Asiatic Researches, vol. iii, p. 183, 8vo. edit.; and Catalogue des mss. Sanscrits, p. 79.

Dr. J. Taylor, *London*, 1812, 8vo. The author is Chrishna Kêsava Misra, (probably only an allegorical name,) who in this work takes a review of, and opposes the various philosophical systems of the Hindoos.

Prabod'h Chandro'daya, that is, the Rising of the Moon of Science, an allegorical drama, after the English version of Dr. J. Taylor, in the Beiträgen zur Alterthumskunde, mit besonderer Rücksicht auf das Morgenland, von J. G. Rhode, *Berlin*, 1820, 8vo; heft ii, p. 41—99.

Schlegel's Ind. Bibliothek, vol. i, p. 36; ii, p. 161.

HISTORICAL DRAMA.

Urvasi Vikrama, or the Hero and the Nymph, by Cálidása.

Vikramorvasi, or *Vikrama* and *Urvasi*, a drama, by Cálidása, (in Sanscrit,) 8vo. 2s. Parbury and Allen's Catalogue. It is one of the plays translated by Mr. Wilson.

Uttara Rama Cheritra, or continuation of the History of *Rama*; a drama in seven acts, by Bhavabhúti, (in Sanscrit,) 8vo. 2s. 6d. Parbury and Allen's Catalogue, 1831.

Uttara Ram Cheritra; containing the history of the family of *Rama*, after the reconquest of Sita, by Cálidása. This piece also is one of those Mr. Wilson translated into English, see above, p. 209[d].

Malavikagni mitra, by Cálidása, published by Mr. Wilson.

Mudra Rakshasa, or the Signet of the Minister; a drama in seven acts, by Visa'kha Datta, (in Sanscrit,) 8vo. 2s. 6d. Parbury and Allen's Catalogue. One of

[d] I have continued this title from Adelung, though it is evident, from the one which precedes it and Professor Wilson's notice at the beginning of his translation of this play, that it is considered to have been written by Bhavabhúti.

the plays translated by Mr. Wilson. See Schlegel's Ind. Bibl. ii, 2, p. 151.

Anarghya-Raghavah, a play by Murâri. See Hamilton's Catal. des mss. Sanscr. No. cxii; Schlegel's Ind. Bibl. ii, 2, p. 160.

Chandrâbhishêkah, the Coronation of *Chandra*, (*Chandraguptar*,) a tragedy. See Asiat. Researches, vol. iv, p. xviii[e]. It is among the manuscripts presented by Sir William Jones to the Royal Society. See Catalogue, No. 52.

Hari-Vansa, relates the history of *Deo-Cal'yun*, from whom Wilford believes Deucalion to be derived. See Asiat. Res. vol. v, p. 507, or p. 288, 8vo. edition.

COMEDIES.

Malati and *Madhava*, or the Stolen Marriage. This is one of the plays translated by Mr. Wilson, previously to which, an outline of the plot and a version of part of the fifth act, introduced by Mr. Colebrooke into his Essay on Sanscrit Prosody (Asiat. Researches, vol. x.), had made it known to the English public. See also Schlegel's Ind. Bibl. ii, 2, p. 150.

This piece was written by Bhavabhúti, who, Mr. Wilson informs us, flourished in the eighth century of the Christian era. It is esteemed one of the best Sanscrit plays. The same author observes, that there is more passion in the thoughts of Bhavabhúti than in those of Cálidása, but less fancy; yet in summing up their respective merits, he considers him entitled to

[e] The following is Sir William Jones's notice of it in the volume of the Asiatic Researches referred to: "A most beautiful poem by Somadeva, comprising a very long chain of instructive and agreeable stories, begins with the famed revolution of Pataliputra, by the murder of king Nanda and his eight sons, and the usurpation of Chandragupta; and the same is the subject of a tragedy in Sanscrit."

even a higher place than his rival as a poet. See Mr. Wilsons's translation, p. 133.

Invocation of *Carálá*, from the *Malati Madhava*, a Hindoo drama, in Asiatic Journal, 1826, July, p. 31.

Lalita Mâdhava, the favourite comedy of Crishna. See Schlegel's Ind. Bibl. ii, 2, p. 160.

The Drama of *Vikrama* and *Urvasi*, or the Hero and the Nymph, a comedy by Cálidása: in English, translated by H. H. Wilson, see above, p. 209; Schlegel's Ind. Bibl. ii, 2, p. 150.

Carmarupa and *Camalata*, an ancient Indian drama, elucidating the customs and manners of the Orientals, translated from the Persian, by Franklin, *London*, 1793, 8vo.

The *Mrichchakati*, or the Toy Cart, a drama, one of the plays translated by Mr. Wilson, who considers it a work of great interest as regards both the literary and national history of the Hindoos. It is announced as the work of a celebrated king, Sudraka, who, according to one account, flourished before the birth of Christ, and, according to another, one hundred and ninety years after it. At whatever time, however, this drama may have been written, it displays a very singular picture of Indian manners and morals, in a plot full of life, character, and incident.

Professor Wilson's translation of it was reviewed at great length in the Calcutta Annual Register, 1826, and in various journals published at the same place, particularly in the India Gazette and John Bull; again in the Asiatic Journal, Jan. 1827. An analysis of the piece also will be found in the Quarterly Review, vol. xlv, p. 43. The Review in the Asiatic Journal was translated into French for the Journal Asiatique, Mars, 1827, etc. It was also published separately under the title of, Sur un Drame Indien, par M. H. H. Wilson, traduit en Français, par M. Dondey-Dupré, fils: see also Schlegel's Ind. Bibl. ii, 2, p. 149. In the Asiat. Journal, 1826, Dec. p. 679, there is the translation of a Simile from the *Mrichchakati*[f].

Ratnâvali, a comedy by Harsha Dewas, king of Cashmire, who is said to have reigned in the eleventh century of the Christian era, translated into English by H. H. Wilson, see above, p. 209. Schlegel's Ind. Bibl. ii, 2, p. 155.

Mahânâtaka, or the great comedy, in Sanscrit and Pracrit, a drama to the honour of Râma, by Hanuman, and published by Madhusudana Misra. See Jones's Oriental mss. No. 47; and Catal. des mss. Sanscr. p. 8; Schlegel's Ind. Bibl. ii, 2, p. 155.

Hâsyarnava, the Sea of Laughter, a farce in three acts, by Jagadiswara. It is a bitter satire on kings and their servants, who are described as profligate scoundrels; and on priests, who are represented as hypocrites. See Sir William Jones's Works, vol. vi, p. 451, Catal. des mss. Sanscr. p. 80, and Schlegel's Ind. Bibl. ii, 2, p. 161.

Dhûrta-Samâgamah, the Assembly of Knaves, a farce in one act. See Schlegel's Ind. Bibl. ii, 2, p. 161.

The following are taken from Professor Wilson's Appendix to his Hindu Theatre.

Mahavira Cheritra, a drama in seven acts, ascribed to Bhavabhúti. The adventures of Rama form the subject of this piece, and the plot is much the same as the story of the *Rámáyana*, but considerably compressed. It possesses the same loftiness of sentiment, excellence of picturesque description, and power of language which distinguish the other works of this author.

[f] In 1826 the first act of this comedy was represented by the pupils of the literature and poetry classes, in the Sanscrit college at Calcutta, with great humour and talent, and is said to have afforded much satisfaction to all present. See Asiat. Journal, 1827, Aug. p. 238.

Veni Samharah, a drama in six acts. The plot of this piece is taken from the *Mahábhárat*. It alludes to the incident of Draupadi's being dragged by the Veni or braid of hair into the public assembly: a disgrace of a heavy nature, and which was most bitterly revenged.

Malavikagnimitra, or *Agnimitra* and *Malavika*, a comedy in five acts, written by Cálidása, but it seems uncertain whether the great poet of that name or another.

Viddha Salabhanjika, or the Statue, a comedy in four acts. This piece is a comedy of domestic intrigue, and gives a not unentertaining picture of the interests and amusements of Hindoo princes in the retirement of their harams.

Prachanda Pandava, or Offended Sons of Pandu, is a *Nataka* (or most regular kind of drama) in two acts. The subject is taken from the *Mahábhárat*; and the piece is written in a simple but powerful style.

Hanumán Nataka, a drama in fourteen acts. This is an imperfect performance by various hands, describing the story of the *Ramayana*. It was composed in the tenth or eleventh century.

Dhananjaya Vijaya, a drama in one act, by Kanchana Achárya.

Anergha Raghava, or *Murari Nataka*, a drama in seven acts. This play is most usually known by the latter appellation, which it derives from the author, whose name was Murari; but the former is the proper title, implying the sacred descendant of Raghu. Rama is the hero of the piece.

Sareda Tilaka, a piece in one act, of a licentious nature.

Yayati Cheritra, a drama in seven acts, by Rudra Deva.

Dutaugada, or the Mission of *Augada*. This consists of only four scenes, taken from the *Ramayana*.

Mrigankalekha, a *Natiká* in four acts, by Viswéswara.

Vidagdha Madhava, a play in seven acts. The subject is taken from the *Bhagavat*, and relates to the loves of Crishna and Ráda. It is in fact the songs of Jayadéva dramatised. See above, p. 212.

Abhirama Mani, a drama in seven acts, by Sundara Misra.

Madhuraniruddha, a drama in eight acts, by Chandra Sekhara, who probably lived in the seventeenth century. It relates the secret loves of Ushá the daughter of Asura Bóna, and Aniruddha the grandson of Crishna, and the defeat and death of the former by that divinity.

Kansa Badha, a drama in seven acts, by Crishna Kavi the son of Nrisintra, the subject of which is the destruction of Kansa by Crishna. It is little more than a re-set of the tenth section of the *Bhágavat Purana*, which gives an account of the early life of the last incarnation of Vishnu as Crishna, thrown into dialogue. It contains but little action, and that inartificially and disjointedly put together. The language is in general good, though highly elaborate. It was probably written about the beginning of the seventeenth century.

Pradyumnha Vijaya, a drama in seven acts, the subject of which is the victory of Pradymnha the son of Crishna, over Vajranábha the sovereign of the Daityas. The story is entirely copied from the *Harivansa*, the last section of the *Mahábhárat*, and is tediously spun out. It is a work of no imagination. Its author is named Sankara Dikshita, who is supposed to have written it about the middle of the last century.

Sri Dama Cheritra. This is a modern play in five acts, by Sáma Rája Dikshita. The subject of it is taken from the tenth section of the *Bhágavat*, and is the elevation of Sidrama or Sudama, the early friend of Crishna, to sudden and unexpected affluence in requital of his attachment to that deity. It contains too much description and too little action; though there is some vivacity in the thoughts, and much melody in the style.

Dhurtta Narttatea, a farce in one act, or two *Sandhis* or portions, by the same author as the preceding play, and of the same date. Its chief object is to ridicule the Saiva ascetics; and though the language is highly laboured, it is neither fanciful nor humorous.

Dhurtta Samagama, an incomplete manuscript, somewhat indelicate, but not devoid of humour. The name of the author does not appear.

Hasyarnava, a comic piece in two acts, the work of a pundit named Jagaddisa. It is a severe, but grossly indelicate satire upon the licentiousness of the Brahmans assuming the character of religious merchants, the encouragement given to vice by princes, the inefficacy of ministers, and the ignorance of physicians and astrologers.

Kautuka Suvaswa, a farce in two acts, being a satire upon princes who addict themselves to idleness and sensuality, and fail to patronise the Brahmans. It contains more humour and less indecency than any of the other farces. It is not supposed to be very ancient.

Chitra Yajna, a drama in five acts, the subject of which is the celebrated legend of Daksha.

Iscias, the heterogenous composition of a pundit of Nadiya about twenty or thirty years ago. It is valuable as conveying some idea of the sort of attempts at dramatic composition made by the present race of

Hindoos in Bengal, which is exactly similar to the *Improvista Commedia* of the Italians.

Some few other pieces are mentioned among the mss. of Sir William Jones, Hamilton's Catalogue des Manuscrits Sanscrits, and Schlegel's Ind. Bibliothek, ii, 2; but they are either included under some other name in the foregoing, or are of little consequence.

TALES.

Sakontala-Natak, a kind of romance, from the drama of the same name. This work was translated from the Sanscrit by an inhabitant of Hindoostan, named Afsous, into his native language, and printed in 1814, at Fort William, in Roman characters. See above, p. 210.

Vrihat Kathá, a collection of Indian stories, translated into English in the Calcutta Quarterly Magazine, and from thence inserted in Blackwood's Edinburgh Magazine, July, 1825. *Upakosa*, one of these, has been translated into German in the Abendzeitung, 1825, No. 209. An Indian abridgement of this voluminous collection, is entitled *Kathâ Sarit Sâgara*, or, the Sea of the Rivers of Stories.

Singaassun Buttressee, or the Thirty-two imaged Throne, Sanscrit, in the Devanâgari character, ornamented with rude coloured drawings illustrative of the story. Manuscript; see Howell and Stewart's Catalogue of Oriental Literature, *London*, 1828.

Batris Singhasan, or Fabulous History of Raja Vikramaditya, as related by the thirty-two statues supping his throne, in Bengali, *Serampoor*, 1808, 8vo. [e]. Le Trône enchanté, conte Indien, traduit du Persan par le Baron Lescallier, *New York*, 1817, 2 vols. large 8vo.

[e] Priced in Parbury and Allen's Catalogue 12s. 6d., where another is mentioned, with plates, 15s., and an edition, *London*, 1816, 8vo. 12s. 6d.

Vásavadattá, by Subandhu, an allegorical romance, setting forth the the loves of Candaspacétu and the princess Vásavadattá, in a very ambiguous style, full of double allusions. See Colebrooke's notice of this work in Asiatic Researches, vol. x[f].

Dasa Cumâra Charita, or Adventures of the Ten Youths, abridged by Apayya.

[f] The opinion of this work, given by Adelung in the text, is quite at variance with that of Colebrooke in the work referred to. The latter says, (Asiatic Researches, vol. x, p. 449, 8vo. edition,) this story is told in elegant language, and intermixed with many flowery descriptions in a poetical style. There is an allusion, however, in Bhavabúti's drama (*Malati madhâvr*, act. ii.) to another tale, of Vásavadattá's having been promised by her father to king Tanjana, and giving herself in marriage to Udayana. I am unable to reconcile this contradiction otherwise than by admitting an identity of name and difference of story. This passage was perhaps misunderstood by the translator, and gave rise to the opinion in the text.

The following is the outline of the story as given by Colebrooke: "Candaspacétu, a young and valiant prince, son of Chintánaní king of Cusumapura, saw in a dream a beautiful maiden, of whom he became desperately enamoured. Impressed with the belief that a person, such as seen by him in his dream, had a real existence, he resolves to travel in search of her, and departs, attended only by his confidant Macaranda. While reposing under a tree in a forest at the foot of the Vind'hya mountains, where they halted, Macaranda overhears two birds conversing; and from their discourse he learns that the princess Vásavadattá, having rejected all the suitors who had been assembled by the king her father for her to make choice of a husband, had seen Candaspacétu in a dream, in which she had even dreamt his name. Her confidant, Tamálica, sent by her in search of the prince, was arrived in the same forest, and is discovered there by Macaranda. She delivers to the prince a letter from the princess, and conducts him to the king's palace. He obtains from the princess the avowal of her love; and her confidant, Calatí reveals to the prince the violence of her passion.

"The lovers depart together: but, passing through the forest he loses her in the night. After long and unsuccessful search, in the course of which he reaches the shore of the sea, the prince, grown desperate through grief, resolves on death. But at the moment when he was about to cast himself into the sea, he hears a voice from heaven, which promises to him the recovery of his mistress, and indicates the means. After some time, Candaspacétu finds a marble statue the precise resemblance of Vásavadattá. It proves to be her; and she quits her marble form and regains

Tale of the Four Simple Brahmans, translated from the Sanscrit, in the Asiatic Journal, 1817, May, p. 437—440. German: die vier einfältigen Brahmanen, in Schlegel's Ind. Bibl. ii, 3, p. 259.

Aventures de *Paramadra,* traduites par l'Abbé Dubois, avec le texte de l'original, *Paris,* 1826.

Beital Pachisi, or the Twenty-five Tales of a Demon, (*Vetala, Betal*). This collection of stories is attributed by some to Sivadasa, and by others to Jambhala Datta, etc. The original Sanscrit is a composition of considerable antiquity, and deservedly popular; it is translated into all the dialects spoken in India. An English version of it, *Beital Pachisi,* or the Twenty-five Tales of a Demon, will be found in the Asiatic Journal, 1816, July, p. 27, etc. Some of these tales are given in Scott's additions to the Arabian Nights, Entertainments.

Suka Saptati, Tales of the Parrot, of which the Persian *Tuti-Nameh* is a translation.

The Four Dumbies, (hard of hearing,) an Indian tale, in Schlegel's Ind. Bibl. ii, 3, p. 259—283.

Loves of *Camarupa* and *Camalatu,* an ancient Indian tale; elucidating the customs and manners of the orientals, translated from the Persian, by W. Franklin, *London,* 1793, 8vo.

Hindee Story-Teller, or Entertaining Expositor, in the Roman, Persian, and Nagree character, by Gilchrist, *Calcutta,* 1802, 8vo.

Gulzar i Hal, the Rosebud of the Moment; a translation from a Sanscrit work, entitled *Parbuden Chanden Oudi,* Persian, ms. See Howell and Stewart's Oriental Catalogue for 1827, p. 91.

animation. She recounts the circumstances under which she was transformed into stone. Having thus fortunately recovered his beloved princess, the prince proceeds to his city, where they pass many years in uninterrupted happiness."

APPENDIX.

To p. 11. For the German scholar, may be added the second chapter of the first volume of the Symbolik und Mythologic der alten Völker besonders der Griechen von Dr. Fried. Creuzer, *Leipzig*, 1819, 8vo. This very learned work contains much valuable matter on the subject to which it more immediately refers; but it likewise gives an interesting view of the ancient authorities, both native and foreign, upon Hindoo learning; and goes deep into the religion of Brahma, as well as the cosmogony, philosophy, sciences and arts of the Hindoos in general. I am therefore surprised that it should have escaped the notice of M. Adelung.

Early in the year 1831, Messrs. Parbury, Allen, and Co., announced the speedy publication of a Dictionary (1 large vol. 4to.), in Bengali, Sanscrit, and English, by the justly celebrated Mr. Haughton. The following is a prospectus of the work: This Dictionary in addition to what is usually contained in similar compilations, will have the words traced to their originals, studiously avoiding whatever is fanciful in the derivation of the *Unádi*, and other Sanscrit words of doubtful origin; a distinction that must increase the value and importance of its derivations. The originals of all words introduced into the Bengali language from the Arabic, Persian, Turkish, Hindustani, and other languages, are likewise given. A copious index is added, which, it is anticipated, will be highly serviceable to the scientific student; but particularly to the Botanist, as every thing which recent investigation has rendered positive has been embodied in this work, and exact references given to the authorities from which they are taken, such as the Asiatic Researches, the Transactions of the Royal Asiatic Society, the Publications of Mr. H. T. Colebrooke, etc.

To p. 54. *Kobita Rutnakur,* or Collection of Sungskrit Proverbs in Popular Use, translated into Bengalee and English, compiled by Neel Rutna Holdar, *Calcutta,* 1830.

To p. 66. Broughton's (Thos.) Selections from the Popular Poetry of the Hindoos, arranged and translated, with a preface on the Literature of the Hindoos, *London,* 1814, 8vo.

Vedan Modi Taringini, or A Description of the Different Religious Sects and Ceremonies of the Hindus, translated from the Sanscrit into English by Maharaja Kalcekishen Bahadur, *Calcutta,* 1831.

The Mythology of the Hindoos, with notices of various Mountain and Island Tribes inhabiting the two Peninsulas of India and the neighbouring Islands; and an Appendix comprising the minor *Avatars,* and the Mythological and Religious terms, etc. etc. of the Hindoos, with plates illustrative of the principal Hindoo Deities, etc., by Charles Coleman, esq., *London,* 1832, 4to.

To p. 136. A neat edition of Menu, with notes, has recently been published at Paris by M. Loiseleur Deslongchamps, which is in a great measure founded on that of Mr. Haughton. A fourth has just appeared at Calcutta under the title of *Manusanhita;* the Institutes of Menu with the Commentary of Kulluka Bhatta, published under the authority of the Committee of Public Instruction, 2 vols. 8vo. 1830-31.

The *Mitakshara,* A Compendium of Hindoo Law, by Vijnanesvara, founded on the texts of Yajnavalkya, edited by Lakshmi Narayana Nyayalankara (in Sanscrit), 1830, 8vo.

To p. 139. *Vyavahara Tatwa*, A Treatise on Judicial Proceedings, by Rhagunandana Bhattácharya, edited by Lakshmi Náráyan Serma (in Sanscrit), 1831, 8vo.

To p. 147. *The Kutbi*, A Treatise on Logic. Asiat. Journal, March, 1817, p. 250.

To p. 167. *The Navakiraha Sakaram*, or Brahmanical Astrological Tables. A drawing of one of these was sent by the Rev. C. T. E. Rhenius, one of the Church Missionaries at Madras, to the Missionary Society; see Asiatic Journal, Nov. 1818, p. 504. It would hardly be worth mentioning here, but that it forms the subject of a curious mistake made by Adelung, who classes it among the Stories, and calls it a Brahmanical Astrological *Tale*.

To p. 169. The Lilavati was translated into Persian by the celebrated Feizi, the brother of Abulfazl, vizier to the emperor Akbar; this version has lately been published at Calcutta.

To p. 186. *Sahitya Derpana*, A Treatise on Rhetorical Composition (in Sanscrit), by Viswanath Kaviraja, 1831, 8vo.

Kavya Prakasa, A Treatise on Poetry and Rhetoric, by Mammata Acharya (in Sanscrit), 1831, 8vo.

To p. 193. *The Rains*, from the *Ritusanhara*, or Seasons of Cálidása, translated into English verse. Asiatic Journal, April 1817, p. 344.

To p. 204. *Hitópadésa*, id est, Institutio Salutaris, Textum codd. mss. collatis recensuerunt, Interpretationem Latinam, et Adnotationes criticas adjecerunt Aug. Gul. A. Schlegel et Christ. Lassen, part i, 1829, part ii, 1831, 4to. *Bonnæ ad Rhenum.*

To p. 210. *Malati and Madhava*, a drama in ten acts, by Bhavabhúti (in Sanscrit), 8vo.; under the authority of the Committee of Public Instruction at Calcutta, 1830.

To p. 214. *Vikrama and Urvasi*, a drama, by Cálidása, printed in Sanscrit also by the same Committee, 1830.

To p. 215. *The Mrichchakati*, a Comedy, by Sudrakar Raja, with a commentary explaining the Pracrit passages (in Sanscrit), *Calcutta*, 1830, 8vo.

In conclusion it may not be considered irrelevant to the object of the present compilation, to notice a kind of literary curiosity in the shape of an original work, composed in Sanscrit, by the very learned Dr. Mill, Principal of Bishop's College at Calcutta. This is entitled *Sri-Chrishtasangita*, or the Sacred History of our Lord Jesus Christ. Book I, comprising his infancy (*Yeshutpattiparva*): and is an attempt to exhibit the historical truths of Christianity in a dress borrowed from the metrical legends of the Hindoos; for which purpose the author has made choice of the plain style and easy versification of the great standard mythological epics of Vyasa and Valmiki. To the whole is subjoined a genealogical and chronological table (also in Sanscrit, and entitled *Chrishtavansavali*,) of our Lord's descent from Adam, *Calcutta*, 1831, 8vo. We may also mention another work by the same author, under the title of Proposed Version of Theological terms, with a view to Uniformity in Translations of the Holy Scriptures, etc. into the various languages of India; part i, Sanscrit, with remarks on Dr. Mill's proposed renderings, by H. H. Wilson, printed at Bishop's College Press, 4to. (no date).

INDEX OF AUTHORS.

INDEX OF WORKS.

CORRIGENDA.

p. 3, note, *read* Raffles's History of Java, vol. ii, p. 369.
p. 19, note, l. 14, For Varanais, *read* Varanasi.
p. 16, l. 7, *read*, of the Greek, Latin, German, and Sclavonic.
p. 41, l. 12, For is, *read* are.
p. 70, l. 20, For propably, *read* probably.
p. 72, last line, For is, *read* are.
p. 77, l. 20—23, *substitute*, *Upanishad*, a commentary upon the *Sama Veda*, in Sanscrit, published by Rammohun Roy, *Calcutta*, 1818, 8vo., printed in Bengali character.
p. 86, l. 9, For Bhânarâ Châryya, *read* Bhāscāracharya.
p. 109, For Dushwanta, *read* Dushmanta, all through the article.
p. 128, l. 18, For Sasta, *read* Sastra.
p. 131, l. 29, For Hared, *read* Nared.
p. 152, l. 24, For Mahesnara, *read* Maheshwara.
p. 163, note, last line but one, For Talmul, *read* Tamul.
p. 176, l. 1, For Kudma, *read* Kurmar.